# TEXTS AND CULTURAL CHANGE IN EARLY
# MODERN ENGLAND

EARLY MODERN LITERATURE IN HISTORY

General Editor: Cedric C. Brown
*Professor of English and Head of Department, University of Reading*

Within the period 1520–1740 this series discusses many kinds of writing, both within and outside the established canon. The volumes may employ different theoretical perspectives, but they share an historical awareness and an interest in seeing their texts in lively negotiation with their own and successive cultures.

*Published titles*

Anna R. Beer
SIR WALTER RALEGH AND HIS READERS IN THE SEVENTEENTH CENTURY: Speaking to the People

Cedric C. Brown and Arthur F. Marotti (*editors*)
TEXTS AND CULTURAL CHANGE IN EARLY MODERN ENGLAND

James Loxley
ROYALISM AND POETRY IN THE ENGLISH CIVIL WARS: The Drawn Sword

Mark Thornton Burnett
MASTERS AND SERVANTS IN ENGLISH RENAISSANCE DRAMA AND CULTURE: Authority and Obedience

The series Early Modern Literature in History is published in association with the Renaissance Texts Research Centre at the University of Reading.

# Texts and Cultural Change in Early Modern England

Edited by

Cedric C. Brown

and

Arthur F. Marotti

First published in Great Britain 1997 by
**MACMILLAN PRESS LTD**
Houndmills, Basingstoke, Hampshire RG21 6XS and London
Companies and representatives throughout the world

A catalogue record for this book is available from the British Library.

ISBN 0–333–66287–3

 First published in the United States of America 1997 by
**ST. MARTIN'S PRESS, INC.,**
Scholarly and Reference Division,
175 Fifth Avenue, New York, N.Y. 10010

ISBN 0–312–17728–3

Library of Congress Cataloging-in-Publication Data
Texts and cultural change in early modern England / edited by Cedric
C. Brown and Arthur F. Marotti.
p. cm. — (Early modern literature in history)
Includes bibliographical references and index.
ISBN 0–312–17728–3 (cloth)
1. English literature—Early modern, 1500–1700—History and
criticism. 2. Social change in literature. 3. Literature and
society—England—History—16th century. 4. Literature and society–
–England—History—17th century. 5. Literature and history–
–England—History. 6. Books and reading—England—History.
7. Social change—England—History. 8. Transmission of texts.
9. Canon (Literature) 10. Literary form. I. Brown, Cedric C.
(Cedric Clive), 1943–   . II. Marotti, Arthur F., 1940–   .
III. Series.
PR428.S64T48 1997
820.9'355—dc21                                            97–24801
                                                              CIP

This book is printed on paper suitable for recycling and made from fully managed and
sustained forest sources.

10   9   8   7   6   5   4   3   2   1
06   05   04   03   02   01   00   99   98   97

Printed and bound in Great Britain by Antony Rowe Ltd, Chippenham, Wiltshire

# Contents

# Acknowledgements

The essay by Janel Mueller is reprinted (with small alterations) from *Representing Women in Renaissance England*, ed. Claude J. Summers and Ted-Larry Pebworth, by permission of the University of Missouri Press. Copyright © 1997 by the Curators of the University of Missouri.

The essay by Richard Dutton is a revised version of that first appearing in *Elizabethan Theater: Essays in Honor of S. Schoenbaum*, ed. R. B. Parker and S. P. Zitner (Delaware: University of Delaware Press, and London: Associated Universities Press, 1996).

Figure 1, 'Persecutiones aduersus Catholicos à Protestantibus Caluinistis exitae in Anglia', is reproduced from Richard Verstegan, *Theatrum Crudelitatum Haereticorum nostri Temporis* (Antuerpiae: Apud Adrianum Huberti, 1587), p. 83, by permission of Special Collections Library, University of Michigan.

Figure 2, the title-page of *Saint Peters complaynt*, is reproduced by permission of The Huntington Library, San Marino, California.

# Notes on Contributors

**Cedric C. Brown**, co-editor of this volume, is Professor and Head of the Department of English at the University of Reading. He has written widely on Milton, including two books, and on poetry, masque and country house entertainment in the seventeenth century. He has also edited several volumes on the politics of early modern literature, and his current work includes a book on the social transmission of poetry texts. He is General Editor of the series *Early Modern Literature in History*.

**Richard Dutton** is Professor of English and Associate Dean for Research (Humanities) at Lancaster University. Recent publications include *Mastering the Revels: the Regulation and Censorship of English Renaissance Drama* (1991), an edition of *Jacobean Civic Pageants* (1995) and *Ben Jonson: Criticism: Authority* (1996). He also wrote *William Shakespeare: A Literary Life* in the Macmillan *Literary Lives* series, of which he is General Editor.

**Paul Hammond** is Professor of Seventeenth-Century English Literature at the University of Leeds. He is the author of *John Oldham and the Renewal of Classical Culture* (1983), and *John Dryden: A Literary Life* (1991), and editor of the first two volumes of *The Poems of John Dryden* (1995) in the Longman Annotated English Poets series. His latest book is *Love between Men in English Literature* (1996). His essay in this volume is part of work in progress on the literature of homosexual relationships in seventeenth-century England.

**Paulina Kewes** is Lecturer in English at the University of Wales, Aberystwyth. She has published articles on late seventeenth-century drama, most recently in *Publishing History* and *The Review of English Studies*, and her book on *Authorship and Appropriation: Conceptions of Playwriting in England, 1660–1710* is forthcoming from Oxford University Press.

**Peter Lindenbaum** is Professor of English Literature at Indiana University. He has written on Sidney, Shakespeare and Milton in *Changing Landscapes: Anti-Pastoral Sentiment in the English Renaissance* (1986), and has more recently been focusing on the ways in which texts present themselves in the seventeenth century.

He is at work on a book-length study of Milton and publishing history.

**Arthur F. Marotti**, co-editor of this volume, is Professor of English at Wayne State University. A former editor of the journal *Criticism*, he is the author of *John Donne: Coterie Poet* (Madison and London, 1986), *Manuscript, Print and the English Renaissance Lyric* (Ithaca, NY and London, 1995) and numerous articles on early modern literature. His current project is a book on *Catholicism, Anti-Catholicism, and Early Modern English Texts*.

**Janel Mueller** is William Rainey Harper Professor of Humanities at the University of Chicago and the editor of *Modern Philology*. Her research interests have centred on English Reformation literature and on earlier English women authors. She is presently editing the writings and correspondence of Katherine Parr, and, in conjunction with Leah Marcus and Mary Beth Rose, preparing an edition of the speeches, selected letters, poems and prayers of Elizabeth I.

**Pamela Neville-Sington** is a historian and bibliographer. She has written *Paradise Dreamed: How Utopian Thinkers Have Changed the Modern World* (1993), an introduction to incunabula, 'A Purchas Bibliography', in *The Purchas Handbook* (Cambridge, forthcoming), and an essay on 'Press, Politics, and Religion', in *The History of the Book in Britain, 1475–1557* (forthcoming). She has also edited and is writing a biography of Fanny Trollope. In the present context, she is working with Anthony Payne on a bibliography of Hakluyt for the Hakluyt Society.

**Lori Humphrey Newcomb** is Assistant Professor at the University of Illinois at Urbana-Champaign. She has published articles on Jacobean popular culture and servant readers, and written on Shakespeare, Mary Wroth and Emanuel Forde. The essay in this volume draws on her forthcoming book-length study, *The Stuff of Fiction: Publishing and Reading Elizabethan Popular Romance, 1585–1800*.

**Sasha Roberts** is a Research Fellow at Roehampton Institute, London, where she also teaches English Renaissance literature. She has published on Shakespeare, Renaissance literature and art, and recently co-edited an anthology on *Women Reading Shakespeare, 1660–1900* (1997), with Ann Thompson. She is currently working on a study of the representation of domestic space in Shakespeare.

# Introduction

When the anonymous Catholic political libel against the Earl of Leicester which first circulated in manuscript in the late 1580s came into print in 1641 as *Leicester's Commonwealth* at the time of the Irish Rebellion and on the eve of the English Civil Wars, that old text clearly meant something very different in its new historical circumstances from the context of Elizabethan Protestant–Catholic propaganda wars and factional struggles at the Elizabethan Court. Similarly, when in 1638 the royalist publisher Humphrey Moseley published the Latin epigrams of Sir Thomas More over a hundred years after their composition, or produced a magnificent folio edition in 1647 of the collection of dramas associated with Francis Beaumont and John Fletcher, old texts were given new life and new meaning in new circumstances. Even works that were much reprinted, like Sidney's *Arcadia*, whether or not their texts were altered, corrupted or accompanied by different paratextual[1] material, inevitably changed because the conditions in which they were reproduced and were received had changed, making them new or different works.

Recognizing these realities, most literary scholars of the last quarter of the twentieth century have questioned, if not assaulted, the older view of literary texts as transhistorical entities whose values lie in the 'universal' meanings they embody.[2] Emphasizing the ways in which texts are historically contingent, both in their original circumstances of production and reception and in their subsequent reproductions, transformations and reception, critics have been alert to large cultural changes and to particular local circumstances which shaped the understanding and interpretation of particular works. Especially in the case of a canonical author like Shakespeare, whose sociocultural status as a sign of Englishness was signalled by his appropriation by a conservative nationalist ideology in the eighteenth, nineteenth and early twentieth centuries,[3] it is important to highlight the relationship of his plays and poems to those cultural changes that made them mean different things in different times to different audiences and readers. In other words, scholars have attended to the phenomenon Maria Corti calls 'desemiotization' – that is, the destruction of a syntax of codes in a cultural system and the creation of a 'new and different type of semiotization',[4] resulting in the production of

1

new texts within the new codes and a different understanding and interpretation of older texts whose survival and readability testify to their adaptability within the historical process.

The essays collected in this volume were presented in their original, shorter forms in the summer of 1995 at the third triennial conference on Literature and History at the University of Reading, England. The general theme of the conference was 'Texts and Cultural Change: History, Politics and Interpretation, 1520–1660',[5] a topic which has been broadened here in its chronological coverage to accommodate texts produced or reproduced beyond the original terminal date. The various narratives about texts in this volume span from mid-Tudor times to the middle of the eighteenth century.

Although the essays in this volume interlock in many rewarding ways, the conference was designed as a whole to study the historical vicissitudes of texts from a variety of critical vantage points. These included sociologically inflected historical bibliography, revisionist textual criticism, sociopolitical interpretation and both intellectual and cultural history. The scholars whose work is represented in this collection – only a fraction of all those who took part in the original international event – all pay particular attention to the materiality and the historicity of the texts they discuss, many of them practising the kind of sociological bibliography D. F. McKenzie has advocated in his broad definition of that discipline,[6] or the kind of local reading that Leah Marcus has attempted and encouraged.[7] These studies could also be said to emerge from a contemporary re-emphasis in literary study on the importance of archival research and detailed scholarly investigation, 'the new erudition', as the editor of a recent issue of the journal *Representations* has called it (though not all of it is new to all).[8] Historical bibliographical work on the media of manuscript and print,[9] in combination with the sociocentric work of textual revisionists,[10] has made more possible culturally defined analyses of manuscript and print embodiments of texts within changing sociocultural conditions of production and reception. Texts have been analysed afresh in their material and historical specificity, viewed in relation to the cultural and ideological changes in which they participated and which they helped to shape.

The scholars in this collection do not speak with a single voice: they are of different ages, come from both sides of the Atlantic and the work of a historian-bibliographer is included among that of the literary or cultural critics. But they all obviously work in a scholarly climate which follows the period of work of New Historicists and cultural materialists and they pick up also on important studies of those who have contributed to our knowledge of the history of the book. There are signs of the literary and cultural theory produced by poststructuralist theorists, including contemporary feminist theory. But these scholars are more empirically oriented, perhaps, than many who do historicist literary study: they are eager to draw on the riches of the archive for their cultural evidence, ready to examine the material characteristics of print or manuscript texts for what they can specifically reveal about the historical semiotic encoding of the texts' production and reception. Their focus is different from those who like to debate the issue of 'subversion' and 'containment'.[11] The scholars represented in this collection have, on the whole, concentrated more on the particular historical moment of each textual production or reproduction in order to delineate the specific sociocultural forces at work in the individual contexts they are analysing. At this level of analysis, some of the larger generalizations about political, social and religious change break down or demand important qualifications. For example, Janel Mueller demonstrates in the first essay that some of the assumptions about the cultural changes wrought by print technology or about the relationship of orality, visuality and print have to be qualified and adjusted in the particular case she examines.

These scholars open up subjects that need more extensive discussion, or allow their surprising discoveries to attract others to new opportunities of research. Although they do not foreground a master-narrative of the development of English society and culture in the early modern period, they do deal with such large-scale cultural changes as the democratization of literacy, the social stratification of taste and changing perceptions of erotic behaviour. Some of their essays follow the reception history of particular works through several historical periods, dealing with such topics as the adaptations and revisions of texts and of their manner of presentation and the changes in the way prose narratives are read in developing bourgeois culture. Other essays concentrate more on the relation of texts to their immediate occasions and specific historical moments. Many of the essays concern publishing history, dealing with censorship, the paratextual shaping of the reading experience and the impact of publishing format on the ways texts were used and interpreted. More simply, Dutton and Brown, one using playtexts, the other funerary elegies, both plead for a greater sensitivity in modern readers to the kinds of difference presented by different versions of texts.

In 'Complications of Intertextuality: John Fisher, Katherine Parr and "The Book of the Crucifix"', Janel Mueller analyses Katherine Parr's *Lamentations of a Sinner* as a text that poses questions about the hermeneutic usefulness of the categories of race, class, gender and generational position – the last a factor she briefly highlights because of its undeserved neglect. Dissatisfied especially with the limitations of a gender-oriented approach, especially in the light of Parr's attempt to create a genderless, generic Christian speaker and the tradition gendering of the Christian soul as female, she argues that religion is a more important factor than gender as a basic determinant of interpretation. Comparing Parr's use of the metaphor of 'the book of the crucifix' to promote Protestant scripture-reading with Bishop John Fisher's earlier use of it to foster a kind of visually-oriented Franciscan spirituality, Mueller notes the different orientations towards the new medium of print – Fisher looking back, in his use of the metaphor, to the illuminated manuscript and medieval religious modes of visual communication and Parr assimilating the metaphor to print culture. In so doing Mueller settles on the religious differences between the Catholic and Protestant writers (despite their shared Erasmian orientation) as crucial markers to which interpreters should attend, treating 'religion ... as exercising a potentially determinative force in human life and its linguistic and social forms, just as race or ethnicity, class and gender (and generation?) are already taken to do' (pp. 29–3). She notes the differences between Catholic and Protestant attitudes towards religious imagery, the sacraments (with their 'attendant modalities of worship' [p. 31]) and the eucharist – all of which were related to their different attitudes towards the new print medium, particularly towards the popular dissemination of the text of the Bible. Since these all had material bases in the culture of the time, they should have been more readily acknowledged in the interpretations of early modern texts by cultural materialist critics, but they have not been because, like most New Historicists, they have tended either to avoid the topic of religion or to treat it as a form of false consciousness in need of social, political and economic decoding.

Religious differences between Catholicism and Protestantism also lie at the heart of the discussion in Arthur F. Marotti's 'Southwell's Remains: Catholicism and Anti-Catholicism in Early

Modern England'. This essay argues that Catholics, during the worst of the persecution in the second half of Queen Elizabeth's reign, a period in which a Protestant, anti-Catholic nationalist ideology was being formed, continued material religious practices such as the collection and devotional use of relics even as they translated Catholic modes of perception and spirituality into the medium of print, an environment in which polemical and propagandistic battles between English Protestantism and international Catholicism took place. Marotti contends that both the martyrdoms of the Jesuits Edmund Campion and Robert Southwell and the writings published by them or printed after their deaths were texts within print culture which carried an oppositional force politically and served to cement the bonds of an imperilled English Catholic community. These 'texts' highlighted, within the medium of print, devotional, social, political differences between, on the one hand, English Catholics and their religion and, on the other, the Protestant state religion and the governmental machinery for enforcing conformity to it. In particular, in focusing on the vocabulary of the relic, the 'remains' of the Catholic martyr, Marotti demonstrates how print culture assimilated some of the power associated with the material practices of relic-collection, preservation and devotion, the kind of force John Milton later struggled to dispel in his *Eikonoklastes*.

In '"A very good trumpet": Richard Hakluyt and the Politics of Overseas Expansion', Pamela Neville-Sington performs an exercise in what she calls 'forensic bibliography' (an application of historical bibliographical methods) to ground Hakluyt's texts in the context of the factional politics of the late Elizabethan period. She associates Hakluyt with those members of the Elizabethan power elite (represented prominently by his patron and dedicatee, Sir Francis Walsingham) who wished to foster overseas exploration and colonization in order to make England less dependent on the larger European trade and its volatile market conditions. Hakluyt's texts thus participated in a cultural change in which England gradually moved towards empire-building. Neville-Sington focuses on the bibliographical traces left by post-publication censorship in the surviving copies of Hakluyt's works, particularly the 1589 and (expanded, three-volume) 1598–1600 editions of his *Principal Navigations*. Examining the politically sensitive material Hakluyt included, such as the accounts of Sir Francis Drake's circumnavigation of the globe and the glorified but largely unsuccessful 1596

Cadiz expedition, she shows how booksellers and readers (including some prominent government officials) conspired, even after censorship forced the excision of sections of the texts, to market and preserve them, binding them into their personal copies. The surviving copies, then, which contain the evidence of censorship and its evasion, preserve not only the signs of the work's original political orientation and sponsorship, but also evidence of the response of the authorities and of the actions individuals producing and consuming the texts took to create the version they wanted to see.

Using historical bibliographical evidence in different ways, Peter Lindenbaum argues in 'Sidney's *Arcadia* as Cultural Monument and Proto-Novel' that, between its first appearance in 1590 and the 1739 edition, Sidney's prose romance underwent a change of use as readers and the publishers who responded to their needs moved from treating the text as a storehouse of moral and political wisdom, memorable sayings and turns of phrase and as a cultural monument to its deceased aristocratic author to reading it novelistically within middle-class culture as a prose narrative. He emphasizes the importance of paratextual elements, examining the marks and annotations to be found in the large Folger Shakespeare Library collection of Sidney editions, relating them to the bibliographical features of the printed editions of the century and one half following the publication of the 1590 *Arcadia*. He pays special attention to the significance of the different (folio, quarto, octavo and duodecimo) formats in which Sidney's work was published, especially to the features of the full-dress 1655 edition, 'to whose condition all the earlier sixteenth- and seventeenth-century editions can be said to have aspired (and subsequent seventeenth-century editions replicated)' [p. 82]. This interesting edition contains the most elaborate supplementary material, including not only an earlier frontispiece, dedication and preface to the reader, but also such new items as an anonymous biography of Sidney and an 'Alphabetical Table, or Clavis, whereby the Reader is let in to view the principal stories contained in the Arcadia as they stand in their proper places'. The cultural change Lindenbaum measures between this edition and the 1739 one produced in three-volume duodecimo form, the format of the eighteenth-century novel, is one that manifested itself in reader behaviour and publishing decisions.

From one famous romance to another. In 'The Triumph of Time: The Fortunate Readers of Robert Greene's *Pandosto*' Lori Newcomb uses the publishing history of the editions, chapbook condensations and ballad form of Greene's enormously popular romance to test the relationship between historical bibliographical data, anecdotal evidence about elite, middle-class and popular reading habits and large-scale cultural change in the early modern period. Greene's text becomes a convenient reference point for a discussion of the social spread of literacy and the attendant processes of what Pierre Bourdieu calls 'distinction',[12] the conservative hierarchization of aesthetic and literary taste (in which, for example, the reading of romance either in its original aristocratically oriented versions or in more popular adaptations and chapbook condensations was stigmatized by associating it with female and servant readers). Newcomb examines anecdotes about popular romance reading which were designed to allay upper-class anxieties about the democratization of literacy and the socioeconomic transgression of class boundaries, testing their accuracy against other social-historical and literary-historical evidence. She notes an irony in the fact that, from Ben Jonson's time through the eighteenth century and beyond, 'those who voiced complaints about the popularity of Greene's romance were themselves highly conscious of their own implication in the commodification of literary texts and in the dissemination of fantasies of [social] mobility' (p. 101). She points out that 'early modern criticism [began] to read popularity among "unfortunate" readers as a crucial marker of aesthetic misfortune – an interpretative assumption that later criticism has tended to share' (p. 99).

Newcomb disputes the contrast in reception-history of the elite audience of Sidney's *Arcadia* and the popular audience of Greene's *Pandosto*, emphasizing their overlap during much of their early history, especially between 1588 and 1680, the period in which the text of *Pandosto* enjoyed an astonishing textual stability as it was reproduced repeatedly in its full form. Although, between 1680 and 1700 the text was marketed 'to multiple audiences on different rungs of the social ladder' (p. 105) in different formats (from the uncut original to the 16-page anonymous chapbook redaction), it was eventually 'pushed out of the elite market' (p. 98) in the eighteenth century when novel writers sought to elevate their enterprise socially and aesthetically above that of the popular romance writer. Newcomb's insightful economic, social and ideological analysis of eighteenth-century literary production and literary criticism situates popular romance in a large field of cultural conflict begun in Greene's, Sidney's and Jonson's time. The implied, actual and imagined readerships of *Pandosto* interacted through its bibliographical and reception histories in ways which reveal the participation of the text in major cultural changes.

In the first of three essays about the writing of Shakespeare, Sasha Roberts argues in 'Editing Sexuality, Narrative and Authorship: The Altered Texts of Shakespeare's *Lucrece*' that the editorial changes to the original textual presentation of Shakespeare's poem can best be understood in two contexts which involve larger cultural developments. The first is implicit in the editorial use of marginal comments, division into chapters with discursive headings and the selective use of italics and of verbal emendations to substitute for the potential Shakespearean equivocal readings of Lucrece's rape and suicide a univocal meaning that affirms her chastity and nobility of motives. The second is that of publishing history, a context in which changes in the status of authorship and prestige of literary texts are reflected in the material presentation of editions of the poem. She notes the significance of the change of title in the sixth (1616) Quarto to *The Rape of Lucrece* and its use of italicization, marginal comments and chapter headings to produce the 'polite' reading of the poem which makes Lucrece chaste, innocent and selfless. Roberts highlights the bibliographical and sociocultural importance of John Stafford's ninth (1655) Quarto, *The Rape of Lucrece, Committed by Tarquin the Sixt; and the Remarkable Judgments that befell him for it. By the incomparable Master of our English Poetry, WILL. SHAKESPEARE Gent.*', which includes a frontispiece portrait depicting Lucrece about to kill herself while Collatine tries to prevent the action, above which is a medallion with the portrait of the author looking straight out at the viewer-reader. Given the political and gender issues embedded in the Lucrece story and its conflict of interpretations, Roberts' account does much to illustrate the ways in which the editorial attempts to control interpretation are situated in an evolving sociocultural context in which authorship, textuality and an ideological 'just-so' story like this one are contested territories.

Richard Dutton's essay on the literary transmission of Shakespeare's plays, 'The Birth of the Author', takes up a bold position: Shakespeare, who as one of the regularly employed 'ordinary poets' of and as a shareholder in a theatrical company was constrained from independently pursuing print publication of his dramas, deliberately circulated reading versions of some of his plays in manuscript form. Working back from Humphrey

Moseley's preface to his great folio edition of Beaumont and Fletcher, where that publisher states that circulating long (manuscript) versions of those authors' dramas were more appealing to readers than the shorter, theatrical versions, Dutton argues that Shakespeare composed long reading texts of his plays for manuscript circulation, much as Jonson did for print. Operating under unusually strict constraints as a shareholder in the Lord Chamberlain's/King's Men, Shakespeare was 'a company man' (p. 161) who would not have taken plays that were company property and profited personally from their printing. Thus, to make reading versions of them available (to meet the demand for such literary commodities), he would have been forced to limit himself to manuscript transmission – as he did with his sonnets.

The evidence Dutton brings to bear is circumstantial, but most suggestive. He argues that there is no reason to assume that Shakespeare did not follow the practice of Beaumont, Fletcher and Middleton, for example, of allowing manuscript versions of his plays to circulate. He interprets Heminge and Condell's preface to the 1623 Folio (a printed text that then would 'have made the manuscripts of his plays seem redundant' [p. 165]) as referring to Shakespeare's assumption of the role of the gentleman writer in a manuscript culture: 'There is substantial evidence of a Shakespeare who regularly wrote, with some facility, plays too long and complex to be staged in the theatre of his day, plays for which the only plausible audience was one of readers. The "good" quartos provide us with the clearest evidence of what those plays were like' (p. 172). Dutton swims against the current tide of Shakespearean editing, represented by the Wells and Taylor Oxford edition,[13] which seeks to present theatrical versions of plays rather than old-fashioned composite texts produced in the name of a kind of textual idealism. He invites us to consider the differences between reading versions and theatrical versions of the Shakespearean dramas and to readjust our interpretive methods accordingly.

The detail of Cedric C. Brown's 'Mending and Bending the Occasional Text: Collegiate Elegies and the Case of "Lycidas"' concerns a reading of the changes in Milton's showpiece elegy for Edward King between the two early printings, that is, in the Cambridge memorial volume of 1637/8 and the Humphrey Moseley collection of Milton's poems in 1645. The issue here is the shift from an institutional volume turning around university conventions and ideals and an author-centred volume published long enough after

the original funerary occasion for reconstructions of the 1637 context
– personal, institutional and national – to be necessary for the reader.
However, the specific issues here are placed in a larger context, to
do with the cultural conventions of funerary writing, especially
within a collegiate situation. Throughout, Brown's concern is to
show how much community orientation matters in such elegies and
many features in 'Lycidas' derive from Milton's artful negotiations
with his rhetorical task. Further, it is shown that the functions of funerary elegy overlap with the epideictic and hortatory characteristics
of funerary oration and sermon, so that the more political features of
Milton's poem, often thought to be intrusive, are in fact elaborations
of the kind of 'laying to heart' enjoined upon audiences, when considerations were often carried beyond personal loss into a prophetic
meaning of the loss to institution, church and state.

Another set of comparisons is also offered, in order better to
place Milton's collegiate elegy, not only against Milton's own
earlier funerary poems, especially 'On the Death of a Fair Infant',
but also the precocious schoolboy elegies of Abraham Cowley,
where cultural and educational expectations are easy to read. The
effect of this comparison is to highlight the difference between the
eager entry of the grammar-school poet into the displays of rhetoric
sanctioned by the funerary occasion and the careful self-positioning
of Milton in 'Lycidas', as he signals a re-entry into collegiate elegy
and its expectations, some years after leaving Cambridge, with an
almost imperious demonstration of rhetorical distinction and vocational exhortation. Many of the passages discussed in Brown's
essay, however, throw light on the communal nature of the memorial enterprise, not so much grieving as asking for grief and a laying
to heart and showing, in the case of the ecclesiastical and political
context, how minutely the text responded to the contemporary situation and therefore had to be altered, or explained, in subsequent
publication when both the urgency of the occasion and the communal expectations were lost. He shows how little the criticism of subsequent centuries absorbed of the communal enterprise and how
much it took from the authorially-centred presentations begun in
1645. Finally, all this material is offered as an example of the way
many systems of communication are waiting to be realized by a
better awareness of the cultural conventions of kinds of occasional
poetry, in which the early modern period is especially rich.

In 'Between the "Triumvirate of Wit" and the Bard: The English
Dramatic Canon, 1660–1720', Paulina Kewes examines the period

in which Shakespeare, Fletcher and Jonson were acknowledged as important 'ancient' (i.e. pre-Restoration) playwrights, but on the whole seen as inferior to 'modern' dramatists like Dryden, Wycherley, Lee and Farquhar. She does not centre her analysis in performance history (though she does use its evidence to confirm her conclusions) and she avoids the 'unrepresentative' opinions expressed by John Dryden and Thomas Rymer in their famous essays on drama. Instead, she looks to the rich, but neglected, evidence found in dramatic catalogues that not only compiled and ranked lists of older and newer plays, but also offered critical judgements about their worth. Attending carefully to their aesthetic standards and culture-specific assumptions, she closely examines such works as Francis Kirkman's *A True, perfect and exact Catalogue* (1661), Edward Phillips' *Theatrum Poetarum* (1675) and Gerard Langbaine's *Momum Triumphans* (1688) and *The Account of the English Dramatick Poets* (1691) (and its revision by Charles Gildon, *The Lives and Characters of the English Dramatick Poets* [1699]). Choosing, then, a cultural moment just before the eighteenth-century elevation of Shakespeare in the canon of English authors, she shows how the texts that he and his dramatic contemporaries wrote could be evaluatively reduced and recoded in an era in which new standards of taste and judgement were applied to poetic productions.

Not only did the plays of Restoration and early eighteenth-century dramatists greatly exceed the revised and unrevised work of Shakespeare, Fletcher and Jonson in the number of theatrical productions, but, if the evaluative works Kewes examines are a good measure of contemporary taste and judgement, they fell considerably in literary esteem in the period under discussion. What is at stake here is not simply a matter of changed historical contexts – the loss, for example, of those political and social contexts that made sense of the themes and conflicts of those dramas – but also a major change in aesthetic canons (conditioned by sociological and ideological changes) and the development of new ways of practising literary history and criticism.

In the course of her discussion, Kewes refers to some of the adaptations of Shakespeare done in the Restoration and early eighteenth-century to accommodate him to contemporary tastes and standards. In his essay, 'Friends or Lovers? Sensitivity to Homosexual Implications in Adaptations of Shakespeare, 1640–1701', Paul Hammond (after some discussion of John Benson's alterations of Shakespeare's *Sonnets*) examines two of these revised texts as registers of changed cultural attitudes toward homoeroticism between Shakespeare's time and the early eighteenth century. He observes that, in his use of terms like 'friend' and 'lover' and in his portrayal of same-sex emotional intimacy, Shakespeare cultivated an imaginative indefinition which suited the less sharp distinctions made in his contemporary world between the homoerotic and the heterosexual. But he concludes, first, from Benson's obvious discomfort with the expressions of same-sex desire and then, later, from George Granville's homophobic 1701 revision of *The Merchant of Venice* (under the title *The Jew of Venice*), Nahum Tate's adaptation of *Coriolanus* (*The Ingratitude of a Commonwealth* [1682]), Thomas Otways' adaptation of *Romeo and Juliet* (*The History and Fall of Caius Marius* [1680]) and Dryden's revision of *Troilus and Cressida* (1679), that changed cultural attitudes towards homoeroticism forced the nervous textual changes that were made. Such 'Restoration adaptations were motivated partly by a concern to protect male friendship from the suspicion of homosexual desire and to preserve the clarity and stability of the definition of masculinity in the face of a new world of homosexual self-definition' (pp. 245–6) in an era which saw the establishment of the 'molly house' and of a homosexual subculture.

Kewes' and Hammond's essays, like Lindenbaum's, Newcomb's and Brown's, move beyond the original 1660 chronological endpoint of the conference for which they were originally drafted. In considering Restoration and eighteenth-century culture, they suggest that the cultural changes affecting texts in the early modern period need to be traced from the sixteenth through to the nineteenth century. Whether one is dealing with large-scale epistemic change, the media shift from manuscript to print culture, the formation of modern individualism, the commodification processes of early capitalism and the growth of bourgeois culture, or the shift from top-down monarchism to more modern forms of representative government, it is clear that the continuities and changes that historians and literary scholars are tracing demand this broader historical framework. The collapsing of the old 'Renaissance', 'Seventeenth-Century' and 'Restoration/Eighteenth-Century' period specializations in literary study into the category of the 'Early Modern' (which in some versions runs from the late Middle Ages through much of the nineteenth century) suggests that scholars are already acknowledging the need to move in this larger field in order to discuss both the historically-specific and the culturally general issues they most engage them. It is hoped that the essays in this collection will stimulate more work of this kind, encouraging the work of those scholars whose passion is for archival research and close attention to the specific material and historical details of this only partially recoverable era.

## NOTES

1. The term is coined by Gerard Genette: see, for example, his 'Introduction to the Paratext', trans. Marie MacLean, *NLH* 22 (Spring 1991): 261–72. Peter Lindenbaum's essay discusses paratextual issues related to the printing of Sidney's *Arcadia*.
2. For example, in the Introduction to his influential anthology, *The New Historicism* (New York and London, 1989), H. Aram Veeser lists as one of the key assumptions of the New Historicists (shared also by cultural materialist critics): 'no discourse, imaginative or archival, gives access to unchanging truths nor expresses inalterable human nature' (p. xi).
3. See Michael Dobson, *The Making of the National Poet: Shakespeare, Adaptation, and Authorship, 1660–1769* (Oxford, 1992), Gary Taylor, *Reinventing Shakespeare: A Cultural History from the Restoration to the Present* (New York, 1989) and Hugh Grady, *The Modernist Shakespeare* (Oxford, 1991).
4. Maria Corti, *An Introduction to Literary Semiotics*, trans. Margherita Bogat and Allen Mandelbaum (Bloomington, IN, 1978), p. 19.
5. Selected papers from the first (1989) conference, 'Politics, Patronage and Literature in England, 1558–1658', edited by Cedric C. Brown, were published in *The Yearbook of English Studies* 21 (1991) and republished selectively in *Patronage, Politics and Literary Traditions in England, 1558–1658* (Detroit, 1991). Some papers from the second (1992) conference, 'Politics in English Culture, 1520–1660', were edited by Cedric C. Brown and published as a special issue of *Criticism* 35 (Summer 1993).
6. D. F. McKenzie, *Bibliography and the Sociology of Texts* (London, 1986).
7. Leah S. Marcus, *Puzzling Shakespeare: Local Reading and its Discontents* (Berkeley, Los Angeles and London, 1988) and *Unediting the Renaissance* (New York and London, 1996).
8. Randolph Starn, 'Introduction: "The New Erudition"', *Representations* 56 (Fall, 1996), 1.
9. See Elizabeth Eisenstein, *The Printing Press as an Agent of Change* ... 2 vols (Cambridge, 1979); Lucien Febvre and Henri-Jean Martin, *The Coming of the Book: The Impact of Printing 1450–1800*, trans. David Gerard, ed. Geoffrey Nowell-Smith and David Wooton (London and Atlantic Highlands, NJ, 1976); Roger Chartier, *The Cultural Uses of Print in Early Modern France*, trans. Lydia Cochrane (Princeton, NJ, 1987) and 'Texts, Printing, Reading', in *The New Cultural History*, ed.

Lynn Hunt (Berkeley and Los Angeles, 1989), pp. 154–75; Mary
Hobbs, *Early Seventeenth-Century Verse Miscellany Manuscripts*
(Aldershot, 1992); Harold Love, *Scribal Publication in Seventeenth-
Century England* (Oxford, 1993); Arthur F. Marotti, *Manuscript, Print
and the English Renaissance Lyric* (Ithaca, NY and London, 1995); and
H. R. Woudhuysen, *Sir Philip Sidney and the Circulation of Manuscripts,
1558–1640* (Oxford, 1996).

10. See Jerome McGann, *A Critique of Modern Textual Criticism* (Chicago,
    1983); Steven Urkowitz, *Shakespeare's Revision of 'King Lear'* (Princeton,
    NJ, 1980); *The Division of the Kingdoms: Shakespeare's Two Versions of
    King Lear*, ed. Gary Taylor and Michael Warren (Oxford, 1983); and
    *New Ways of Looking at Old Texts: Papers of the Renaissance English Text
    Society, 1985–1991*, ed. W. Speed Hill (Binghamton, NY, 1993).

11. Arguments between New Historicist and cultural materialist critics
    have led to some political posturing but not much affected critical
    practice. A useful political critique of new historicism is provided in
    the anti-regiocentric and historically particular method advocated by
    James Holston in 'Ranting at the New Historicism', *ELH* 19 (1989):
    189–225.

12. Pierre Bourdieu, *Distinction: A Social Critique of the Judgement of Taste*
    (London, 1984).

13. *The Complete Oxford Shakespeare*, ed. Stanley Wells and Gary Taylor
    (Oxford, 1987).

# 1

# Complications of Intertextuality: John Fisher, Katherine Parr and 'The Book of the Crucifix'

## Janel Mueller

The level of current interest in interpreting texts as registers of cultural change in early modern England bespeaks an increasingly shared perspective in literary studies which again seeks to take history seriously. As we literary-historical types now go about our usual business of intertextuality – analysing texts in relation other texts – we avoid dealing solely in textual formulations of our concerns. For, unless they are tethered to extralinguistic referents of context, relations among texts seemingly cannot be freed from the spectre of an indefinite regress of signifiers in play. Many of us have accordingly turned to an almost hallowed triad – race (or ethnicity), class and gender – as anchors for our work on historical texts in historical contexts. Taken over from our social science colleagues in the current vogue of interdisciplinary method-swapping, these factors look so promising because race, class and gender are powerfully material in their bases and potently ideological in their social encodings and decodings.

Thus we routinely suppose that if we analyse texts for what we call their race, class or gender 'inscriptions' and interpret them accordingly, we will be able to surmount disjunctions between world and word, between material facts and ideas in literature, and manage to make our criticism and historical work be about something that can count as real. We further assume that race, class and gender, as fundamental constituents of human lives in social relations, will unfailingly leave significant markings in a text; or, what amounts to nearly the same thing in practice, we assume that the markings of race, class and gender will yield significance more basic, more primary, than for example that conveyed by way of the verbal and cognitive effects of rhetoric or poetics. To this triad of race, class and gender I want to join the powerful factor of a writer's generation, his or her biological and social moment, for we now know from historical linguistics that generationally diffused variation is the chief motor of language change.[1] Why should the situation not be similar with literary change, something that we have much trouble accounting for?

The 'we' locutions that I have been using are not disingenuous. These reflections indicate lines that my own critical thinking has taken and I am aware of a number of colleagues who have been moving in this same direction. Nevertheless, I have come to regard the material that I present in this paper as something of a test case or a limit instance of the capacity of gender – particularly as now theorized – to anchor the literary-historical work that I have been doing on women in English Protestantism. I begin by explaining my concrete difficulties in a specific case and the available interpretative options as I saw them. I end with some reflections on what for me remains a conjoint dilemma of methodology and interpretation: how to decide which factor to treat as determinative when more than one option seems available and what interpretative difference it makes to decide one way or the other.

The heart of my material is an odd metaphor, 'the book of the crucifix', which is arguably by traditional rhetorical criteria even a catachresis (an outright violation of figurative language). The oddity of this metaphor consists in its conflation of long-divergent, even long-opposed domains in Christian symbolics: on one hand, the book as the Bible, Holy Writ, the acme of verbal truth; on the other, the crucifix as the simulacrum of Christ's bloody, suffering body, the most sacred object, the acme of non-verbal truth. I first encountered the metaphor of 'the book of the crucifix' in the sustained use that Katherine Parr makes of it in her religious prose work, *The Lamentation of a Sinner*, published in November 1547.

Katherine Parr was Henry VIII's last Queen and his widow; also in earlier years an intimate of Henry's daughter, Princess Mary. Thanks to arrangements made with Catherine of Aragon by Parr's mother, one of the Queen's ladies, to enroll her daughter along with Princess Mary under the tutelage of Juan Luis Vives, she received the most advanced Christian humanist education then thought suitable for a Tudor royal female and the other children admitted to her nursery.[2] But, however well lettered and latined she was, such a female education did not constitute a sufficient incentive to authorship (as opposed to translation or patronage) for any woman of the earlier Tudor – that is, the pre-Elizabethan – period. In that period the catalysts for female authorship were education to a point of secure literacy – not necessarily including Latin, as in Parr's case – and the *sine qua non*, a conversion to Protestantism, with its emphasis on the equality of all souls before God and its urgent imperative to share the soul-saving news of the Gospel in order to make other Christians aware of their own accountability to God for their spiritual state.[3]

If the categories of the compilation and the familiar letter are excluded, Katherine Parr is the first certain instance in English of a woman writer.[4] Her first work, *Prayers or Meditations*, minutely modifies excerpts from Book 3 of Thomas à Kempis's *Imitation of Christ* in Richard Whitford's English translation published in about 1530. The end result moves Parr beyond adaptative translation into original composition while still holding to enough common ground in Christian orthodoxy to satisfy her religiously conservative husband, Henry VIII.[5] The publication of Parr's *Prayers or Meditations* in June 1545 with the King's authorization thus predates by more than a year the clandestine publication of Anne Askew's *First* (1546) and *Latter Examination* (1547). Askew, a member of Parr's circle of ladies, records the investigation and condemnation for Protestant heresies that brought her to death at the stake.[6] Understandably Parr would withhold her account of her own conversion to an objectionably Lutheran strain of Protestantism from the notice of a violent husband who was sure to disapprove. She published her *Lamentation of a Sinner* at the safe interval of nine months after Henry VIII's death.[7]

The intense self-reckoning into which Parr plunges in her *Lamentation* makes clear that her book owes its existence to another book, which she terms 'the booke of the crucifixe'. She declares:

> This crucifix is the boke, wherin God hath included all thinges and hath most compendiously written therein, all truth, profitable and necessary for our salvacion. Therfore let us indevour our selfes to studye thys booke, that we (beyng lightened with the spirite of god) may geve hym thankes for so great a benefite. (*L*, sig. Ciir-v).

As she proceeds, Parr elaborates the metaphoric relation between 'book' and not so much 'the crucifix' as 'the crucifixion' – the significance of the action of Christ's love for human souls rather than the material image or icon of it. 'Inwardlye to behold Christ crucified upon the crosse', says Parr, 'is the best and godliest med-itacion that can be' (*L*, sig. Bviiiᵛ). 'To learne to knowe truly our owne sinnes, is to study in the booke of the crucifixe, by continuall conversacion in fayth... . If we looke further in thys booke, we shall see Christes greate victory upon the crosse' (*L*, sigs. Ciiʳ⁻ᵛ). 'We may see also in Christe crucified, the bewtie of the soule, better then in all the bookes of the worlde. For who that with lively fayth, seeth and feleth in spirite, that Christe the sonne of god, is dead for the satisfiying and the purifiyng of the soule, shall se that his soule, is appoynted for the very tabernacle and mansion of the … majestie and honour of god' (*L*, sigs. Bviiiᵛ–Ciʳ).

This odd metaphor of the book of the crucifix or crucifixion becomes the vehicle for Parr's figuration of a true apprehension of Christian faith as a process of intently reading the one message that really matters for the relation between Christ and the soul. When I began to consider how to interpret this metaphor, I recognized that I was working with a crucial stretch of text. As a first move, I took the feminist scholar's turn towards autobiography as the likeliest form that gender marking would assume in a woman author's text. I hypothesized a scenario in which the 'book of the crucifix' was a metaphor coalescing those definitive developments in Katherine Parr's experience that brought her to the authorship of her *Lamentation*. These developments would include her superb educa-tion; the authority that as Queen of England she learned to exercise through writing – in particular, the letters and proclamations that she issued when Henry appointed her Regent while he undertook the reconquest of lost English territories in France in the summer and autumn of 1544; and, finally, her conversion as a mature woman from the Catholicism of her girlhood to a Protestantism rendered unmistakable by her embrace of justification by faith (this last apparently a consequence of the daily consultations that Henry required her to have with Thomas Cranmer, Archbishop of Canterbury and ranking member of the Privy Council, while she acted as Regent).[8]

On further reflection I imagined that, while a gender factor might account for the bookish character of the metaphor, a gener-ational factor might account for its oddity. The mixed modalities of Parr's 'book of the crucifix' might be read as a mark of the transitional mentality of a person born about 1513, before the printing press had gathered much momentum as a cultural medium, but so placed as to witness at first hand its steadily expanding force and impact. Moreover, the components of the metaphor – half text, half image – might be interpreted as trace elements in the experience of an adult convert to Protestantism, that religion of the Book *par excellence*, who in growing up had been habituated to older visual modes and to the use of images in Catholic worship. However, for all of these imagined autobiographical resonances, confirming the factors of gender and generation – Parr's historical specificity – to hold as determinants of my proposed interpretation, there was a condition that the metaphor of 'the book of the crucifix' really had to fulfil. It had to be Parr's own creation. I wanted to believe that it was, of course, and yet I suspected that it might not be.

While working on my 1988 article on *The Lamentation of a Sinner*, I hoped to resolve my uncertainty about the originality of Parr's metaphor, but my findings were negative. I found some weak support for my hunch that the book of the crucifix was a metaphorical oddity of early modern date because none of the indices to writers of the Church in either the Latin or the Greek series of the Migne *Patrologia* included 'book' among the profuse imagistic equivalences that they listed for Christ's cross.[9] Moreover, since the *Lamentation* begins with Parr's account of coming to awareness of her justification by faith in Christ and thus offers the first conversion narrative in English, I looked in Luther, Tyndale and other early Tudor Protestants for adumbrations of her metaphor of the book of the crucifix. But there too I turned up nothing significantly similar.[10] The closest I came overall in that research was a passage in Erasmus's *Enchiridion Militis Christiani* (written 1501, published 1503, 1st enlarged edn, 1518), a book which Parr is known to have owned. Erasmian piety, moreover, is the best publicized of Parr's prominent interests as Queen.[11] In his seventeenth rule Erasmus advises

> that thou mayest with ... profyte, in thy mynde recorde the mistery of the cross: It shalbe hovefull that every man prepare unto hym selfe a certayne way and godly crafte ... Suche may the crafte be / that in crucifyeng of every one of thyne affectyons, thou mayste applye that parte of the crosse whiche most spe-

cially therto agreeth. For there is not at all any maner eyther temptacion eyther adversyte, whiche hath not his proper remedy in the crosse.[12]

This passage focuses the extremities of inward spirituality and struggle on the figure of Christ crucified, as Parr does in the first-person soul-searching that opens her *Lamentation*, but Erasmus offers no intimation of a book of the crucifix. Could I conclude that the metaphor was Parr's own? Clearly not. I could only conclude that gender and generation had not been ruled out as its possible autobiographical determinants.

In due course I discovered the exact formulation, 'the book of the crucifix', in a sermon by John Fisher, Bishop of Rochester, who together with Thomas More was beheaded as a traitor in 1535 for refusing to swear the Oath of Supremacy. The sermon containing the metaphor was preached on an unspecified Good Friday, for which no scholar has been able to fix a year. However, a passing reference to 'the B. of R. Innocent' (if this phrasing can be trusted to be Fisher's own and not a printer's interpolation) seems to me to provide reasonable grounds for dating the sermon to the period 1531–4, a time when the nomenclature 'bishop of Rome' would have been *de rigueur* for any public reference in England to a pope and when Fisher himself was shifting from acquiescence to resistance regarding Henry VIII's claimed governorship of the English Church.[13] When and how Parr became acquainted with Fisher's Good Friday sermon is unknown; its transmission and eventual printing are as uncertain as the year that he preached it. If she heard it between 1531 and 1534 when she was the wife of John Neville, Lord Latimer, a ranking peer in Parliament, she would just have turned 20 years of age and have been a Catholic at that time. But it is easy to see why this Good Friday sermon attracted her attention and stayed in her memory, for it is a conceptually ingenious and spiritually stirring composition.[14]

At no juncture in Fisher's long preaching career, from about 1501 until its abrupt suspension when he was arraigned for treason in 1534, was it permissible to own or read an English Bible without authorization from one's bishop; such was the perceived strength of the menace that Lollardy still posed to Catholic orthodoxy.[15] In keeping with these historically specific constraints, Fisher maintains that the crucifix will serve as well to arouse a right response as the scripture for Good Friday will. He will infuse the physical object with signification drawn from two verses of the Old Testament reading assigned for that day in the liturgy. The words will literally be read onto the object of devotion, thus merging the biblical text into the ceremonial action of the rite for Good Friday – the veneration of the crucifix standardly mounted on the grille or screen separating the church nave from the choir and its altar. So Fisher opens by signalling his interpretative intervention that will make a book of a crucifix:

> The Prophet Ezechyell telleth that hee sawe a booke spread before him, the which was written both within and without … . This booke to our purpose may bee taken unto us, the Crucifixe, the which doubtlesse is a merveylouse booke, as wee shall shewe heereafter. (*S*, 388)

Fisher offers an object of devotion – 'the image of the Crucifixe' – as a substitute equivalent to scripture in evoking Christ's consummate love for humankind:

> Who that will exercise this lesson, he shall … come to a great knowledge both of Christ & of him selfe. A man may easily say & thinke with him selfe (beholding in his hart the Image of the Crucifixe), who arte thou and who am I.

This question, says Fisher, was posed by St Francis of Assisi, in whose exemplary spirituality 'meditation and imagination' were 'so earnest and so continuall, that the token of the five woundes of Christ, were imprinted and ingraved in thys holy Sancytes bodye' (*S*, 391). Thus promoting the Franciscan spirituality that figures prominently in English religion during Henry's reign, Fisher admits that the devotions of ordinary Christians cannot 'attayne' such 'hygh fruite' as the stigmata. Yet ordinary Christians can take the crucifix, as a book for their instruction, to their hearts:

> Thus who that list with a meeke harte and a true fayth, to muse and to marvayle of this most wonderfull booke (I say of the Crucifixe) hee shall come to more fruitefull knowledge, then many other which dayly studie upon their common bookes. This booke may suffice for the studie of a true christian man, all the dayes of his life. In this boke he may finde all things that be necessarie to the health of his soule. (*S*, 390)

At length, when closing his sermon, Fisher steers away from any possible construing of his book of the crucifix as a call for popular scripture-reading, instead renewing his exhortation to imitate St Francis's devotion to the crucifix as physical object:

> Thus … it is an easie thyng for any man or woman to make these two questions wyth them selfe. O my Lorde that wouldest dye for me upon a Cross, how noble and excelent art thou? & agayne, how wretched and myserable am I? (*S*, 391–2)

After I found the book of the crucifix metaphor in Fisher, my feminist scholar's hypothesis about its uniquely autobiographical expressiveness for Katherine Parr lay pretty much in ruins. She had not created her key metaphor. Fisher ostensibly had. He seems to imply this when he introduces it: 'This booke *to our purpose may bee taken unto us*, the Crucifixe, the which doubtlesse is a merveylouse booke, as wee shall shewe heereafter' (my emphasis). But I had another problem and that was the utter paucity of other auto-referential markings in Parr's text. Even if I shifted my interpretative focus away from the book of the crucifix metaphor – the site, for me, of paramount intensity and expressiveness – there was only one certain self-identification of the first-person speaker in the entire *Lamentation*. This was Parr's passing reference to 'king Henry the eight, my most sovraigne favourable lord and husband' in the course of hailing him as a Moses who had brought God's English people out of bondage to the papal 'Pharao', 'Bishop of Rome' (*L*, sig. Dvi[r]).[16] Confronting the hard textual facts, I considered whether I could salvage autobiographical significance for Parr's *Lamentation* by pursuing a generational difference even if I had to give up a gendered one. Could the oddity of the metaphor in question be usefully tracked to an origin in an early, transitional phase of modern print culture?

Fisher was born about 1469, six years before William Caxton set up the first English printing press in Westminster, making him Parr's senior by two generations (44 years). Perhaps Fisher could be situated as an exponent of the late medieval manuscript culture in which he came to adulthood and in which the Lollards' fervour for judging all things by God's book continued to be rigorously suppressed. Would a corresponding generational placement of Katherine Parr throw significant light on what she did with Fisher's metaphor? Certainly, the circumstances prompting Fisher's coinage had radically altered by the time Parr used it to figure her justification by faith. Fisher himself had been discredited as a spokesman for Catholic orthodoxy to the extent of suffering a traitor's death. What is more, vernacular scripture reading was so far from being illegal by 1538–40 that Henry VIII, at that date, was mandating that the so-called Great Bible, whose publication he had authorized, be made available for public reading in the parish churches of the realm.

To work towards an interpretation in terms of a generational divide, I realized, would prioritize the differences between Fisher's text and Parr's. There is conspicuous evidence that Fisher envisaged his book of the crucifix as an artifact dating from before the era of print. He exhibits a truly metaphysical ingenuity as he details why he calls the crucifix a book. A book has 'boardes' (still a current term for 'hard covers' among bibliographers), leaves, lines, writings and 'letters booth small and great'. The two planks of Christ's cross are the 'boardes' of the book of the crucifix, on which its leaves, 'the armes, the handes, legges and feete, with the other members of his most precious and blessed body' are spread. No 'Parchement skynne' was ever so stretched and hung up to dry in order to make a writing surface as Christ's body was stretched and laid out upon the cross. And on its spread skin the lines to be read are the marks of the whip lashes, the red letters his blood, the blue letters his bruises, the five capital letters the great wounds in his two hands, his two feet and his side, 'for bycause no parte of thys booke shoulde bee unwritten' (*S*, 393, 394, 395, 396). Fisher develops his extended conceit of the crucifix as an illuminated manuscript. He then proceeds to read this manneristically drawn image, so evocative of figure groupings in early sixteenth-century Netherlandish and Rhineland paintings of Christ's crucifixion and deposition from the cross, as a 'wryting' of 'lamentation' (*S*, 397).

Parr inflects the text in a systematically different fashion. While the *Lamentation* engages as lavishly as the Good Friday sermon does in a rhetoric of emotion – apostrophe, rhetorical questions, serial parallelisms, stark antitheses – her treatment of the crucifixion never becomes graphic and pictorial like his; instead, it remains consistently theological and phenomenological. Parr opens with 'lamentation', the key word of her title and unfolds her concomitant shame, confusion, misery, perversity and presumption as she develops her self-accusation of being altogether insensible of Christ as her crucified saviour – being, that is, without the faith that justifies:

I did as much as was in me, to obfuscate and darken the great benefite of Christes passion: ... And therfore I count my selfe one of the moste wicked and myserable sinners, bycause I have ben so much contrary to Christ my saviour.... . What cause nowe have I to lament, mourne, sigh and wepe for my life and time so evil spent? (*L*, sigs. Av^r-v, Aviiᵛ)

Parr's turn from phenomenology to theology proceeds through reiterations of Tyndale's key term for scripture, the 'promises', to explain 'what maketh me so bolde and hardy, to presume to come to the lord ... who is only the Advocat and mediatour betwene god and man to helpe and relyve me, ... beyng so greate a Sinner' – 'trulye nothinge, but hys owne woorde', 'the promise of Christ'. 'He promiseth and bindeth him selfe by hys worde, ... to all them that aske hym with true fayth: ... For fayth is the foundacion and grounde ... : and therfore I wil saye, Lord encreace my fayth' (*L*, sigs. Bii^r-v, Biiiᵛ).[17] She shifts to merge theology with phenomenology in giving this account of the advent of her justifying faith:

I never had this unspeakeable and most high charitie and abundant love of god, printed and fixed in my heart dulye, tyll it pleased god of hys mere grace, mercy and pitie, to open myne eyes, makyng me to see and beholde with the eye of lively fayth, Christ crucified to be myne only saviour and redemer. For then I beganne (and not before) to perceyve and ... knowe Christ my Saviour and redemer. (*L*, sig. Bvᵛ)

'Therfore inwardlye to behold Christ crucified upon the crosse, is the best and godliest meditacion that can be,' Parr affirms and precisely at this point introduces her metaphor:

Therfore to learne to knowe truly ... is to study in the booke of the crucifixe, by continuall conversacion in fayth: ... this crucifix is the boke, wherin God hath ... most compendiously written ... all truth profitable and necessary for our salvacion. (*L*, sigs. Bviiiᵛ, Ciiʳ)

Viewed along a generational divide, it is Fisher who returns the book of the crucifix to earlier roots in Franciscan devotion, there seeking to renew the mystical rapture of the saint with his divinely conferred stigmata as a talisman against the continuing danger of Bible-reading by the laity.[18] It is Parr who brings the book of the crucifix into Protestant print culture, promoting Bible-reading by the laity through her equation of this metaphor with the promises of the Gospel, apprehended in Tyndalian fashion as the felt truth of one's personal salvation. With these findings, however, I found myself confronting another question. Could I sustain the premium on difference that resulted from emphasizing the generational factor and yet claim to have fairly interpreted what, intertextually considered, is a relation of verbal identity – the same words, 'book of the crucifix'? I had yet taken no critical notice of the measure of likeness between Fisher's and Parr's texts, so I began to examine how far this extended. Beyond the verbal identity of the key metaphor, I found that other likenesses were generated by a further intertextual relation: their shared recourse to Erasmian motifs and themes. This material promotes perceptions of continuity in Fisher's and Parr's religious experience by documenting, for each, a pair of connections with the two best-known works of Erasmus in England, the *Enchiridion Militis Christiani* and the *Paraclesis*.

In the *Enchiridion*, a book which Fisher as well as Parr is recorded as owning,[19] Erasmus variously calls the saving act of divine love that is Christ's death upon the cross 'philosophia Christi' and 'a Christian man's book'. Fisher's Good Friday sermon echoes the one formulation, referring to the crucifixion as 'another higher Philosophie which is above nature', 'the very Philosophie of Christian people'.[20] Parr echoes the alternative Erasmian formulation because she refuses to refer to Christian faith as philosophy, in keeping with the Protestant categorization of philosophy as 'carnall and humane reasons' (*L*, sig. Aviv). After invoking St Paul, who called Christ 'the wisedome of god', she can join with Erasmus in identifying personal, experiential knowledge of 'Christ crucified' with what is learned from study in 'a christian mans boke'  the titular metaphor of the *Enchiridion Militis Christiani* – and then turn directly to identify this with 'the booke of the crucifixe' (*L*, sig. Civ–Ciir).

The second instance where Erasmus serves as intertext is the notable passage in *Paraclesis* which exhorts vernacular reading of scripture upon all ranks of society, high and low, men and women, not even excluding the ploughboy in the field. Steering clear of Bible-reading, Fisher urges devotion to the crucifix as the truest employment of all Christians: 'every person both ryche and poore', 'the poor laborer ... when he is at plough earyng his grounde and when hee goeth to hys pastures to see hys Cattayle', 'the rich man ... in his business ... . And the poore women also ... when they be spinning... . The ryche weomen also in everie lawfull occupation that they have to doe' (*S*, 391–2).[21] For her part, when Parr climaxes her *Lamentation* with a comprehensive vision of 'all sortes of people' who 'loke to theyr owne vocacion and ordeyne the same according to Christes doctrine' (*L*, sig. Gii$^{r-v}$) – citing preachers, laymen, fathers, mothers, children, servants, matrons and young women – she echoes the same passage in *Paraclesis*. And since 'Christes doctrine', the Bible, is the book supremely emphasized by Erasmus and Parr, it is they who draw closest in this second intertextual tie. Thus, despite marked local differences in their respective appropriations, an intertextual approach to interpretation leaves Fisher and Parr looking significantly alike in aspiring towards a Christian universalism that Erasmus had conceptualized for them both.[22]

So much for what might be done respectively to interpret Fisher's and Parr's books of the crucifix by emphasizing a generational factor on the one hand, and intertextual relations – a key metaphor compounded with Erasmian affinities – on the other. Clearly there is a complex weave of differences and similarities here. Is the one to count as more significant than the other? And, if so, on what grounds should the judgment be staked – on intrinsic grounds of content or on extrinsic evaluation of the methodology employed? For example, since intertextual relations are classed with the history of ideas, now much discredited for failure to reckon with concrete social realities, we are likely to prefer a generational factor that deals more directly with them.[23] But this very mention of dealing with one's objects of interpretation raises yet another question for me. Can I really claim that a two-generation gap in age and experience in Henrician England accounts accurately and adequately for the characterization I have just given of Fisher's and Parr's metaphors? This is what I need to claim if I am to assign this factor the role of a basic determinant in my interpretation. As I began by stating, it is reassuring to think that our current approaches to texts by way of race, class or gender (or generation) are anchored by the combined weight of materiality and ideology and are thereby well grounded. But what if our interpretations by way of any or all of these factors come up short, as I think this one of mine manifestly does?

I would want to claim that a more primary determinant of the difference between Fisher's and Parr's metaphors is the emergent (and here clearly detectable) difference between a Catholic and a Protestant. The cutting edge is provided by Parr's central insistence on justification by faith – a tenet that the Council of Trent, which began meeting in 1548 to codify Roman Catholic orthodoxy, found unassimilable from first to last.[24] Add to that the fact that the two are historical contemporaries who deal in older and newer ways with the book of the crucifix and the authority of Erasmus – this gives us the generational factor, but not as primary. Then add that the two are a man and a woman – this gives us the factor of gender compounded with the further difference between Fisher's celibate state and Parr's married one, but still without a discernible effect on their divergent handlings of the book of the crucifix metaphor. Then add that the two are a Queen and a Bishop, a cleric and a layperson respectively – this gives us two more rank or status factors that criss-cross gender by assigning different values to Parr and Fisher, but still without discernible impact on the textual difference, the metaphor in question. Yet what of the difference that seems to me so determinative here, the difference between a Catholic and a Protestant? It is obvious that religion presently has no theoretical standing comparable to that of race, class or gender as a primary determinant of interpretation. If religion goes anywhere in current categories, it is lumped (like intertextuality) with the history of ideas.[25] So where does my interpretation leave me if I aspire to make it in newer methodological terms? At the close of this essay I shall return to the question of constituting religion as a fourth primary determinant.

Here, however, I want to reflect on how troubling the recognized primary determinant of gender, in particular, has become for me in the interpretation of religious texts by women authors, particularly. In my earlier article I argued that Parr's *Lamentation* challenges and baffles the prediction of feminist methodology that the fact of a woman author will eventuate in significant, gender-specific textual markings. For, apart from an arguably feminine-sounding disclaimer that 'I have certeynly no curious learning to defende ... but a simple zele and earnest love to the truth, inspired of god, who promiseth to powre his spirite upon al flesshe: which I have by the grace of god (whom I moste humblie honour) felt in my selfe to be true' and the aforementioned brief reference to Henry VIII as 'my most sovraigne favourable lord and husband' (*L*, sigs. Bvii<sup>r</sup>-v, Dvi<sup>r</sup>),

Parr's 'I' renders her gender all but undetectable. At best, gender in the two texts in question is a matter of inference from authorial positioning: Fisher's enactment of the male-only office of preacher as he publicly instructs the people with the words of the prophet Ezekiel, Parr's private self-accounting with no overtones of a public context or a judgement on others. It is the unsparing honesty and lack of individuation in that self-accounting, moreover, for which William Cecil's prefatory letter to the *Lamentation* most highly praises Parr as author, noting that she asks and makes no allowances for her gender or her royal rank.[26]

Instead, Parr deploys her 'I's and 'me's', to construct what I have termed a generic and genderless Christian response to the message of salvation through faith in Christ crucified. 'Truly I have taken no lytle small thing upon me, firste to set furth my whole stubbernes and contempt in wordes, the which is incomprehensible in thought (as it is in the Psalme) who understandeth hys faultes?' she exclaims, assimilating the pronoun 'his' to her case (*L*, sig. Ai^v). Again, she laments in a similar gender elision, 'And I most presumptuously thinking nothing of Christ crucified, went about to set furth mine owne righteousnes, saying with the proude Pharisey. Good lord I thanke the, I am not like other men' (*L*, sig. Avi^r). Thus, as I formerly read Parr's conversion narrative, its first-person author compiles the traits of an Everyman-Everywoman, a generic Christian soul: blind ignorance, cold and dead knowledge, a stone-hard heart softening into penitential lament, a dejected conscience suddenly overcome and joyed by the gift of divine love and forgiveness.[27] I tied these generic traits in with the other, considerable evidence in the *Lamentation* of the universalism – the attempt to reclaim the etymology and the lower-case 'c' for 'catholicism' – and the personalism that energized early Protestants in their conviction that all souls are equal before God and that every soul is individually accountable to God. Parr conceives and casts herself as a subject for discourse on the shared grounds of humanity confronting divinity. Such (as mine is), she implies, are all souls; such (as mine is) is the human soul.

Since recent theoretical developments have split off social positionality (masculine and feminine roles) from biology (sexed bodies) in defining gender as a determinant for interpretation, I am compelled to question from a number of angles my earlier claim that the 'I' characterized and voiced in Parr's *Lamentation* is a genderless, generic Christian soul. In the first place, on the theoretical front where I began, if gender positionality is split off from sexed bodies, does gender as a primary determinant retain any measure of its theoretically desirable materiality, or only its ideological charge?[28] And if only the latter, what are the implications for gender as an alleged primary determinant of experience and the language used to talk about experience? Does splitting gender from anatomy plunge us back into the regresses of verbal indeterminacy from which we have sought and thought to free ourselves?

If gender is to figure now as a relational position, moreover, who can dispute the old dictum that all souls are feminine – or shall we say feminized? – when they register a personal relation to God? (that is, the Judeo-Christian God). Some of the wealth of evidence for this dictum is familiar and scriptural: the erotic love between Christ and his bride, the soul, in the traditional allegorization of the Song of Solomon; the prophet Hosea's figuration of the idolatry of his fellow Jews in the lineaments of his own adulterous wife. Where, I want to know, does the splitting of gender from biological sex leave us in interpreting devotional and mystical texts written in the first person – texts in which religious affect predominates – no matter who their authors? Are such texts to be treated as gendered feminine? as generically feminine? as confounding gender difference because this determinant only operates meaningfully in human social relations, and not in relations between humans and the divine? Caroline Bynum, who has done more than anyone to advance thinking on these questions, shows their extreme intractability by gesturing in opposite directions on the same page. On the one hand, she signals 'the feminist insight that all human beings are "gendered" – that is, that there is no such thing as generic *homo religiosus*' – and on the other proclaims: 'Gender-related symbols, in their full complexity, may refer to gender in ways that affirm or reverse it, support or question it; or they may, in their basic meaning, have little at all to do with male or female roles. Thus our analysis admits that gender-related symbols are sometimes "about" values other than gender.'[29]

In my view, the trouble that I have faced in seeking to analyse and interpret such sites of primary significance as the book of the crucifix metaphor is likely to be alleviated only by making a case for religion – understood, in the present case of Fisher and Parr, in terms of Catholicism and Protestantism – as exercising a potentially determinative force in human life and its linguistic and social forms, just as race or ethnicity, class and gender (and generation?)

are already taken to do. If religion is accorded such equal status, it will emerge as a primary determinant in certain contexts, just as the others do. At present these primaries appear an ill-sorted lot, showing how rough and unready the state of theorizing about them is. None the less, it seems clearly desirable to me that materiality be predicated as a feature of all of them and be explicitly specified for all of them – religion too, if it is to be accorded the status of a primary determinant.[30] It seems equally clear to me that much more explicit allowance for historical and situational variation must be made regarding the material component of each recognized primary determinant in interpretation. If this is done, then it may prove possible, for any given determinant, to correlate a decline in its material manifestation and perceptibility with a reduction in its capacity for determination. In the late twentieth century, blue-jeaned everybodies apparently bear witness to the waning power of class distinctions, while developing surgical and endocrinological procedures for transsexuality may weaken the power of gender as a primary sociobiological determinant. As for religion in our own Western culture and era, two among many indications of its potential to figure as a primary determinant include the strongly materialized practices that mark conflicting stands on the issue of legalized abortion and the distinctive clothing worn by such diverse groups as orthodox Jews, the Amish and members of the Nation of Islam and other Muslims.

If allowance for historical and situational variation is extended to Tudor England, we find class as a factor of primary difference being read as materially encoded in sumptuary laws and a network of protocols of deference and precedence, not in bodily features as such. This is why pretenders like Perkin Warbeck could be genuinely dangerous, if the pretences materialized in their dress and bearing were convincing. Similarly, gender as a factor of primary difference in Tudor England was read as materially encoded in female bodies viewed as male ones fallen short of fulfilment.[31] This is why the accession of Elizabeth I to the throne of England, for example, required to be explained as a special providence of God, with divine right merely a secondary consideration.[32] Religion might be argued to read as a factor of primary difference in sixteenth-century England on analogous material grounds: its sharply rival sets of objectifications of the holy.

Positing religion as such a materialized factor would immediately pick out as significant the contrasting object referents for

Fisher's and Parr's books of the crucifix, both as exemplifications of the phenomenon and as sites where the determinative strength of the factor of religion thus materialized can be weighed interpretively. More broadly, positing religion as a materialized factor might help to make legible and intelligible certain currently under-emphasized aspects of massively deployed social energies in six-teenth- and earlier seventeenth-century England. Although iconoclasm has drawn appreciable scholarly attention,[33] the long-sustained contestations over sacramental dogma and its attendant modalities of worship (themselves encoded in and as bodily practices) have not yet done so. I am thinking not only of the centrality of John Foxe's *Acts and Monuments* to Reformation English culture, but also of the voluminous book wars fought over transubstantiation by generation after generation: Thomas More against John Frith, Stephen Gardiner against Nicholas Ridley and Thomas Cranmer, Thomas Harding against John Jewel.

By the same token turned to its obverse face, can we then proceed, as I suggested above, to theorize that race or class or gender or generation or religion lose force as primary determinants in specific historical and situational contexts when and if they diminish (or lose) their material component? Clearly there is more hard work to be done at a fundamental level before we can feel sanguine about making our criticism and historical work be about something that counts as real. Towards what I am inclined to regard as not just the desideratum but the necessity of theoretically constituting religion on a par with the triad of race, class and gender as a material determinant of human experience and expression, however, the way at present looks long and hard – given the sweeping negativism of Freudian and post-Freudian, Marxian and modern secular predispositions regarding religion. But I am prepared to make a start.

## NOTES

1.  In my view too little notice has been given to Richard Helgerson's *Self-Crowned Laureates: Spenser, Jonson, Milton and the Literary System* (Berkeley and London, 1983), with its cogent definition of 'the literary system' in terms of generational patterns. Robert O. Evans has my thanks for calling my attention to the pioneering work of Anthony Esler, *The Aspiring Mind of the Elizabethan Younger Generation* (Durham, NC, 1966).

2.  For these biographical particulars, see Anthony Martienssen, *Queen Katherine Parr* (London and New York, 1973), pp. 18–28.

3.  See the treatment of the (uneven) gradation from translation to original authorship in Elaine Beilin, *Redeeming Eve: Women Writers of the English Renaissance* (Princeton, NJ, 1987), chs. 1–3 and the essays on Margaret More Roper, Elizabeth Tudor and Anne Askew, in Margaret P. Hannay, ed., *Silent But for the Word: Tudor Women as Patrons, Translators and Writers of Religious Works* (Kent, OH, 1985).

4.  Julian of Norwich's scholarly editors take the view that she dictated her *Showings of Divine Love* (*c.* 1393), while the *Book of Margery Kempe* (*c.* 1436–8) was unquestionably dictated by its illiterate author. See Edmund Colledge and James Walsh, eds, *A Book of Showings to the Anchoress Julian of Norwich* (Toronto, 1978), Vol. I: Introduction; and *The Book of Margery Kempe*, ed. Sanford B. Meech, with annotation by Hope Emily Allen, EETS orig. ser. 212 (London, 1940), p. 153, for an extended passage in which Margery's scribe asserts his presence and describes his misgivings about some of what she dictates to him. The *Book of St Albans* (1486), attributed in its earliest printings to Dame Juliana Berners, traditionally identified as the prioress of the nunnery of Sopwell in Hertfordshire, contains treatises on hawking, hunting and heraldry which have been analysed as compilations by different hands. See *The Boke of Saint Albans by Dame Juliana Berners*, ed. William Blades (London, 1901), pp. 6–14.

5.  See my 'Devotion as Difference: Intertextuality in Queen Katherine Parr's *Prayers or Meditations* (1545)', *Huntington Library Quarterly* 53 (1990): 171–97.

6.  On the relation between Askew and Parr, see Martienssen, 189–223, building on John Foxe, 'The Trouble of Queene Katherine Parre', *Actes and Monuments* (London, 1570), 2: 1422–5. On the historical significance of this case, see Paula McQuade, '"Except that they had offended the Lawe": Gender and Jurisprudence in *The Examinations of Anne Askew*', *Literature & History*, 3rd ser., 3.2 (1994): 1–14 and Elaine Beilin's edition of Askew's *Examinations*, forthcoming in the Oxford University Press series, *Women Writers in English, 1350–1850*.

7.  Henry VIII died in January 1547. Parr's reference to him as an English Moses who has led God's people out of captivity to Pharaoh, the bishop of Rome, clearly indicates that the King is still alive (Katherine Parr, *The lamentacion of a sinner, made by the most vertuous Ladie, Quene Caterin, ...* (London, 1547), sigs. Dv$^v$–Dvi$^r$). Further citations will be abbreviated *L* and incorporated parenthetically in my text. For discussion, see Janel Mueller, 'A Tudor Queen Finds Voice: Katherine Parr's *Lamentation of a Sinner*', in Heather Dubrow and Richard Strier, eds, *The Historical Renaissance: New Essays on Tudor and Stuart Literature and Culture* (Chicago, 1988) pp. 15–47.

8.  Martienssen, pp. 180, 200–5; for discussion, see Mueller, 'A Tudor Queen Finds Voice', 28–33.

9.  To illustrate the relative remoteness of any analogues: Christ is called a 'book' (liber) by Rabanus Maurus (*PL*, vol. 112, col. 987) and by St Bruno the Carthusian (*PL*, vol. 152, cols 545, 805); he is

called 'a book written within and without' (liber scriptus intus et foris) by Adam Scotus, echoing Ezekiel 2:10 (*PL*, vol. 198, col. 774). Of the cross, Alcuin pronounces that it 'is a sign, the sign of the living God' (signum Dei vivi, crucis est signum) (*PL*, vol. 100, col. 1129).

10. Luther comes closest, yet not very close, in articles 20 and 21 of his *Heidelberg Disputation* (May 1518): 'He deserves to be called a theologian ... who comprehends the visible and manifest things of God seen through suffering and the cross' (*Luther's Works*, ed. Helmut T. Lehmann and Harold J. Grimm [Philadelphia, 1957], 31: 52–3).

11. F. Rose-Troup, 'Two Book Bills of Katherine Parr', *The Library*, 3rd ser., 2 (1911): 40–8; James K. McConica, *English Humanists and Reformation Politics* (Oxford, 1965), ch. 7; John N. King, 'Patronage and Piety: The Influence of Catherine Parr', in Hannay, ed., *Silent but for the Word*, p. 48.

12. Erasmus, *Enchiridion Militis Christiani: An English Version*, ed. Anne M. O'Donnell, S.N.D., Early English Text Society. o.s., no. 282 (Oxford, 1981): 178–9. In quoting I have modernized s and u/v and expanded printers' contractions.

13. Convocation first acceded to the royal supremacy in February 1531 after Fisher managed to lodge his famous qualification 'as far as Christ's law allows' and the formal submission of the clergy to the King's headship took place in May 1532, presumably with Fisher's mounting discomfiture. When the Act of Supremacy began to be enforced by oath in the spring of 1534, Fisher explicitly refused to take the oath and was confined to the Tower of London in April. He was executed on 22 June 1535, with More following him to the block on 6 July. See John Guy, *Tudor England* (Oxford, 1988), pp. 128, 131, 135 and Richard Rex, *The Theology of John Fisher* (Cambridge, 1991), p. 9.

14. The *Short-Title Catalogue* lists one edition only (STC 10899) of *A spirituall consolation, written by John Fyssher to hys sister Elizabeth*, to which *A sermon ... very aptely applyed unto the passion of Christ: preached upon a good Friday* is appended in continuous pagination. The ascription of printer and date [W. Carter, 1578?] is derived from the annotated catalogue by A. F. Allison and D. M. Rogers, *The Contemporary Printed Literature of the English Counter-Reformation between 1558 and 1640*, vol. 2 (Aldershot, 1994), where this item is no. 273. This Good Friday sermon has attracted much less critical attention than others by Fisher – his defiance of Luther, his memorial sermon on Henry VII and his series on the Penitential Psalms, for example. Rex, *Theology of John Fisher*, p. 217, notes the cursory discussions by J. W. Blench and Edward Surtz, S. J., but offers only a brief synopsis of his own (46–9).

15. For an authoritative account of Lollardy, see Anne Hudson, *The Premature Reformation* (Oxford, 1988).

16. See, further, my remarks on how Parr 'screens topicality, polemic and personality from her text' and the mutedness of her gender identification (explicit only in her name on the title-page until her late reference to her royal husband), in Mueller, 'A Tudor Queen Finds Voice', 41–2.

17. Compare William Tyndale in *The Parable of the Wicked Mammon* (1529): 'See therefore thou have God's promises in thine heart ... The promises, when they are believed, are they that justify; for they bring the Spirit, which looseth the heart, ... and certifieth us of the goodwill of God unto usward.... Christ is our Redeemer, Saviour, peace, atonement and satisfaction; and hath made amends or satisfaction to Godward for all the sin which they that repent (consenting to the law and believing the promises) do, have done or shall do.... For in the faith which we have in Christ and in God's promises find we mercy, life, favour and peace' (*Doctrinal Treatises and Introductions to Various Portions of the Holy Scriptures*, ed. Henry Walter, Parker Society vol. 25 [Cambridge, 1848], pp. 48, 52, 47).

18. Both Fisher's reference to beholding the image of the crucifix in one's heart and Erasmus's notion of recording the mystery of the cross 'in thy mind' (cited above, p. 5) have affinities with the important devotional trope of 'the book of the heart', the subject of a book-in-progress by Eric Jager.

19. On the importance of the *Enchiridion* as the best single source for Erasmus's conception of the Christian life, see Preserved Smith, *Erasmus: A Study of His Life, Ideals and Place in History* (New York, 1923), pp. 55, 58; John Joseph Mangan, *Life, Character and Influence of Desiderius Erasmus of Rotterdam* (New York, 1927): 1:174; and Johan Huizinga, *Erasmus and the Age of Reformation*, trans. F. Hopman (New York, 1924; New York, 1957), p. 54. Rex, *Theology of John Fisher*, 47, records that Fisher owned a copy of the *Enchiridion*. For Parr, see n. 11.

20. John Fisher, *A Sermon verie fruitfull, godly and learned, upon thys sentence of the Prophet Ezechiell, Lamentationes, Carmen, ...* in *The English Works of John Fisher*, Part I, ed. John E. B. Mayor, Early English Text Society, e. s. no. 27: 389. Subsequent references will be abbreviated *S* and incorporated parenthetically in my text. In quoting I have modernized s and u/v and expanded printers' contractions.

21. I am not implying that Fisher was disingenuous, for current political circumstances sufficed to deter him from any overt endorsement of Erasmus's scripturalist brief in *Paraclesis*. As Rex remarks, 'Fisher seems to have accorded a higher place to scripture and the vernacular in the Christian religion than we have been accustomed to expect of the late medieval English hierarchy' (*Theology of John Fisher*, p. 48; cf. pp. 158–60).

22. Any adequate assessment of the Erasmian likenesses-within-difference that link Fisher's and Parr's texts would, however, also need to reckon with appropriations of *Paraclesis* by Tyndale in his English translation of the work and by Thomas Cromwell and Thomas Cranmer in citing it to defend their vernacular scripturalist program. Parr is not likely to have been ignorant of any of these at the time she wrote her *Lamentation*.

23. For a probing discussion of problems of methodology and subject-matter, see Dominick La Capra, *Rethinking Intellectual History: Texts, Contexts, Language* (Ithaca, NY, 1983), ch. 1.

24. On the importance of justification by faith as a confessional difference as early as the 1540s, see William P. Haugaard, 'Katherine Parr: The Religious Convictions of a Renaissance Queen', *Renaissance Quarterly*, 22 (1969): 346–59.

25. For a sharply reasoned, historically acute argument that religion was the principal category in which sixteenth- and seventeenth-century authors 'thought through' a whole range of vital concerns, see Debora K. Shuger's *Habits of Thought in the English Renaissance* (Berkeley and Los Angeles, 1990).

26. In Cecil's words, 'This good lady thought no shame to detect her sinne, to obteyne remission: no vilenes, to become nothing, to be a membre of him, which is al thinges i[n] all: no folye to forget the wisdome of the worlde, to lerne the Simplicitie of the gospel: at the last, no displeasauntnes to submyt her selfe to the scole of the Crosse, the learning of the crucifixe, the booke of our redempcion, the very obsolute library of goddes mercye and wisdome' (*L*, pp. 8–9). In connection with the lack of gendering in Parr's *Lamentation*, it is difficult to argue for a feminine tactic of silence employed to minimize the presumptive scandal of a Queen of England abasing herself in print, when Cecil praises her outspokeness about her spiritual state.

27. Barbara Kiefer Lewalski, *Protestant Poetics and the Seventeenth Century Religious Lyric* (Princeton, NJ, 1979), provides a pathbreaking account of the composite features of this Protestant subjectivity, revising that of Louis L. Martz in *The Poetry of Meditation: A Study in English Religious Literature of the Seventeenth Century*, rev. edn (New Haven, CT, 1962).

28. See, especially, Judith P. Butler's *Gender Trouble: Feminism and the Subversion of Identity* (New York, 1990) and *Bodies That Matter: On the Discursive Limits of 'Sex'* (New York, 1993).

29. Caroline Walker Bynum, 'Introduction: The Complexity of Symbols', in *Gender and Religion: On the Complexity of Symbols*, ed. Caroline Walker Bynum, Stevan Harrell and Paula Richman (Boston, 1986), p. 2.

30. Admittedly, Louis Althusser has provided for the determining force of ideas in the cultural-materialist process by offering a fundamental revision of the Marxian binary of 'base' and 'superstructure'. His influential work on 'ideological state apparatuses', a category which easily accommodates the political mandates of Reformation and Counter-Reformation Christianity, permits cultural potency to be claimed for religion without invoking considerations of materiality. However, it seems obvious to me that race or ethnicity, class, gender and generation have attained the status of primary determinants because, in large measure, they register perceptually as physical facts about human beings. I want to pursue the possibility that religion can be put on the same footing.

31. See Thomas Laqueur, *Making Sex: Body and Gender from the Greeks to Freud* (Cambridge, MA, 1990), ch. 2.

32. See Constance Jordan, *Renaissance Feminism: Literary Texts and Political Models* (Ithaca, NY, 1990), pp. 131, 202.

33.  This literature notably includes Margaret Aston, *England's Iconoclasts* (New York, 1988), John R. Phillips, The *Reformation of Images* (Chicago, 1970) and Eamon Duffy, *The Stripping of the Altars: Traditional Religion in England, ca. 1400–ca. 1580* (New Haven, CT, 1992), as well as work on literary implications, especially in Milton studies: see Lana Cable, *Carnal Rhetoric: Milton's Iconoclasm and the Poetics of Desire* (Durham, NC, 1995), Ernest B. Gilman, *Down Went Dagon: Iconoclasm and Poetry in the English Reformation* (Chicago, 1986) and David Loewenstein, *Milton and the Drama of History: Historical Vision, Iconoclasm and the Literary Imagination* (New York, 1990).

# 2

# Southwell's Remains: Catholicism and Anti-Catholicism in Early Modern England

## Arthur F. Marotti

There is tremendous talk here of Jesuits and more fables perhaps are told about them than were told of old about monsters. For as to the origin of these men, their way of life, their institute, their morals and teaching, their plans and actions, stories of all sorts are spread abroad, not only in private conversation but also in public sermons and printed books and these contradict one another and have a striking resemblance to dreams.

> Robert Persons to Alfonso Agazzari, August 1581[1]

> But now he's gone and my idolatrous fancy
> Must sanctify his relics.

Shakespeare, *Alls Well That Ends Well*, 1.1.100–1

English nationalism rests on a foundation of anti-Catholicism. In the sixteenth and seventeenth centuries English identity was defined as Protestant, so Roman Catholicism, especially in its post-Tridentine, Jesuit manifestations was cast as the hated and dangerous antagonist, most fearfully embodied in a papacy that claimed the right to depose monarchs. Politically intrusive popes' vision of *international* order directly conflicted with the kind of political autonomy implicit in the ideology of the newly emerging nation-state. As the model of a polity, the Protestant nation contrasted most vividly with a transnational entity such as the Holy Roman Empire, just as in reform theology the spiritually enlightened, scripture-reading 'godly' believer contrasted with the 'superstitious' devotee of a corporate Catholicism in which spiritual authorization always came (in mediated form) from above through a hierarchical Church, an institution deformed through centuries of bureaucratic overgrowth and non-scripturally-based traditions. From the time of Queen Elizabeth's accession in 1558 to that of the Glorious Revolution of 1688, Catholicism was for the majority of nationalistic English both an enemy within and an enemy without. A vocabulary of anti-Catholicism or anti-Popery was developed and deployed for a wide variety of national and international political circumstances, becoming immersed finally in the post-1688 era in a Whig narrative of English history.[2]

In the early modern era, a number of religiously coded events helped shape English nationhood and the narrative accounts of English history: these include the Northern Rebellion of 1569,[3] the Spanish Armada of 1588, the Gunpowder Plot of 1605, the proposed Spanish match for James I's son Charles in the early 1620s, the Irish Rebellion of 1641, the 'Popish Plot' of the late 1670s and the Glorious Revolution of 1688. The failures of the Northern Rebellion, the Spanish Armada and Gunpowder Plot were absorbed into a Providential narrative of deliverance in which God periodically saved an elect Protestant nation from the assaults of the forces of the Antichrist, the last transformed into a national holiday of thanksgiving, Gunpowder Treason Day or Guy Fawkes Day.[4]

The late-feudal rebellion of the Northern Earls in 1569 was more a local and conservative aristocratic backlash against the continuing Tudor centralizing of power and the elevation of 'new men' in the growing bureaucratic nation-state,[5] but it was portrayed as primarily a Catholic threat, retrospectively connected to Pope Pius V's 1570 Bull of Excommunication of Queen Elizabeth, which absolved her Catholic subjects of allegiance to her and thus led to the strong link between Catholicism and treason, emphasized in the later proclamations and statutes directed against priests (especially missionary priests) and the recusant Catholic laity who assisted them. There were numerous seminary priests in England in the 1570s (joining the older surviving Marian Catholic clergy), but the first Jesuits did not arrive until the 1580s (unfortunately on the heels of the Spanish-assisted Irish Rebellion of 1579). In the context of the

Papal Bull and the danger of a Catholic uprising or assassination plot, these more militantly Catholic missionaries provoked a wave of anti-Catholic legislation and persecution. For example, Elizabeth's royal proclamation 'Declaring Jesuits and Non-Returning Seminarians Traitors' states:

> ... it hath manifestly and plainly appeared unto her highness and her council, as well by many examinations as by sundry of their own letters and confessions, besides the late manifest attempts of the like companions directed by the pope out of the number of the said seminaries and Jesuits broken out to actual rebellion in Ireland, that the very end and purpose of these Jesuits, seminary men and such like priests ... is not only to prepare sundry her majesty's subjects inclinable to disloyalty to be apt to give aid to foreign invasion and to stir up rebellion within the same, but also (that most perilous is) to deprive her majesty (under whom and by whose provident government, with God's assistance, these realms have been so long and so happily kept and continued in great plenty, peace and security) of her life, crown and dignity.[6]

Although in the 1580s and 1590s, only about twenty Jesuits came to England, one would think from the government's actions and from the rash of anti-Jesuit polemical activity that a secret army of thousands had landed on England's shores to prepare the way for foreign invasion.[7]

The first Jesuit priests to arrive in England as missionaries in 1580 were Robert Persons and Edmund Campion: the former became the polemical nemesis of English Protestantism – excoriated, in the words of one impassioned antagonist, for example, as 'a notorious lyer, a brasen faced Fryer, a known cozener, a sacreligious Bastard, an incestuous villain, a cursed Fairie bratte and bloudthirsty traytor';[8] the latter was a martyr who haunted the Elizabethan Protestant establishment. Campion's arrest in 1581 was a high-profile one, partly because two of his prose works were perceived as arrogantly aggressive polemical assaults on English Protestantism. The first of these was Campion's hastily composed letter to Queen Elizabeth's Privy Council defending his mission as non-political, a work he did not wish to circulate until his arrest, but which quickly found its way to its original addressees. It came to be known as

'The Brag' because Campion announced himself able and ready
defend the truths of Roman Catholicism in debate with Protestant
adversaries:

> I do ask, to the glory of God, with all humility and under your
> correction, three sorts of indifferent and quiet audiences: the first
> before your Honours, wherein I will discourse of religion, so far
> as it touches the commonweal and your nobilities; the second,
> whereof I make more account, before the Doctors and Masters
> and chosen men of both Universities, wherein I undertake to
> avow the faith of our Catholic Church by proofs innumerable,
> Scriptures, Councils, Fathers, History, natural and moral reasons;
> the third before the lawyers, spiritual and temporal, wherein I
> will justify the said faith by the common wisdom of the laws
> standing yet in force and practice.[9]

Campion's 'Brag' elicited a strong reaction from the authorities,
both in their subsequent treatment of him as a prisoner and in their
printed propaganda. The zealous Protestant minister William
Charke's *Answer to a Seditious Pamphlet by a Jesuite* (1580) responds
to the manuscript circulation of 'The Brag' which, for him, constituted 'Libels, abusing the name and holy authority of the [Privy]
Counsell' (Aiii). Charke worries about the vulnerability of
Protestants to the rhetoric of clever Jesuits: he fears the peace of
gospel-loving Christians might be disturbed by disputation with
the religious enemy. At the same time, he associates Protestantism
with the life of the spirit (and the scriptural word) and Catholicism
with 'the feeling and wisdom of a natural man' (ciiii$^v$), a religion
designed to 'snare the heart of a carnall man, bewitching it with so
great glistering of the painted harlot' (Bviii) and other sensual baits.
*The Great bragge and challenge of M. Champion a Jesuite ... lately
arrived in Englande, contayning nyne articles here severallye laide down
... confuted & aunswered by Meredith Hanmer* (1581) associates the
Jesuit threat with that of the Family of Love and Anabaptists, suggesting as well that Jesuits were involved in homosexual practices.
Robert Persons' *Brief Censure uppon two books written in answer to
M. Edmond Campion's offer of disputation* (1581) was issued within
days of Hanmer's pamphlet by the secret Green Street press.[10]
Referring to Hanmer's book and to his own *Brief Discours contayn-
ing certayne Reasons why Catholiques refuse to go to Church* (1580),
Persons wrote to Alfonso Agazzari, the Rector of the English

College at Rome (17 November 1580), in a bit of self-promotion: 'Nothing is spoken of here now but the Jesuits, especially after the recent publication of two books in English, which nearly everybody thinks were written by them, one in defence of the imprisoned Catholics, the other controverting the calumnies against the Society of Jesus contained in two books written by Protestants; and it is almost unbelieveable what a stir has been caused by these rejoinders.'[11] In another letter to Agazzari, Persons emphasized the importance of Catholics' using the press to counter the arguments of English Protestants,

> to ensure that the heretics should not be able to publish anything without its being almost immediately attacked more vigorously. Charke and Hanmer, Calvinist ministers ... wrote against Campion, abusing in wonderful fashion the whole Jesuit order and condemning expressly the life of Ignatius Loyola. But within ten days there appeared a short criticism by an unknown author ..., which taxed those ministers with so many lies that both they and their followers were mightily ashamed.[12]

Campion's secretly printed defence of Catholicism, *Rationes Decem* (1581), copies of which mysteriously appeared on the benches of St Mary's Church in Oxford, provoked the Bishop of London to instruct the Regius Professors of Divinity at Oxford and Cambridge, Laurence Humphrey and William Whitaker, to compose the first two (of several) Protestant refutations.[13] Both 'The Brag' and *Rationes Decem* prompted Campion's captors and torturers to arrange four 'conferences' in the Tower in which he was forced, with no other resources than a Bible, his associate Ralph Sherwin and the depleted energies of his racked body and mind, to dispute questions of religion with a team of Protestant theologians well equipped with notes and reference materials meetings quickly publicized in print in accounts by his adversaries.[14]

After Campion's death, Thomas Alfield's narrative of the execution appeared anonymously in February 1582 as *A true reporte of the death & martyrdome of M. Campion Jesuite and preiste, & M. Sherwin, & M. Bryan preistes ... Observid and written by a Catholike preist ...* . This work answered 'a most infamous libel, entitled, *An Advertisement and defense for truth against her backbyters and specially against the whispering favorers and colorers of Campions ... treasons* (A4ᵛ).[15] Like Campion himself in his 'Brag', Alfield argued that 'meerely and

only religion, no treason, no unduetifulness to our Prince, no disobedience to her temporal lawe' (B3) lay behind the actions of the
missionaries.

This work's dramatic account of Campion's execution, including
his dialogue with his persecutors, who tried one final time to get
him to confess treason, includes a report of a strange event connected with the execution of Campion's fellow martyr, the seminary priest Alexander Bryant: '[he] after his beheading, himself
dismembred, his hart bowels and intrels burned, to the gret admiration of some, being layd upon the blocke his bellye downward,
lifted up his whole body then remayning from the grounde' (D2ᵛ).[16]
In his consolatory *Triumph over Death* (1595), Robert Southwell later
referred, in a collection of examples of supposed divine punishments exacted against Protestant persecutors, to 'the wonderful
stay and standing of the Thames the same day that Father *Campion*
and his companye were martyred to the great marvayle of the
Cittizens and maryners' (Bb3ᵛ).[17] Both accounts reflect the Catholic
belief in miracles, associated by Protestants with the practices of
magic and other forms of trickery associated with the 'old religion'.
Such faith in the physical manifestations of the spiritual underlay
the Catholic reverence for saints' relics. Referring to the martyrs of
1581 and 1582, William Allen remarks:

> ... for the Catholikes, of Italie, Spaine, Fraunce and namely
> (which is lesse to be marveled at) of England, more then the
> weight in golde ... is offered for any peece of their reliques, either
> of their bodies, haire, bones or garments, yea of any thing that
> hath any spot or staine of their innocent and sacred bloud.
> Wherein surely great diligence and honorable zeale hath been
> shewed by divers noble gentlemen & verteous [sic] people, that
> have to their great daunger obtained some good peeces of them,
> to satisfie presently the godly greedy appetite of holy persons of
> divers nations making extreeme sute for them.
>
> Marry that is most notable and memorable, that divers devoute
> people of our nation that can get no part of their sacred reliques,
> yet come as it were on pilgrimage to the places where their quar-
> ters or heades be set up, under pretence of gasing and asking
> whose heades or bodies they be and what traitors they were, ...
> there, to do their devotion & praiers unto them, whose lives they
> knew to be so innocent and deathes so glorious befor God and
> the world.[18]

Henry More's later account of the English Jesuit mission describes the way in which people who sought relics behaved at the execution of Campion, Sherwin and Bryant:

> While these martyrs were being torn asunder, the Catholics did their best to retrieve at least a few of their remains. But their enemies exercised great care to prevent this. One young gentleman, however, pushing through the people around him, let his handkerchief fall in order to get it soaked in Campion's blood, or at least that it might collect a few drops. But his attempt was instantly noticed and he was seized and put in gaol. All the same, while he was being arrested, another took the opportunity in the general confusion to cut off Campion's finger and make off with it. That, too, was observed, but ... it proved impossible to find the man who did it. Another young man secretly offered £20 of our money to the executioner for a single joint of Father Campion's finger, but he did not dare to give it. Their clothes were much sought after by Catholics, ... but so far they have not been able to get anything. It is thought that their enemies tried to burn everything so that nothing should fall into the hands of the Catholics.[19]

Given the talismanic power Catholics attributed to saints' relics,[20] it is not surprising that both sophisticated and unsophisticated Catholics, at the execution scene and afterwards, acted as they did. But, in this case, as in others, some Protestants were also strongly affected by the spectacle. Henry Walpole, then a Protestant gentleman attending Campion's execution out of curiosity, after being splashed with some of Campion's blood, supposedly had a conversion experience which led him to join the Jesuits and finally experience the same sort of martyrdom in 1595.[21]

It is clear that Campion, like so many other missionaries, came to England expecting, if not desiring, to be martyred. In his unfinished biography of his former colleague, Robert Persons quotes Campion's revealing remark about his decision to dress in humble rather than elegant attire: 'he would say that to him that went to be hanged in England any kind of apparel was sufficient'. He also notes that Campion took as his alias the name 'Edmonds in remembrance of St Edmond King and Martyr of England whom he desired to imitate'.[22]

The martyred Campion's body was instantly sacralized at Tyburn – not only for Catholics, but, given the powerful

Protestant discourse of martyrdom that was such an essential feature of nascent English nationalism, for a larger community as well.[23] Any time there was a public execution of a Catholic priest or layman, the government created a situation in which spectators might sympathize, admire and, in some cases, be moved to emulate the victims and react negatively to the power that condemned and killed them. Francis Bacon advised Queen Elizabeth not to hang Catholics for their religion because of the sympathy it won them: 'they should never have the honour to take any pretence of martyrdom in England, where the fulness of blood and greatness of heart is such that they will even for shameful things go bravely to death, much more when they think themselves to climb heaven; and this vice of obstinacy seems to the people a divine consistency; so that for my part I wish no lessening of their number but by preaching and by education of the younger sort under schoolmasters.'[24] Francis Walsingham realized that executing Catholics 'draweth some to affect their religion, upon conceit that such an extraordinary contempt of death cannot but proceed from above ...'.[25] Robert Cotton made a pragmatic appeal for leniency towards Catholics: in a work whose belated 1641 publication coincided with the Irish Rebellion, Cotton argued against making Catholics into martyrs because 'there are too many of the blind *Communality*, altogether *Popish*, though not reconciled *Papists*, who, in their foolish ignorance, will say, it is pitty any should dye for their Conscience, though indeed they make honourable amends for their Treason'.[26]

Torturing and executing Catholic priests, then, conferred martyr status on them not only within Catholicism,[27] but also in the eyes of the English public at large. The authorized spectacle of public execution, mutilation, dismemberment and the display of the heads and quartered bodies of supposed traitors on London Bridge and the gates of the city of London was designed to proclaim the morally sanctioned power of the state over the bodies of those who would destroy it, but all this could be reinterpreted in a martyrological context to yield a very different message. In a poem appended to the *True Report* of Campion's execution, the writer testifies to the politically oppositional meaning Catholics could find in such state theatricalism:

> We can not feare a mortal torment, wee,
> this Martirs blood hath moistned all our harts,

whose partid quartirs when we chaunce to see,
we lerne to play the constant christians part,
his head doth speake, & heavenly precepts give,
how we that looke should frame our selves to live.

(E4)

In another poem from this pamphlet, 'A Dialogue betwene a Catholike and Consolation', the writer similarly states:

His quarters hong on every gate do showe,
his doctrine sound throgh countries far & neare,
his head set up so high doth call for moe
to fight the fight which he endured here,
the faith thus planted thus restord must be,
take up thy crosse said Christ and folow me.

(F4)[28]

After Henry Garnet was hanged for supposed complicity in the Gunpowder Plot, his head was perceived as an instrument of miraculous pedagogy by those who observed it. One Catholic reported:

After that Father Henrie Garnett, Superior of the Societie of Jhesus in England, was executed ... in the year 1606, his head appeared in that lively colour as it seemed to retaine the same hue and shew of life which yt had before itt was cutt off, soe as both heretiques and Cathollyques were astonished thereat and soe much the more, in that according to custom beinge cast into hoate water itt receaved no alteration at all; as neyther it did after yt was placed upon London Bridge and sett upp there uppon a pole. Whereupon there was such resort of people for the space of six weeks as that was admirable ... Whereuppon the magistrates of the citye and counsaile confounded with the miracle and displeased with the continuall resort of people to beholde the unexpected event, gave order that the heade should be put soe as the face should be turned uppwardes and the people thereby not able to vewe the face as they had been accustomed. There have been soe manie to see it at once sometymes, what from the bridge, what from places near thereunto, as from the water and houses, as divers there present have thought them to have been to the number of 400 or 500 persons.[29]

Relics were dangerous (like Lenin's embalmed body now in the 'former Soviet Union') – a source of power not sanctioned by state authority, in the case of executed Catholics a focus for an alternative allegiance, not just to the foreign pope, but, more generally, to a religious and personal devotional order outside the officially sanctioned one. Like those of Garnet or other Catholic martyrs, the physical 'remains' of Edmund Campion delivered a strong political message.

In print culture, however, Campion's 'remains' were present in both his own polemical discourse and in the language of his enemies and interpreters. In a passage excised by censorship from the second edition of Holinshed's *Chronicles* (1587), the writer complains about Catholic propaganda evoked by the deaths of Campion and of the other two priests:

> No sooner had justice given the blow of execution and cut off the foresaid offendors from their cause, which they falslie gave out to be religion, dispersed abroad their libels of most impudent devise, tending to the justifieng of the malefactors innocencie, to the heinous and unrecompensable defamation of the course of justice and judgement against them commensed and finished: in somuch that speaking of the daie whereon they died, they blushed not to intitle them martyrs... . Thus slanderouslie against the administration of justice scattered these vipers brood their lieng reports, therein to the skies advancing the children of iniquitie as spotlesse; yea forging most monstrous fables, put them in print...[30]

In Holinshed, what follows immediately upon this account of Campion's death is the discussion of another politically sensitive topic, the winding down of Queen Elizabeth's negotiations to marry the French Catholic Duke of Alençon. The uncut 1587 edition has several pages that were censored after publication because the near-match of the Protestant Queen with a Catholic spouse (bitterly opposed by the more radical Protestants on the Privy Council and by many of Elizabeth's other subjects) was brought into an uncomfortable association with the business of executing missionary priests. In the cut version of Holinshed, the Duke is introduced only at the point of his departure from England.[31] The best Catholic was a departing one – one dying or setting sail.

In one of his more manically exaggerated letters to Agazzari, Robert Persons reported on the benefits of the execution of Campion, Sherwin and Bryant for the Catholic cause:

> ... the enemy are evidently enraged that the death of the last martyrs has inflicted such a great blow on their cause... . Walsingham declared lately that it would have been better for the Queen to have spent 40,000 gold pieces than to kill publicly those priests. And in truth the effect has been that we have all Protestants, who are of more moderate temper, very much on our side... . All with one voice, our enemies as well as ourselves, declare that if their lives had been prolonged to their hundreth year they could not have benefited their cause as much as has their short life, but glorious death. Many have stood firm, fearless and loyal after it, who had been timid before; some there have been who have joined the Catholic Church; countless numbers of the opposite party have begun to have doubts; and all the Catholics who are in chains and undergoing persecution bear it with such joy and exultation that they do not feel anything that they are suffering... . our persecutors are almost bursting with indignation and wrath. Countless is the number of books, dialogues, treatises, poems, satires, which have been composed and published, some in print, some in manuscript in praise of these martyrs and in blame of their adversaries.[32]

From both Continental and secret English presses, Catholic polemicists were quick to make the case for their side.[33] Among these works are (in addition to Allen's *A Brief Historie*), Persons' *An Epistle of the Persecution of Catholickes in England* (1582)[34] and Richard Verstegan's later *Theatrum Crudelitatum haereticorum nostri temporis* (Antwerp, 1587) – the last a gruesomely illustrated series of vignettes of both Continental and English persecution running from Henry VIII's time into the 1580s.[35] Verstegan's work includes the following: a Henrician composite scene of ecclesiastical despoilation – a life-size cross being chopped and pulled down, a fire burning Catholic books, vandals dismantling two church structures (one an abbey) and a church being burned;[36] the executions of Sir Thomas More and Bishop John Fisher (25); the execution of

Carthusian monks – depicted as a progress from hauling the victims on a hurdle to the place of execution and hanging them, to dismembering them and burning the body parts (27); the hanging of the Franciscan John Forest, accompanied by the image of St David in the fire and abbots and religious authorities strangled, eviscerated and dismembered (29); many scenes of Continental French and Low Countries' persecutions (31–68), including one scene of Dutch Protestants' using human heads in a game of boules; a general illustration of Elizabethan persecution in which are shown a vestment-wearing cleric, a noblewoman and a gentleman being thrown in prison, a Catholic home raided and despoiled at night, torch-bearing pursuivants on horseback capturing their prey and Catholic prisoners, bound together, being moved from one horrid place of imprisonment to another (71); a scene in which one man is being racked, four prisoners peer out from behind bars, armed men are moving menacingly towards a church and the cramped prison cell called 'Little-Ease' is depicted (73); a scene of various noble and base Catholics in prison (including the supposedly murdered Henry Percy, Earl of Northumberland) – one prone, emaciated man naked in his cell, another compressed into a ball in a hoop device, another man in bed being awakened by torch-bearing men at night and other Catholics in prison in leg-irons (75); an illustration of Henry Huntingdon's cruel persecution in the North, exemplified by the pressing to death of Margaret Clitherow, the suspension of a priest upside down in the stocks in a way that forces him to be choked by his own excrement, a picture of a fetid dungeon in which Catholics are suffocating from the bad air and the general crowding of English prisons with Catholics (77); scenes of abuses of justice showing a Catholic priest having his ears perforated, a Catholic being whipped behind a cart, a Catholic sewn into a bear-skin and baited by dogs and Catholics hauled before tribunals along with common felons (79); a scene of Irish persecution in which two bishops and a monk are hanged and a bishop in the stocks has his feet held to the fire (81); a scene showing Jesuits, secular priests, nobles and other Catholics dragged to the place of execution, one man being shown a body being dismembered to terrorize him into recanting and Catholics being hanged and dismembered, their decapitated heads and body parts then set up on display on the gates of the city of London (83) (Figure 1); and, finally, the scene of the execution of Mary, Queen of Scots (85). The last two scenes allude to the heightened political tension of the 1580s just before the Armada. Verstegan's visually enhanced propaganda constituted a Catholic recapturing of martyrological discourse from Protestant writers like John Foxe; his book circulated on the Continent to the disadvantage of the English government.[37]

In the light of the outpouring of Catholic polemic and propaganda following Campion's execution, Laurence Humphrey of Oxford wrote to the Earl of Leicester:

> ... the ghost of the dead Campion has given me more trouble than the Rationes of the living, – not only because he has left his poison behind him, like the fabled Bonasus, which in its flight burns up its pursuers with its droppings, but much more because his friends dig him up from his grave, defend his cause, and write his epitaph in English, French and Latin. It used to be said, 'Dead men bite not'; and yet Campion dead bites with his friends' teeth ...; for as fresh heads grow on the hydra when the old are cut off, as wave succeeds wave, as a harvest of new men rose from the seed of the dragon's teeth, so one labour of ours only begets another and still another; and in the place of the single Campion, champions upon champions have swarmed to keep us engaged.[38]

Defending the official Elizabethan position, Lord Burghley published in 1583 his justification of the harsh treatment of Catholic missionaries in both *A declaration of the favourable dealing of her Majesties Commissioners* ... and *The Execution of Justice in England*, works that in turn were answered by *William Allen's Defence of English Catholiques* (1584), itself answered by Thomas Bilson's *True Difference betweene Christian Subjection and Unchristian Rebellion* (1585). Nicholas Sanders' posthumously published historical account of the English 'schism', *De Origine ac Progressu Schismatis Anglicani*, was obviously one of the most disturbing Catholic printed texts, if the English government's questioning of arrested missionaries is any indication.[39] Surprisingly, it took until 1593 for a printed reply to be published.[40] Clearly, in the years leading up to the (suspiciously engineered) Babington Plot, the consequent execution of Mary, Queen of Scots (1587) and the Spanish Armada (1588), the persecution of Catholics and the execution of Catholic missionaries and those who assisted them were deeply enmeshed in a national and international struggle for moral and religious

Fig. 1 'Persecutiones aduersus Catholicos à Protestantibus Caluinistis exitae in Anglia' from Verstegan's, *Theatrum Crudelitatum Haereticorum nostri Temporis*

legitimacy. Campion was only one Catholic victim among many, but his case highlights the larger context.

In some ways, Robert Southwell, S. J. was an even more disturbing figure than Campion for the Elizabethan (and Jacobean) government, both before and after his death. Less polemically confrontational than his predecessor or than the indefatigable Persons, Southwell 'published' a number of his writings in both manuscript and print before his arrest in 1592 – the printed books issued by a secret press hidden in the Countess of Arundel's house, the manuscript verse and prose works travelling the networks of Catholic manuscript transmission. One of these pieces, *An Humble Supplication to Her Majestie*, is an eloquent plea for toleration of Catholics written in reponse to the 1591 royal proclamation establishing commissions to hunt down seminary priests and Jesuits.[41]

Southwell's execution at Tyburn was one of the most dramatic of the Elizabethan era. The narrative of his movement from Newgate Prison, to the scaffold, to the dismembering table involves several details that sacralize the body of the priest-martyr. Southwell apparently gave his cap to the Keeper of Newgate prison who treated it, in effect, as a relic: 'which cap the Keeper, albeit a Protestant, maketh such account of that he can be brought by no means to forgo it'.[42] When Southwell got to the place of execution after being dragged on a hurdle through the muddy streets, he cleaned his face with a cloth which he then threw to someone in the crowd. As he wrote in one of his letters describing Southwell's experiences, Henry Garnet noted that this cloth was in his own possession (as a valued object).[43] The third holy object was the rosary Southwell threw from the scaffold to a friend.[44] The live martyr and his dead body were both treated by the executioner with unusual respect. Garnet noted that the hangman did not follow the custom of cutting down the hanging man before he was dead in order to perform the disembowelling on a live body, but instead

> pulled on his legs – an act of courtesy and humanity that is unusual. One of the executioners several times made to cut the rope, but was stopped by the Lord [Montjoy] and by the whole crowd, which cried out three times: 'Let him be, let him be'. The executioner took him down with great reverence and carried him in his own arms, assisted by his companions, to the place where

he was to be quartered, whereas in all other cases it is the custom to drag [the bodies] brutally along the ground. When he was being disembowelled, his heart leaped into the hands of the executioner. All those who stood around spoke of him with respect and there was none to cry 'Traitor' according to custom.[45]

One contemporary narrative describes how some people in the crowd 'dipped handkerchiefs in the sprayed blood and offered [the hangman] money for a piece of bone or a lock of hair',[46] desiring, as did some of the spectators at Campion's execution, relics of the deceased martyr.

Relics, of course, were one of the strong markers of difference between Catholicism and Protestantism. In England, the late Henrician assault on shrines and relics was part of a power contest between the state and the papacy.[47] In one of the first proclamations of her reign, Queen Elizabeth, repeating the language of some of Henry VIII's proclamations, ordered her clergy 'to the intent that all superstition and hypocrisy crept into divers men's hearts may vanish away, they shall not set forth or extol the dignity of any images, relics, or miracles, but, declaring the abuse of the same, they shall teach that all goodness, health and grace ought to be both asked and looked for only of God as of the very author and giver of the same and of none other'.[48] This proclamation ordered officials to 'take away, utterly extinct and destroy all shrines, covering of shrines, all tables, candlesticks, trindles and rolls of wax, pictures, paintings and all other monuments of feigned miracles, pilgrimages, walls, glasses, window, or elsewhere within their churches and houses ...'[49] To this day, the official centre of the English Church, Canterbury Cathedral, is marked by an absence, the space formerly occupied by the relics and shrine of Thomas à Becket.

Robert Southwell's remains or relics include the quarters of his dismembered body displayed on the gates of the city of London, his head mounted on a pole on London Bridge and the bloodstains obtained by devout coreligionists and sympathizers at Tyburn. Anticipating his own death, Southwell had referred to the power ascribed to a martyr's physical remains in his *Epistle of Comfort*, when he addressed Protestant persecutors of Catholics: 'Our prisons preach, our punishments converte, our deade quarters and bones confound youre heresye: You have laboured to suppresse us this 29. yeeares: and yet of our ashes spring others and our dead bones, as *Exechiell* prophesied, are come to be *exercitus grandis* a huge army.'[50] Southwell's most important remains, however, were his writings, several of which were rushed into print in 1595, the year of his execution: two editions of *Saint Peters Complaynt. With other Poems; Moeoniae. or Certaine excellent Poems and spirituall Hymnes: Omitted in the last Impression of Peters Complaint; The Triumphs over Death and A Short Rule to the Good Life.* A Humble *Supplication* was published in 1600, but deliberately misdated as 1595 in order to associate it with Southwell's execution.[51] All these books and the other posthumously printed and reprinted verse and prose were the relics of the martyr the general public could most easily possess; they became part of a growing body of politically oppositionist recusant writing dealing with the faith, practices and sufferings of the persecuted Catholic minority. Take, for example, the prose elegy Southwell wrote in 1591 to console the imprisoned Philip Howard, Earl of Arundel, on the occasion of the death of his sister Lady Margaret, wife of Robert Sackville (later Earl of Dorset). This was published as *The Triumphs over Death: or, A Consolatorie Epistle for afflicted mindes, in the affects of dying friends.... by R. S. the Author of S. Peters Complaint, and Moeoniae his other Hymnes* (1595 and 1596). Since Howard and Southwell were both dead by the end of 1595 they, along with Lady Margaret, could take their places within the larger context of Catholic suffering and persecution evoked by such a printed work.

When he dedicated his collection of Southwell's writings to Richard, Earl of Dorset, in 1620, the publisher William Leake used revealing language in referring to his having 'first collected these dismembred parcels into one body and published them in an entire edition',[52] associating the body parts of the poet-martyr (a Christian Orpheus, as it were) with his scattered literary remains.[53]

The association of an author's body with his body of work, however, was more than a witty turn of phrase. It was historically grounded in the cultural conflicts and discourses of early modern England, related, for example, to the media shift from Catholic visual imagery and oral communication on the one hand, to Protestant fetishizing of the word and the book (most centrally the vernacular Bible). After Catholic relics came under attack, from the late 1530s, when the shrine of Thomas à Becket was destroyed and the saint's bones scattered, the reverence for relics began to migrate into print culture, where the remains of a person were verbal.[54]

Although one of the long-term effects of print culture was the fostering of abstraction, the unbodying of the word – that is, the creation of the Cartesian mind-body split that characterizes modernity,[55] early in the era of print the connection between books and the body was stressed. The corpse of the author and the *corpus* of his work were in closer imaginative proximity: hence even as reformist a Protestant as Milton could call 'a good book ... the precious lifeblood of a master spirit, embalmed and treasured up on purpose to a a life beyond life'.[56] As the historical bibliographer D. F. McKenzie has remarked: 'The common use of the word "Remaines" as a term for posthumous works ambiguously suggests both the items remaining to be published and, as the earthly relics of a departed soul, the close identity of a man's body and his printed works.'[57] Addressing the Countess of Pembroke, the sister of the deceased poet, Samuel Daniel referred to Sir Philip Sidney's poems as 'holy Reliques'[58] (of a Protestant kind). It is interesting to note that Southwell's famous apologetic epistle to his Protestant father was published, with a misattribution of authorship, in a book entitled *Remains of Sir Walter Raleigh* (1664).[59]

Southwell's literary remains were visibly Catholic ones, though they were subjected to a degree of Protestantizing. Gabriel Cawood's edition of *Saint Peters complaynt. With other Poems* (1595) was clearly marketed as a Catholic text. The religious ornament at the top of the title page (Figure 2) depicts a man and a woman kneeling in prayer looking upwards towards a highlighted 'J[esus] H[ominorum] S[alvator]'. Between them is a table on which are the eucharistic symbols of chalice and host as well as what appear to be representations of the three nails of Christ's cross (always found along with the 'JHS' in the Jesuit emblem). The figures are flanked, as James McDonald has described them, by 'doves with hearts for heads' over which are 'crowns of thorns'.[60] The title-page, then, proclaims its connection with the martyrdom of the Jesuit poet whose work it contains. The whole volume takes its name from the title of its longest poem, 'St Peter's Complaint' – which suggests, perhaps, a connection between the martyrdom of the first pope and that of Elizabethan Catholics. Cawood printed only 20 of the 52 poems found (in the usual order) in the circulating manuscripts of Southwell's verse, but some works may be missing, not because of their political sensitivity but rather because Cawood had only the last part of the collection in its typical manuscript order and included whatever he possessed rather than omitting any poems deliberately.[61]

Fig. 2   Title-page of *Saint Peters complaynt*

Despite the signals of the poems' Catholic authorship and content, Cawood's and other early editions did not contain some of the more politically disturbing Catholic material found in the manuscript-circulated versions of Southwell's verse. For example, Southwell's poem on Mary Queen of Scots, 'Decease release', was not included, the fourth stanza of which reads:

> Alive a Queen, now dead I am a Sainte,
> Once Mary calld, my name nowe Martyr is,
> From earthly raigne debarred by restraint,
> In liew whereof I raigne in heavenly blisse.

Also, since Protestant apologists connected Queen Elizabeth and King John as royal victims of papal excommunications, it is not surprising that another politically sensitive poem was also excluded, 'I dye without desert', a piece found in the Folger manuscript of Southwell's verse with the heading 'Arthur Earle of Britaine murthered by his uncle King John'.[62] Finally, given Protestant/Catholic conflicts over the meaning of the Eucharist, it makes sense that 'Of the Blessed Sacrament of the Aulter' had to wait until 1616 to appear in print in the Continental edition of Southwell's work issued by the Jesuit press at St Omer's.

The 1599[63] Edinburgh edition of Southwell's poems by the 'Printer to the Kings Majestie', Robert Waldgrave, clearly Protestantized the verse: for example, it drastically cut back the references to the Virgin Mary and added marginal annotations to 'Saint Peter's Complaint' which use the Protestant names of the Old Testament books.[64] William Barrett's 1620 London edition of *St. Peters Complaint, Mary Magdalens Funeral Teares, With Other Workes* also Protestantized Southwell's text somewhat, particularly in its alteration of his translation of Thomas Aquinas's poem on the eucharist, 'An holy Hymne'.[65] Such religious revision, as Edmund Bunny's enormously popular (Protestant, expurgated) version of Robert Persons's *The first booke of the Christian exercise, appertyning to resolution* (1582) testifies,[66] helped Catholic texts reach and win great approval from a large Protestant English readership. Sometimes, of course, the Protestantizing of a text necessitated radical changes: Alison Shell points out that the Catholic William Byrd 'published a musical setting of some verses on the death of the martyr Edmund Campion with all the references to Campion excised and the praise of "the Martirs of auncient times" substituted'.[67]

In late Elizabethan England Catholic devotional and poetic texts could be admired by those who did not share the authors' religious commitments. John Harington of Stepney copied (from manuscript) the poem about Campion's execution found in the Catholic *True Report* into his manuscript poetical anthology, as did John Lilliat into his, the former supposedly regarding it as 'the best English verse ... that ever he read', the latter labelling the piece 'A good verse, upon a badd Matter'.[68] The prison poem written by the Catholic Chidiock Tichborne, 'My prime of youth is but a frost of cares', was very popular in manuscript transmission and was, surprisingly, printed in a volume entitled *Verses of Prayse and Joye writen upon her majesties preservation*, a 1586 book celebrating the foiling of the Babington Plot.[69] Ben Jonson expressed to William Drummond of Hawthornden his extraordinary admiration for one of Southwell's poems: 'That Southwell was hanged yett so he had written that piece of his the burning babe he would have been content to destroy many of his [poems]'.[70] Even Francis Bacon, whose essay 'On Superstition' is a compendium of anti-Catholic charges, recommended Southwell's *An Humble Supplication* to his brother Anthony soon after its publication: 'I send you the supplication which Mr. Topcliffe lent me. It is curiously written and worth the writing out for the art; though the argument be bad.'[71] Despite confessional differences and the atmosphere of polemical viciousness within print culture, the literary remains of a Catholic author could be both preserved *and venerated*.

## NOTES

1. L. Hicks, S. J. (ed.), *Letters and Memorials of Father Robert Persons, S.J.*, vol. 1, Catholic Record Soc. vol. 39 (London, 1942), p. 83 (cited hereafter as 'Persons, *Letters*').
2. See Peter Lake, 'Anti-Popery: The Structure of a Prejudice', in *Conflict in Early Stuart England: Studies in Religion and Politics 1603–1642*, ed Richard Cust and Ann Hughes (London and New York, 1989), pp. 72–106. A 1689 Act of Parliament made it illegal for a Catholic or anyone married to a Catholic to ascend the throne.
3. This caused 'An Homilie Against Disobedience and Wilfull Rebellion' to be added to the official Church of England *Book of Homilies* along with 'A Thanksgiving for the Suppression of the Last Rebellion' which concludes the volume.
4. See David Cressy, *Bonfires and Bells: National Memory and the Protestant Calendar in Elizabethan and Stuart England* (London, 1989); William

Haller, *The Elect Nation: The Meaning and Relevance of Foxe's Book of Martyrs* (New York, 1963); and Christopher Hill, *Antichrist in Seventeenth-Century England* (London, 1971).

5.  See Carol Z. Wiener, 'The Beleaguered Isle: A Study of Elizabethan and Early Jacobean Anti-Catholicism', *Past and Present* 51 (May 1971): 31–3.

6.  *Tudor Royal Proclamations*, ed. Paul L. Hughes and James F. Larkin, 3 vols (New Haven, CT and London, 1964–9), 2:490.

7.  Bernard Basset, *The English Jesuits From Campion to Martindale* (New York, 1967), p. 109, writes: 'Of the 182 men and women executed as Catholics under Queen Elizabeth, eleven at most could be classed as Jesuits. Of these only Campion, Walpole and Southwell were Jesuit trained... . On Fr William Holt's reckoning in 1596, six hundred priests had been sent into England in thirty-eight years. The Jesuits, after sixteen years in England, could claim, at most, twenty-five of these.' See the recent account of the English Jesuit mission in Thomas M. McCoog, S. J., *The Society of Jesus in Ireland, Scotland and England 1541–1588: 'Our Way of Proceeding?'* (Leiden, New York, Cologne, 1996).

8.  Thomas Bell, *The Golden Balance of Tryall ... . Whereunto is also annexed a Counterblast against a masked Companion, terming himself E.O... .* (1603), M3ᵛ. See Victor Houliston, 'The Fabrication of the Myth of Father Parsons', *Recusant History* 22.2 (October 1994): 141–51. Persons kept the heat up over several decades, beginning with his 1580 pamphlet defending recusancy, which elicited three swift responses by Protestant antagonists. See Peter Milward, *Religious Controversies of the Elizabethan Age: A Survey of Printed Sources* (London, 1977), p. 52.

9.  Quoted in Basset, 455. Persons similarly composed a letter to the London magistrates defending himself and the Jesuit mission. In it, he too arrogantly challenged his Protestant adversaries to theological debate: 'I demand to be allowed to defend this faith ... *your ignorant Ministers have never dared to submit to the test of any disputation...* . I beg most earnestly that either here or elsewhere at your pleasure I may join battle in some kind of disputation with some of your ministers or prelates... . in this cause I challenge the lot of them ...' (English trans. in Persons, *Letters*, p. 39) For a discussion of Campion's and Persons' challenges, see Thomas M. McCoog, S. J., *The Society of Jesus*, p. 148; '"Playing the Champion": The Role of Disputation in the Jesuit Mission', in *The Reckoned Expense: Edmund Campion and the Early English Jesuits ...*, ed.Thomas M. McCoog, S. J. (Woodbridge, England and Rochester, NY, 1996), pp. 119–29; and '"The Flower of Oxford": The Role of Edmund Campion in Early Recusant Polemics', *Sixteenth Century Journal* 24 (1993): 899–913.

10.  Persons, *Letters*, p. 63n.

11.  Ibid., p. 64.

12.  Ibid., p. 84.

13.  See Milward, pp. 57–8.

14.  See McCoog, '"Playing the Champion"', pp. 135–6. Richard Simpson, *Edmund Campion: a Biography* (London, 1867), p. 369, notes that

Campion made converts during the debates, including Philip Howard, Earl of Arundel. On the four conferences, see Simpson, pp. 363–78. Persons wrote: 'truly it can scarcely be told how much good these disputations have done and are doing every day. And if [Campion] dies for that cause they will certainly do still more good. For they are the common talk … of everybody, not only of Catholics, but of our enemies also; and always to the great honour of Fr. Campion' (*Letters*, p. 119). Milward, p. 60, cites *A true report of the Disputation of rather private Conference* … (1583) and *The three last dayes conferences had in the Tower with Edmund Campion Jesuite* … (1583).

15. Helen C. White, *Tudor Books of Saints and Martyrs* (Madison, 1963), p. 212, notes that the story of Campion's capture had already been put in print by the man who betrayed him, George Eliot, in *A Very True Report of the Apprehension and Taking of that Arche Papist Edmond Campion* … (1581). The rabidly anti-Catholic Anthony Munday's *A Discoverie of Edmund Campion and his Confederates* … appeared shortly after the executions in January, 1582 (White, p. 215).

16. Allen includes the same story in *A Brief Historie of the Glorious Martyrdom of xii. Reverend Priests* (1582), distancing himself in his final remark: '[he] after his beheading, him self dismembred, his hart, bowels and intrailes burned, to the great admiration of some, being laid upon the blocke his belly downeward, lifted up his whole body then remayning from the ground: and this I adde upon report of others, not mine owne sight' (fiv^v).

17. White (p. 248) cites Southwell's story of how one of the judges at Campion's sentencing found one of his gloves bloody when he pulled it off (in *An Epistle of Comfort* [Paris, n.d. (c. 1587–8)], Bb3).

18. William Allen, *Briefe Historie*, cvii^v.

19. *The Elizabethan Jesuits: Historia Missionis Anglicanae Societatis Jesu* (1660) of Henry More, ed. and trans. Francis Edwards, S. J. (London and Chichester, 1981), p. 137. Citing Simpson's biography of Campion, Elizabeth Hanson discusses the obtaining of Campion's finger as a relic in 'Torture and Truth in Renaissance England', *Representations* 34 (Spring 1991): 68. Supposedly one of Campion's arms was taken from the city gate and Persons paid money for the halter, which he kept with him and died wearing around his neck (Simpson, pp. 466–7). Mary, Queen of Scots is alleged to have owned a reliquary that contained relics of Campion (ibid., p. 468).

20. For a discussion of relics and their uses in folk medicine, exorcisms and other official and non-official religious practices, see Keith Thomas, *Religion and the Decline of Magic* (New York, 1971), pp. 26–31, 44–5, 53 and passim and Robert Whiting, *The Blind Devotion of the People: Popular Religion and the English Reformation* (Cambridge, 1989), pp. 56–9. The anti-Catholic and anti-Puritan Samuel Harsnett's *A Declaration of Egregious Popish Impostures* mocks the use of relics of Campion and his fellows in ritual exorcisms, especially of Campion's thumb (in F. W. Brownlow, ed., *Shakespeare, Harsnett and the Devils of Denham* [Newark, London and Toronto, 1993], pp. 294–7). John Gee, *The Foot out of the Snare* (1624), sarcastically retails some of the stories

of cures, exclaiming 'What prodigies are these? ... Are they not forg-
eries? that shame not to affirme, that the bones of a Traytor can raise a
dead man, as did Elias his bones? or that the flesh of Campian, could
performe that which was so much admired in our Saviour himselfe,
when hee was amongst us ...' (pp. 43–4).

21. See Simpson, pp. 322, 385, cited in Ruth Hughey, *The Arundel
Harington Manuscript of Tudor Poetry*, 2 vols (Columbus, 1960), 2:60.
Hughey discusses the poem Walpole wrote about Campion, which
was appended to Alfield's account of the execution, a piece for which
Stephen Vallenger (who claimed authorship) had his ears cut off and
was thrown in prison, where he died (Garnet, Letter to Aquaviva, 20
June 1595 – Archivum Romanum Societatis Jesu [hereafter 'ARSJ']
*Anglia.* 31, fols 93–105, transcript and translation in Garnet letter file in
English Jesuit Archive, London).

22. Robert Persons, *Of the Life and Martyrdom of Father Edmund Campian*,
ed. Br. H. Foley, *Letters and Notices* (December 1877) (n.p.: Manresa
Press, 1877), p. 2. Southwell wrote to the Jesuit General, Claudio
Aquaviva, in 1585 from the English College at Rome, hoping to be
sent on the English mission, 'which promises the highest hope of
martyrdom' (23 January 1585, ARSJ. Rome, Fondo Gesuitico 651/648
in Thomas M. McCoog, S. J., 'The Letters of Robert Southwell, S. J.',
*Archivum Historicum Societatis Jesu* 63 [1994]: 103 – translation
separately provided in typescript by Fr. McCoog, to whom I am
grateful).

23. See J. T. Rhodes, 'English Books of Martyrs and Saints of the Late
Sixteenth and Early Seventeenth Centuries', *Recusant History* 22.1
(May 1994): 7–25 and John Knott, *Discourses of Martyrdom in English
Literature, 1563–1694* (Cambridge, 1993).

24. Quoted in Simpson, p. 463. See the account of the sympathetic
popular response to an execution of some newly converted Catholics
in William Weston, *The Autobiography of an Elizabethan*, trans. Philip
Caraman (London, New York, Toronto, 1955), pp. 154–5.

25. 1586 letter quoted in Christopher Devlin, *The Life of Robert Southwell
Poet and Martyr* (London, 1956), p. 139. Lord Burghley's secret memo-
randum, *An Antidote against Jesuitism* (Petyt MSS, ser. 538, vol. 43, fols
304ff) printed in James Spedding, *The Letters and Life of Francis Bacon*
(London, 1861), 1:47–56, discussed in Devlin, Appendix B, makes the
same point.

26. *Serious Considerations for repressing of the increase of Jesuites, priests and
Papists, without shedding Blood* (1641), p. 32.

27. Although those executed for their faith were popularly called
'martyrs' and their remains venerated like those of saints, Rome was
reluctant to canonize martyr-saints in this period (see Peter Burke,
'How to Be a Counter-Reformation Saint', in *The Historical
Anthropology of Early Modern Italy ...* [Cambridge, 1987], p. 56). It took
until the late twentieth century for the English martyrs either to be
beatified or canonized: Philip Howard, Earl of Arundel, for example,
was canonized in 1970 along with 39 other English and Welsh martyrs
(see Francis W. Steer, 'St Philip Howard, Arundel and the Howard

Connexion in Sussex', in *Studies in Sussex Church History*, ed. M. J. Kitch [Falmer, 1981], pp. 209–22).

28. For an anti-Catholic ballad treating the execution of Campion, Sherwin and Bryant, see Hyder Rollins (ed.), *Old English Ballads, 1553–1625* (Cambridge, 1920), p. 64: 'A Triumph for true Subjects and a Terrour unto al Traitours ...'.

29. *Records of the English Province of the Society of Jesus*, ed. Henry Foley, S. J., 7 vols (London, 1877–83), 4:129–30; citing 'Papers relating to the English Jesuits', BL MS Add. 21203, Plut. clii.F. This account describes a halo round Garnet's head. John Gerard's account of the Gunpowder Plot reports miraculous occurrences associated with Garnet's death, including the 'miracle of the straw', the appearance of a miniature image of him in a speck of his blood fallen on to wheat straw during his dismemberment: in *The Condition of Catholics under James I: Father Gerard's Narrative of the Gunpowder Plot*, ed. John Morris, S. J. (London, 1871), pp. 296–307. Also Philip Caraman, *Henry Garnet 1555–1606 and the Gunpowder Plot* (New York, 1964), pp. 443–7. The straw was debunked in Robert Pricket's poem, *The Jesuits Miracles, or new Popish Wonders* ... (1607), which has an engraving of it as a frontispiece. John Gee, *The Foot out of the Snare* (1624), p. 66, also debunks it and the claim that 'the very sight of Garnets straw hath made (at least) five hundred in our kingdom good Catholiques' and mocks the use of Campion's relics for cures.

30. Raphael Holinshed, *The First and Second Volumes of the Chronicles of England* ... (1587), p. 1329. (I cite the Huntington Library copy, which contains pages [1328–31] excised from most other copies of the edition.) On the 'castrations' of the 1587 Holinshed, see Annabel Patterson, *Reading Holinshed's Chronicles* (Chicago and London, 1994), pp. 234–9, 253–63. In his 17 November 1580 letter to the Rector of the English College at Rome, Persons not only mentions the Spanish invasion force sent to Ireland, the influence of the Catholic Lord d'Aubigny over James VI of Scotland and Spain's conquest of Portugal, but also the collapse of the French marriage negotiations: 'suspicion as to the good faith of the French after the rejection of the marriage proposals' in conjunction with 'the coming of the Jesuits to this island' (*Letters*, p. 57) troubled the authorities. In a letter of 14 June 1581 to Pope Gregory XIII, Persons explicitly connects the French party's leaving London with the fate of English Catholics: 'To-day the French representatives left London: it is commonly thought that nothing was accomplished ... . We are in daily expectation of a new and bitter storm of persecution' (ibid., p. 66). Cf. McCoog, *The Society of Jesus*, p. 156.

31. Holinshed, p. 1330.

32. Persons, *Letters*, p. 133.

33. On Catholic martyrologies from the time of Campion's execution, see White, pp. 217–39 and Thomas H. Clancy, S. J., *Papist Pamphleteers: The Allen-Persons Party and the Political Thought of the Counter-Reformation in England, 1572–1615* (Chicago, 1964), pp. 126–42. Michael E. Williams, 'Campion and the English Continental Seminaries', in *The*

*Reckoned Expense*, ed. McCoog, pp. 285–99, discusses the use of
Catholic martyrologies as fund-raisers for English Continental seminaries. I am grateful to Fr. McCoog for letting me see this essay in
manuscript.

34. This work was originally published in Latin, then translated into
French (Milward, p. 65). Milward points out the 'literature of consolation' that grew out of this included Southwell's *Epistle of Comfort*. For
the centrality of consolation for Jesuits and its special meaning see
John W. O'Malley, *The First Jesuits* (Cambridge, MA and London,
1993), pp. 19–20.

35. Elizabeth Hanson (p. 59) cites these as examples of the way 'racking
[and execution] of Catholics were placed within the discourse of
martyrology'. Milward also notes (p. 61): 'The smallest details of
Campion's arrest, imprisonment in the Tower, tortures, trial and execution, were controverted in innumerable pamphlets on either side.'

36. Verstegan, p. 23; further page numbers cited in text.

37. As White notes, such Latin works about the English persecution were
aimed at a Continental and educated, rather than an English and
popular, audience. The book she suggests (p. 232) as the nearest to
Foxe's *Book of Martyrs* is John Gibbons' *Concertatio Ecclesiae Catholicae
in Anglia* ... (Trier, 1583; second [expanded] edition, 1588). Frescoes of
the English martyrdoms were painted on the walls of the English
College, Rome and reproduced in *Ecclesiae Anglicanae Trophaea* (Rome,
1589).

38. Dedication to *Jesuitismi*, quoted in Simpson, p. 462.

39. This became, as Milward notes (p. 71), 'the most popular book on
England in sixteenth-century Europe, going into fifteen editions – including translations into French, Spanish, Italian and German –
within ten years of its first appearance.'

40. *Anti Sanderus. Duos continens Dialogos* ... See Milward, p. 72.

41. Hughes and Larkin, 3: 86–93. See Nancy Pollard Brown, 'Robert
Southwell: The Mission of the Written Word', in *The Reckoned Expense*,
ed. McCoog, pp. 193–213. For an excellent discussion of Catholic inte-
riority and the topic of toleration dealt with in Southwell's *Humble
Supplication*, his letter to Robert Cecil and in Campion's 'Brag', see
Ronald J. Corthell, '"The Secrecy of man": Recusant Discourse and the
Elizabethan Subject', *ELR* 19 (Autumn 1989): 272–90.

42. See Garnet's 'A brief discourse of the condemnation and execution of
Mr. Robert Southwell, priest of the Society of Jesus', in Foley, 1: 373.

43. Letter to Aquaviva of 7 March 1595 (ARSJ.Rome.Angl. Hist. II.107 –
transcription of the Italian and English translation in Jesuit
Archives, London, kindly made available to me by Thomas
McCoog, S. J., who is editing Garnet's letters for publication). In a
letter to Persons (9 April 1598), Garnet also mentions that he had
had the copy of the Breviary Southwell used during his imprisonment and sent it to Alfonso Agazzari (Stonyhurst Coll. P.551, ARSJ
Angl.38.II, fol. 182).

44. See Basset, p. 119.

45. Garnet to Aquaviva, 7 March 1595. I have changed McCoog's translation slightly, to correct the reference to Montjoy from Montague ('Montago' in the Italian).

46. Quoted in Devlin, p. 324. Brown, 'Robert Southwell: The Mission of the Written Word', p. 212, notes that the Countess of Arundel 'had a relic [of Southwell], one of the bones of his feet and wore it constantly, exerting herself in every possible way to follow his edicts'. The author of *A Yorkshire Recusant's Relation* (printed in John Morris (ed.), *The Troubles of Our Catholic Forefathers*, vol. 3 [London, 1877]) refers to the desire to prevent Catholics from collecting relics from executions: 'they use singular diligence and wariness in martyring us, that no part of blood, or flesh, or garment, or anything belonging to the martyr be either unburnt or escape their hands... . The apparel the murderers take and disperse, the pins, points, buttons and all, lest Catholics get them and use them for relics' (pp. 98–9).

47. On the suppression of relics in the English Reformation, see Eamon Duffy, *The Stripping of the Altars: Traditional Religion in England, 1400–1580* (New Haven, CT and London, 1992), pp. 384–5, 390, 407–15 and passim and Whiting, pp. 72–74. Duffy notes (p. 47) that 'A major feast of England's most important saint, Thomas Becket, [was] the translation of his relics ...' For a good discussion of Becket's shrine and how 'the metaphorics of the relic were transformed', see Clark Hulse, 'Dead Man's Treasure: The Cult of Thomas More', in *The Production of Renaissance Culture*, ed. David Lee Miller, Sharon O'Dair and Harold Weber (Ithaca, NY and London, 1994), pp. 190–225. The rediscovery in 1578 of the Roman catacombs with their rich treasure of relics of early Christian saints and martyrs created fresh interest in relics.

48. Hughes and Larkin, 2: 118.

49. Ibid., p. 123.

50. *An Epistle of Comfort to the Reverend Priestes, & to the Honorable Worshipful, & Other of the Laye Sort* ... (1587), Aa7. In one of his letters, however, Southwell refuses to dignify the remains of a contemporary radical Protestant martyr: 'At Norwich in England, a certain leader of a new sect, until a short time ago a tanner ... held that neither Christ nor the Holy Spirit was God; that Christ was not born of the Virgin Mary; that no one should swear for any reason whatever; that there should be no magistrates in a Christian republic; ... This man, after having been condemned to death by persons almost like himself, was shortly afterward burned – [while displaying] wonderful, as they say, obstinacy and the perverse appearance of piety. But shortly after, neither the fellow's bones nor his very ashes could be found so eagerly did the foes of pious relics try to get these faeces' (Southwell to Aquaviva, 26 August 1587, ARSJ. Fondo Gesuitico 651/648, in McCoog, 'Letters of Robert Southwell', 106, translation separately provided by the editor). Erasmus satirically treats all relics as excremental (see 'A Pilgrimage for Religion's Sake', in *Ten Colloquies of Erasmus*, trans. Craig R. Thompson [New York, 1957], pp. 56–91).

51. See James H. McDonald, *The Poems and Prose Writings of Robert Southwell, S. J.: A Bibliographical Study* (Oxford, 1937). The printing of this work may have been allowed in order to foment further dissension between the Jesuits and the anti-Jesuit Catholics during the 'Appellant Controversy' prompted by the appointment of George Blackwell as 'Archpriest' for England (White, p. 257). See Garnet's letter to Persons (5 May 1602) in which he indicates he tried to prevent the publication because it might 'breed new troubles' and further anti-Jesuit hostility among the more accommodationist Catholics (Stonyhurst Coll.P.547).

52. Quoted in McDonald, p. 95.

53. Haviland's 1630 edition of *St. Peters Complaint, Mary Magdalens Funerall Teares, With Other Workes* has, on the title-page of some surviving copies, a portrait of Southwell furnished with this Latin inscription reminding the reader of the martyr's dismemberment: 'P. Robertus Southuell Soc. Jesu Londini pro Cath. fide suspensus et sectus. 3.mar.1595' (McDonald, p. 99): 'Father Robert Southwell of the Society of Jesus, hanged and dismembered in London for the Catholic faith, 3 March 1595'.

54. Hulse discusses (p. 219) how, in the case of Sir Thomas More, not only writings, but also biographies and portraits of the saint, became 'substitute relics'.

55. See Walter Ong, *Orality and Literacy: The Technologizing of the Word* (London and New York, 1982).

56. *Areopagitica*, in John Milton, *Complete Poems and Major Prose*, ed. Merritt Y. Hughes (New York, 1957), p. 720.

57. 'Typography and Meaning: The Case of William Congreve', in *The Book and the Book Trade in Eighteenth-Century Europe*, ed. Giles Barber and Bernhard Fabian (Hamburg, 1981), pp. 93–4. McKenzie illustrates the person/book connection in Shakespearean imagery from *Othello, Twelfth Night, Troilus and Cressida, Richard II, Coriolanus* and *The Winter's Tale*.

58. Samuel Daniel, *Poems and A Defence of Ryme*, ed. Arthur Colby Sprague (Chicago, 1930), p. 9.

59. Brown notes that Southwell's letter followed Ralegh's own *Instructions to His Son* in this publication (Nancy Pollard Brown and James H. McDoland, eds, Robert Southwell, *Two Letters and Short Rules of a Good Life* [Charlottesville, 1973], xlviii–ix). On the surviving manuscript and print versions of Southwell's letter to his father, see Brown, 'Robert Southwell: The Mission of the Written Word', 206–7. Other titles using the same metaphor include: *Reliquiae sacrae Carolinae* ... (1648); *Reliquiae Wottonianae* ... (1651); *J. Cleaveland Revived: ... with some other exquisite remains of the most eminent wits* ... (1659); Simon Ford, *Londini quod reliquum, or, Londons remains* (1667, following the fire of 1666); Joseph Glanvill, *Some Discourses, Sermons and Remains* (1681); *Golden remains of Sir George Freeman* ... (1682); *The Works of Mr. John Oldham: together with his remains* (1686); *Some genuine remains of the late pious and learned John Lightfoot D.D.* (1700).

60.  McDonald, p. 77. He notices (p. 91) that the 1616 St. Omer's edition of *S. Peters Complaint and Saint Mary Magdalens Funerall Teares* has 'the emblem of the Society of Jesus ... the letters "I H S", surmounted by a cross rising from the cross-piece of the "H"; below the letters, three nails; around the letters and the nails, a radiance of light'. (This is similar to the ornament at the top of the Cawood title-page.)

61.  McDonald remarks (p. 77): 'Apart from *Saint Peters Complaint* most of the poems he printed occur toward the end of the manuscripts.'

62.  Folger Shakespeare Library, Harmsworth MS.

63.  McDonald, pp. 82–3, suggests this is a likely date.

64.  Ibid., pp. 82, 85.

65.  Ibid., p. 98. White notes (p. 270) that in *Moeoniae*, in the cycle on Mary and her Son, the printer did not include poems found in manuscript on 'The Death of Our Ladie' and 'The Assumption of Our Lady'. See Brown, 'Robert Southwell: The Mission of the Written Word', 200, 204, 206–7, on the attempts to suppress the Catholic content and make the writings more acceptable to Protestant readers.

66.  The Continental Catholic press issued the work as *A Christian Directorie* (1585) after Bunny's version had appeared. See Milward, pp. 73–6; also Victor Houliston, 'Why Robert Persons Would not be Pacified: Edmund Bunny's Theft of The Book of Resolution', in McCoog (ed.), *Reckoned Expense*, pp. 159–77.

67.  'Catholic Texts and Anti-Catholic Prejudice in the 17th-century Book Trade', in *Censorship and the Control of Print in England and France, 1600–1900*, ed. Robin Myers and Michael Harris (Winchester, 1992), p. 53.

68.  See Hughey, 1: 106–11 and 2: 57–66 and Edward Doughtie (ed.), *Liber Lilliati: Elizabethan Verse and Song* (Bodleian MS Rawlinson Poetry 148) (Newark, London and Toronto, 1985), p. 83. Harington's opinion was reported by his son, Sir John Harington of Kelston (Hughey, 2: 63).

69.  I note both this and the previous poem in my recent book, *Manuscript, Print and the English Renaissance Lyric* (Ithaca, NY and London, 1995), p. 6.

70.  Cited in McDonald, 134. Leah Marcus points out that the cult of the infant Jesus, which Southwell brought to England, represents a response to the Calvinist view of fallen nature and the corrupt child (*Childhood and Cultural Despair: A Theme and Variations in Seventeenth-Century Literature* [Pittsburgh, 1978], pp. 70–1)

71.  Letter of 5 May 1601; cited in McDonald, 134. White, pp. 270–4, notes the imitation of Southwell's poetry and of *Marie Magdalens Funeral Teares* by non-Catholic writers like Nicholas Breton (in *Marie Magdalens Love* [London, 1595] and *Auspicante Jehova. Maries Exercise* [London, 1597]); and Gervase Markham (in *The Teares of the Beloved* [London, 1600]).

# 3

# 'A very good trumpet': Richard Hakluyt and the Politics of Overseas Expansion[1]

## Pamela Neville-Sington

Not long ago, as we were driving back to Boston after a weekend in Cape Cod, I happened to spot 'Plimoth Plantation' on the map. I realized that, rather surprisingly, I had never been dragged there as a child, so I convinced my sceptical British husband to make a detour. We arrived to find the Pilgrim Fathers in Disney fashion, frozen in time – in the year 1627 to be precise. The volunteers, sporting early seventeenth-century attire, went about their daily chores among the reconstructed village, speaking in contemporary dialects and expecting their visitors to do the same. Most people, especially those with children, wanted to know all about that first harsh winter of 1620–1, the Indians and Thanksgiving. When I began asking questions about the settlers' financial arrangements with London merchants, a torrent of well-informed abuse came forth from the cantankerous Pilgrim John Billington. My husband, who had thoroughly entered into the spirit of things, asked: 'Master Billington, have ye read Hakluyt?' Billington's eyes nearly popped out of his head. 'Oh, aye, I know Hakluyt. How have thee come by this man?' I think my seventeenth-century speech must have broken down somewhat as I explained that I was compiling a bibliography of works by the Elizabethan geographer Richard Hakluyt. 'It is a shame Elder Brewster is not with us this day' (the plantation was being manned by a skeleton crew as we were there off-season) 'for he hast a tome by Hakluyt in his library.' It was my turn to show surprise. Could he tell me anything more? Billington stared at me, started to speak, but stopped in mid-sentence, shook

66

his head in apparent frustration and strolled away. I was left wondering where Billington got his information.

While we were pondering the situation over a late lunch in the Plimoth Plantation cafeteria, a man in jeans, sneakers and T-shirt came bounding up to our table. He introduced himself as Bob, alias John Billington, and explained that he wanted to tell me more about Brewster's copy of Hakluyt, but had found it impossible while stuck in the year 1627. Safely back in 1994, he was able to direct me to the inventory of Brewster's library, made at the time of his death in 1644 and reproduced in an early issue of *The Mayflower Descendant*.[2] I made it to the small local library in Plymouth before closing time and was able to add another copy of Hakluyt's *Divers Voyages* to my list. Sadly, its present whereabouts are not known.

One could say that Bob had read Hakluyt in two different guises, as a modern historian in 1994 and as a Pilgrim Father. The twentieth-century persona had used Hakluyt's published collections of voyages as a guide to the attitudes and behaviour of an early seventeenth-century colonist, from his vocabulary and syntax to the kind of information – and misinformation – which settlers had taken with them to the New World. The seventeenth-century persona had scoured the eye-witness accounts gathered by Hakluyt for vital information on the climate, flora, fauna, native peoples and natural resources which one might encounter in America.

Today literary scholars and historians are often concerned with the difficult task of trying to understand how contemporary readers received a text. What were the forces in Elizabethan England, for example, which acted upon authors and editors and how did readers react to their works? One approach to this question, which is often neglected, is to examine closely the actual books which contemporary readers held in their hands: this can reveal interesting clues about an audience's relationship to a specific text. Richard Hakluyt makes for a very interesting case study in what one might call forensic bibliography. Placed in their geopolitical context, Hakluyt's publications reveal complex layers of meaning dictated by vested private interests, government policy and factions at court.

Richard Hakluyt, born in 1552, came from a family mainly of lawyers and merchants. He himself trained as a priest while studying geography at Oxford. He published three collections of voyages: the *Divers Voyages* of 1582, a small octavo pamphlet concerned exclusively with North America; the *Principall Navigations* of 1589, a folio volume gathering together accounts of all the English voyages of exploration to date and his major work, the *Principal Navigations* of 1598–1600, three large volumes of voyages which covered the known world. Hakluyt was a conscientious editor and an historian's dream, for he was careful to collect contemporary accounts drawn from first-hand experience and, what is more, he printed a number of texts translated into English from Spanish, Portuguese, Dutch, French, Latin and Italian.

Hakluyt was first and foremost a propagandist for long-distance trade and colonization, something which was obvious to his contemporaries. Sir Philip Sidney called the geographer's first work, the *Divers Voyages*, 'a very good trumpet' for Sir Humphrey Gilbert's 1583 expedition to explore and colonize North America. In the prefatory letter to Sidney, the book's dedicatee, Hakluyt sets out a coherent policy of overseas expansion. He writes that 'there is a time for all men' and since it was 'the Portingales time to be out of date' following the recent union with Spain, England must take the initiative and acquire territory in the 'fertill and temperate places' of the New World. The 'desire to advance the honour of our Countrie which ought to bee in every good man' demands it, as does the sight of prisons 'filled with able men to serve their Countrie, which for smal robberies are dayly hanged up in great numbers'.[3] The other undesirables who were to set sail with Gilbert to the New World were members of the Catholic gentry who had sworn not 'to do anything to Elizabeth's prejudice'.[4] At the back of the *Divers Voyages* Hakluyt lists the numerous commodities 'growing in part of America, not presently inhabited by any Christians from Florida Northward'. Access to these commodities together with the market created by the colonists and natives would make England completely self-sufficient.

In advocating this course, Hakluyt was reflecting the philosophy of a faction within government which believed that the country's interests would be best served if England became an autarky, with its balance of trade no longer dependent upon the fluctuating markets of northern Europe. The Lord Treasurer, Burghley, culled the records, ancient and modern, for statistics to show the downward spiral of England's trading position.[5] To persuade ministers and merchants alike that colonization was the answer, Hakluyt gathered all the information on explorations, past and present, that he could find among company records, government documents and sailors' first-hand accounts, both English and foreign.

These eye-witness descriptions of long sea voyages were of considerable strategic value, for they offered otherwise inexperienced English sailors practical navigational information. Hakluyt knew that ignorance of foreign waters led to disaster at sea. He later explained:

albeit my worke do carry the title of The English voyages, aswell in regard that the greatest part theirs and that my travaile was chiefly undertaken for preservation of their memorable actions, yet where our owne mens experience is defective, there I have bene careful to supply the same with the best and chiefest relations of strangers.[6]

The creation of the Muscovy and Levant Companies and major voyages of Fenton, Frobisher and Drake had all taken place by 1582, when the *Divers Voyages* appeared in print. Hakluyt could, therefore, assert with some justification that the time was never better to explore North America. A copy of this now rare pamphlet in the Free Library of Philadelphia suggests that some had at the time found Hakluyt's arguments convincing. A contemporary title-page inscription shows that Sir Edmund Brudenell of Northamptonshire bought his copy of *Divers Voyages* on 22 May 1582, the day after the work had been entered in the Stationers' Register. Within a few weeks Brudenell had signed up with a number of Catholic associates for Gilbert's enterprise.[7]

However, as Hakluyt would have been the first to admit, in 1582, compared to her Continental rivals, England did not know nearly enough about America.[8] Hakluyt considered joining two different expeditions to the New World. But, in the end, he decided to explore America by going to France. Why France? In the words of one historian, 'he went there because he could not go to Spain.' And 'if France was thus nearer to Spain than England, it was also in a sense nearer to America', for the French, too, albeit on a much smaller scale than Spain, had explored America, particularly the northern coast and planted colonies.[9]

Hakluyt's tour of duty with the English ambassador in France from 1583 to 1588, serving as chaplain, courier and intelligence agent, broadened his outlook as well as enriching his collection of sources. In Paris he frequented the exiled court of Don Antonio of Portugal. He described to his paymaster back in London, Sir Francis Walsingham, his encounters with five or six of [Don Antonio's] best captains and pilots... . The number of Portugals which hang upon the poor king are about an hundred or sixscore; divers of them are lately come out of the East India, overland.[10]

In this same letter addressed to Walsingham, we find mention of Hakluyt's most important contact in France, the Royal Cosmographer André Thevet. Soon after his arrival, Hakluyt sought out Thevet, whom he undoubtedly admired: he had used his work as a source for the *Divers Voyages*. Thevet, born in about 1516, was much the older of the two and had published several large tomes on geography. Perhaps most important in Hakluyt's eyes, he had actually travelled to at least some of the places he wrote about, the 'French Antarctic', that is Brazil and the Levant – though these were voyages made back in the 1550s. It is evident that for a time Thevet, who had access to valuable material, took Hakluyt into his confidence; after all, both were men of the cloth who had devoted themselves to the study of geography. Also, Thevet was, as Frank Lestringant remarks, something of a megalo-maniac:[11] like all collectors, he enjoyed showing off his treasures. So he fed Hakluyt priceless manuscripts, including the Aztec Codex Mendoza, as well as information about the voyages to the New World which the French Crown was considering at the time.[12]

Another manuscript which Thevet loaned to Hakluyt was the most important source to date on the French in America, René de Laudonnière's eye-witness account of the French colony in Florida which had been brutally stamped out by the Spanish in 1565. However, Thevet had sat on this document for 20 years. Admittedly it was not the sort of story to inspire the French to further exploits, but his motives were probably more complicated. The Catholic priest may not have wanted to make martyrs of Laudonnière's Huguenot colonists in Florida. And, although he prided himself on his title as Royal Cosmographer to four Valois kings, by the 1580s Thevet was leaning towards the Catholic League, which put him in the Spanish camp.

It soon became clear that although Thevet and Hakluyt had met as geographical allies they would part as fierce political enemies. When Hakluyt appeared on Thevet's doorstep to return the Laudonnière manuscript and to present him with a copy of the book which he had had printed from it, the old cosmographer called Hakluyt and his fellow editor, Martin Basanier, plagiarists and imposters and accused them of sinister enterprises and villany.[13] Hakluyt later offered his opinion that the Florida manuscript 'by the malice of some too much affectioned to the Spanish faction, had bene above twentie yeeres suppressed'.[14] Hakluyt remained steadfast in his purpose: to make Laudonnière's account widely available to his fellow countrymen he published an English translation in London in 1587.[15] He had gone to France as a naive enthusiast of exploration, but this episode seems to have taught him that geography could not be separated from politics. He was to become very adept at trimming his sails to the political winds, as we shall see.

In France Hakluyt had taken on board just how far England was lagging behind in the exploration of new worlds: as he writes, he

> both heard in speech and read in books other nations miraculously extolled for their discoveries and notable enterprises by sea, but the English of all others for their sluggish security and continuall neglect of the like attempts [are] ... either ignominiously reported, or exceedingly condemned.

England's reputation on the seas had to be bolstered, both at home and abroad and the defeat of the Spanish Armada in the summer of 1588 gave Hakluyt the opportunity. He returned to England at the end of that year to oversee the publication of the first edition of the *Principall navigations, voyages and discoveries of the English nation, ... to the most remote and farthest distant quarters of the earth at any time within the compasse of these 1500 yeers.*

Although the English nation had united against the Spanish threat in 1588, internal conflicts continued throughout Elizabeth's reign over long-term policies as well as short-term interests. Where did England's economic future lie, in Europe or overseas? A familiar dilemma. What should be the official stance on the maverick privateers? Personal battles were also being fought at court, principally between Sir Robert Cecil and the Earl of Essex. Beneath the larger themes of nationalism and exploration in the *Principall Navigations*, one can discern Hakluyt's own opinions in these matters as well as the inner conflicts which he experienced over certain issues. He was also well aware of the fact that the material he chose to print had to meet with the approval of the censors.

Hakluyt called the *Principall Navigations* of 1589 'a burden, in consideration that these voyages lay so dispersed, scattered and hidden in severall hucksters hands.'[16] He did, however, have help from several interested parties. The main sponsor of this volume was the Secretary of State, Sir Francis Walsingham, who, as Hakluyt wrote, had 'a speciall care of … the advancing of navigation, the very walles of this our Island, as the oracle is reported to have spoken of the sea forces of Athens.'[17] Walsingham gave Hakluyt access to government documents, personally licensed the book for publication and accepted Hakluyt's dedication.[18] Hakluyt's other main source of material was the trading companies, which were always seeking government support for their enterprises abroad. He tells us that he delved into the Levant merchants' records and had the run of their (disorganized) offices.[19] He also had access to the archives of the Muscovy Company, for which he had been acting as an advisor.

Despite his impeccable sources, Hakluyt still fell foul of the censors. This was all too easy to do since they did not read the material in question until after at least some, if not all, the copies had been printed and were ready to go on sale. Existing copies of the *Principall Navigations* provide us with the evidence. A word of caution here: it is always safest to confine one's examination to those copies which are still in their contemporary bindings: these are unlikely to have been sophisticated – or mutilated – by subsequent booksellers and owners.

The changes which officials demanded concern two separate accounts. The first, Sir Jerome Bowes' description of his 1583–4 embassy to Russia, is found in the *Principall Navigations* in two different versions: a rather candid report of the goings-on at the Russian Court and a shorter, watered-down version, 'printed this second time, according to the true copie I received of a gentleman that sent in the same voyage, for the correction of the errours in the former impression.'[20] Presumably it was thought that the ambassador's original report was not conducive to good Anglo-Russian relations and the Muscovy Company, or Walsingham, or Walsingham at the Company's request, ordered that it be revised. The printers on the whole complied and two-thirds of the 30 copies in original bindings have the reworked text. Although the volume of trade with Russia was not great, the country supplied the cordage vital to England's maritime fleet.[21]

The second change concerns an account of Sir Francis Drake's circumnavigation of 1577–80. The preliminary leaves, that is, the dedicatory letter, preface and title-page, were always the last part of a book to be printed. In his 'Preface to the Reader' which Hakluyt set at the front of the *Principall Navigations*, he states that he had deliberately not included an account of the famous circumnavigation in order 'not to anticipate or prevent another mans paines and charge in drawing all the services of that worthie Knight [Drake] into one volume'. However, the projected volume extolling Drake's escapades at sea did not appear; instead, three-quarters of the extant copies of the *Principall Navigations* contain twelve unnumbered pages describing Drake's world voyage.[22] Perhaps officials refused to license the Drake volume and Hakluyt, getting wind of the suppression, slipped a brief account of the circumnavigation in at the last minute. It is even possible that Walsingham, wanting to give this notorious privateer as little publicity as possible, especially after his disastrous Portugal expedition the previous summer, suggested that Hakluyt make this late addition to his text in order to assuage the public's thirst for news of Drake's greatest achievement.

Hakluyt was no doubt happy to include such a popular item as the world voyage in the *Principall Navigations*; yet like the government, but not for all the same reasons, he had mixed feelings concerning Drake and his mates. Queen Elizabeth was furious when these English 'sea dogs' preferred to plunder Spanish ships rather than carry out proper naval campaigns. More fundamentally, as Pauline Croft remarks, 'there was a clash of economic interests at the heart of Elizabethan foreign policy'. Many merchants and politicians feared that the provocative exploits of the privateers would upset the vital trade with Spain and the rest of Europe, especially in wool.[23]

Hakluyt, as we have seen, did not think that England's economic future lay with Europe and in the *Principall Navigations* he sought to undermine the importance of trade with the Continent. Although the Merchant Adventurers had dominated the European cloth trade since the Middle Ages and were by far the single largest and most powerful trading company in London in this period, Hakluyt fails to make a single reference to the Adventurers' often impressive exploits abroad, thus marginalizing them in his readers' imaginations.[24] Yet in his mind the privateers, intent only on short-term gain, were no better than the Merchant Adventurers, with their dependence on trade with Europe: both diverted resources and attention away from the exploration of long-distance trade routes and the settlement of colonies abroad. A Dutchman, whom Hakluyt had been advising on a passage to the East, remarked in 1595 that the English geographer 'has been the instructor of all these English voyages of discovery, but now they are all out to get a scanty profit from war and grieve him'.[25]

However, Hakluyt, writing under the shadow of a 19-year-long undeclared war with Spain, was above all a patriot and a pragmatist. He was no lover of the Spanish and welcomed the opportunity to 'annoy them, if they drive and urge us by their sullen insolencies'.[26] He also realized, as did Queen Elizabeth, that the exploits of Drake at sea were better than nothing, for those Spanish ships captured not only gave up their gold, but also their maps, journals and other secrets of navigation.

Thus far, we have seen how publications were subject to political pressures which inevitably led to last-minute revisions and additions. But how aware was the public of censorship and its implications? I have recently come across interesting evidence which suggests that readers in Elizabethan England were really quite sophisticated in this regard.

With the second, expanded edition of the *Principal Navigations*, published in three volumes between 1598 and 1600, Hakluyt sought to mark England's growing international prestige as a maritime power and to spur her on to empire. These volumes are organized geographically: thus, volume one looked north and northeast, volume two south and southeast and volume three westward. Hakluyt's main patron, Walsingham, had died in 1590. The geographer showed his political acumen by dedicating the first volume of the expanded *Principal Navigations* to Charles, second Lord Howard of Effingham, Lord Admiral of England, ally of the Lord Treasurer, Burghley and hero of the Spanish Armada. Effingham had also been one of the heroes, along with the Earl of Essex, of a more recent naval battle, the siege of Cadiz in 1596. In his dedicatory letter to Effingham, date 7 October 1598, Hakluyt explains that he decided, probably quite late in the day, to place the accounts of both the Spanish Armada and 'Voyage to Cadiz' at the end of volume one of the *Principal Navigations*:

> Both of which, albeit they ought of right to have bene placed among the Southerne voyage of our nation [that is, in volume

two]: yet partly to satisfie the importunitie of some of my special friends and partly, not longer to deprive the diligent Reader of two such woorthy and long-expected discourses; I have made bold to straine a litle curtesie with that methode which I first propounded unto my selfe.

Hakluyt and his unidentified 'special friends' were taking a calculated risk. As far as the government and especially Elizabeth, were concerned, the Cadiz expedition had been a very unsatisfactory affair: the damage done to the Spanish fleet as a whole had been minimal, opportunities had been missed and very little plunder had made its way into the royal coffers. Furthermore, rivalries had developed among the expedition's leaders, Effingham, Essex, Vere and Ralegh, in sharing out the glory and the blame. Not because of any treasonable content, but simply to stifle these controversies, the Archbishop of Canterbury, George Whitgift, as directed by the Privy Council, banned the publication of all discourses on Cadiz.[27]

Perhaps Hakluyt felt that an anonymous eight-page account of the Cadiz voyage tacked on to a much larger work would escape censorship: he certainly knew that it would made the volume hugely popular. No such luck: the 'Voyage to Cadiz' was quickly suppressed. Sir Robert Cecil, son of the recently deceased Lord Burghley and heir to his position as Elizabeth's chief minister, almost certainly took exception to the account's glorification of the Earl of Essex, his main rival at court.

The bibliographical evidence, though confused, indicates the sequence of events. Again, restricting ourselves to contemporary bindings, of the 69 copies of the *Principal Navigations*, half have the title-page dated 1598 in the first volume, advertising 'the famous victorie atchieved at the citie of Cadiz'. However, a third of those dated 1598 do not contain the Cadiz account. It seems likely, then, that the censors objected to the inclusion of the 'Voyage to Cadiz' very soon after the volume went on sale in December; they then ordered that the offending pages be suppressed and a new title-page run off, leaving out any mention of the Cadiz voyage. The printers complied within a month or so, that is by January or February and 34 of the 69 copies of volume one in contemporary bindings have this new title-page, dated 1599.

But, there is still a mystery here, for half of these censored volumes with the 1599 title-page nevertheless include the forbidden Cadiz leaves. Hitherto bibliographers have assumed that this was just another instance of pandemonium in the printer's shop, with well-meaning but overworked printers letting uncensored copies slip through. But, looking at the books themselves, it becomes clear that the presence of the Cadiz leaves in so many copies is due mainly to the initiative of Hakluyt's readers. The leaves in question have clearly been added separately, for they are shorter and often more ragged than the rest of the text and sometimes the stubs of the original leaves are visible.

What must have happened is this: the printers, at the censors' instance, had cut out the Cadiz leaves from those copies which were in the shop at the time. However, these by now infamous leaves were not thrown away: paper was too valuable a commodity and could be used as binders' waste. In any case, the booksellers apparently had no intention of ditching such a popular item and they proved extremely cunning in getting the Cadiz leaves past the authorities. Those in the know or good customers who were buying the officially sanctioned first volume must have been offered the excised leaves under the counter. Since at this time books were usually sold unbound, the book owner could have at some later date, perhaps when the coast was clear following Elizabeth's death, have had the censored leaves, no doubt the worse for wear, bound in their original place at the end of the volume.[28]

Hakluyt's readers understood the process of censorship and could accurately 'read' the political situation. In their response they could be resourceful. The case of the Cadiz leaves certainly shows that booksellers and their customers were able to discriminate between treasonable and pretty innocuous material and that they were prepared to take steps to circumvent the censors. Among contemporaries who owned copies of the *Principal Navigations* with the suppressed 'Voyage to Cadiz' were government officials who should have known better, such as Sir Robert Cecil and Archbishop Whitgift; noblemen like the young John Harington, Baron of Exton, who did not live beyond his 21st year and John, Lord Lumley, whose copy found its way into the young Prince Henry's library; lawyers, for example one Dixie Hickman of Gray's Inn; country parsons like Richard Punder; scholars such as Henry Savile; the adventurer Thomas Shirley; and, as one would expect, a member of the Virginia Company, George Wilmer, gentleman, of Stratford Le Bow, Middlesex.[29] In part constructed by its readers, one could say that the *Principal Navigations* was an early forerunner of the interactive text.

Hakluyt was not, as most scholars perceive him today, a simple chronicler of England's heroic exploits at sea, nor was he a mere trumpet for individual ventures abroad. Although he himself never sailed further than France, he was an active – and necessarily nimble – player in the politics of overseas expansion during Elizabeth's reign.

## NOTES

1.  The research for this paper is part of a larger work to be published by the Hakluyt Society, *A Bibliography of Richard Hakluyt 1552–1616* by Pamela Neville-Sington and Anthony Payne. It will revise, update and expand the bibliographical sections of *The Hakluyt Handbook*, ed. D. B. Quinn, 2 vols (London, 1974). The present author would like to thank Dr Pauline Croft for her suggestions at an early stage and Anthony Payne for his advice and comments throughout.

2.  'Elder William Brewster's Inventory and the Settlement of his Estate', transcribed by G. E. Bowman, *The Mayflower Descendant*, III (1901). Although the inventory lists only the author's name ('Hacklett'), the valuation of the book at two shillings suggests that Brewster owned the *Divers Voyages* and not the much larger and, therefore, more costly *Principal Navigations*.

3.  In Tudor England young people were also perceived as a threat. In the 1590s Arthur Dent denounced those 'many lozy losels and luskish youths both in towns and villages [who] ... do nothing all the day long but walk the streets, sit upon the stalls and frequent taverns and alehouses.' See Ilana Krausman Ben-Amos, *Adolescence and Youth in Early Modern England* (New Haven, CT, 1995) and the review by Peter Clark, *TLS* (10 March 1995) 14.

4.  D. B. Quinn, ed., *The Voyages and Colonising Enterprises of Sir Humphrey Gilbert*, 2 vols (London, 1940) I, p. 72.

5.  Laurence Stone, 'Elizabethan Overseas Trade', *Economic History Review*, 2nd ser., II: 1 (1949–50) 30–58. In *John Dee: The Politics of Reading and Writing in the English Renaissance* (Amherst, MA, 1995), W. H. Sherman remarks that the concept of a balance of trade was something of an obsession in the late Tudor period. In many respects, Dee anticipated Hakluyt. 'In a series of maps, treatises and conferences from the 1550s to the 1590s, Dee developed an expansionist program which he called "This British discovery and recovery enterprise".' However, most of Dee's works remained in manuscript and were read by a relatively small – but select – group at the English Court: 'They informed policies more than they spread doctrines' (p. 149). Hakluyt, too, attempted to 'inform policy' when in 1584 he presented Queen Elizabeth with a manuscript entitled 'A particuler discourse concerninge the greate necessitie and manifolde commodyties that are like to growe to this Realme of Englande by the westerne

discoveries lately attempted', better known as the 'Discourse on Western planting'. See the recent edition by D. B. Quinn and A. M. Quinn (London, 1993).

6. *Principall Navigations*, vol. III.

7. D. B. Quinn, *Richard Hakluyt, Editor: A Study Introductory of the Facsimile Edition of Richard Hakluyt's 'Divers Voyages', 1582* (Amsterdam, 1967) pp. 32–3; E. Arber, *A Transcript of the Register of the Company of Stationers, 1554–1640*, 5 vols, repr. ed. (Gloucester, MA, 1967) II: 411. In St John's College, Oxford, there is a copy of the *Divers Voyages* in a contemporary binding with the initials 'P S' which may have originally belonged to Sir Philip Sidney. It seems that by dedicating his work to Sidney, Hakluyt hoped to bring the adventurer on board the expedition: Sidney did not actually invest in Sir Humphrey's venture until 7 July 1582. Quinn, *Richard Hakluyt, Editor*, p. 27; Quinn, *Gilbert*, II, pp. 245–78. We would like to thank Prof. H. R. Woudhuysen for his correspondence on this matter.

8. *Principal Navigations* (1598–1600), vol. I, dedication to Lord Howard.

9. G. B. Parks, *Richard Hakluyt and the English Voyages* (New York, 1928), pp. 100–1.

10. Richard Hakluyt to Sir Francis Walsingham, 7 January 1584; E. G. R. Taylor, *The Original Writings & Correspondence of the Two Richard Hakluyts*, 2 vols (London, 1935), p. 206.

11. Frank Lestringant, *Mapping the Renaissance World: The Geographical Imagination in the Age of Discovery*, trans. David Fausett (Cambridge, 1994), p. 7. See also *Le Huguenot et le Sauvage: L'Amerique et la Controversé Coloniale, en France, au Temps des Guerres de Religion (1555–1589)* (Paris, 1990).

12. See this same letter from Hakluyt to Walsingham cited above. The Codex Mendoza passed from Hakluyt to Samuel Purchas, author of *Purchas his Pilgrimes* (1625); it is now part of the Bodleian Library's collection.

13. Thevet, 'La grand insulaire' (1587), Bibliothèque Nationale, MS Fonds français 15452, f. 177v.

14. Dedicatory letter to Sir Robert Cecil in *Principal Navigations*, vol. II.

15. For this episode, see Lestringant, *Le Huguenot et le Sauvage*, pp. 163–82 and passim. Hakluyt also eventually rumbled that Thevet was a cosmographer of the old school, who mixed fact with fiction. In the second edition of the *Principal Navigations* Hakluyt includes a description of the Canary Islands occasioned, its author Thomas Nichols writes, 'by the great untruths, in a booke called the New found world Antarctike set out by a French man called Andrew Thevet' (*Principal Navigations*, II: 3 (second numeration); quoted in Lestringant, *Mapping the Renaissance World*, xii).

16. Dedicatory letter to Walsingham, *Principall Navigations* (1589).

17. Idem.

18. Arber, *Stationers' Register*, II, p. 529. See also W. W. Greg, *Licensers for the Press, &c. to 1640* (Oxford, 1962) pp. 93–4.

19. Parks, *Hakluyt*, p. 180.

20. *Principall Navigations*, p. 491.

21. Giles Fletcher's book *Of the Russe Common wealth* (1591) was suppressed for the same reason. See D. B. Quinn, Introduction to Hakluyt, *The Principall Navigations Voiages and Discoveries of the English Nation ... 1589* (Cambridge, 1965), xxiii–iv; T. S. Willan, *The Early History of the Russia Company, 1553–1603* (Manchester, 1956), pp. 177–8. Two years earlier some passages in the second edition of Holinshed's *Chronicles* (1587) had likewise fallen foul of the censors after publication. John Whitgift, Archbishop of Canterbury, ordered 'the staye of furder sale and uttering of the same bookes untill they shall be reviewed and reformyd' (Annabel Patterson, *Reading Holinshed's 'Chronicles'* (Chicago and London, 1994), pp. 237–8).

22. More than half the copies in contemporary bindings include both the revised account of Bowes' embassy to Russia and Drake's circumnavigation.

23. Pauline Croft, 'English Commerce with Spain and the Armada War, 1558–1603', in M. J. Rodriguez-Salgado and S. Adams, eds., *England, Spain and the Gran Armada 1585–1604* (Edinburgh, 1991), pp. 236–63, esp. p. 239.

24. G. D. Ramsay, 'Clothworkers, Merchant Adventurers and Richard Hakluyt', *EHR*, XCII (1977) 504–21; see also Robert Brenner, *Merchants and Revolution: Commercial Change, Political Conflict and London's Overseas Traders, 1550–1653* (Cambridge 1993).

25. Parks, *Hakluyt*, 145.

26. *Principal Navigations*, vol. III, dedication to Cecil. This passage begins: 'Moreover, because since our warres with Spaine, by the taking of their ships and shacking of their townes and cities, most of all their secrets of the West Indies and every part thereof are fallen into our peoples hands (which in former time were for the most part unknowen unto us) ...'

27. R. B. Wernham, *The Return of the Armadas: The Last Years of the Elizabethan War against Spain 1595–1603* (Oxford, 1994), pp. 121ff. Apparently, this account was based on one by Dr Roger Marbecke (BL Sloane MS 226).

28. In at least three of the volumes with the earlier 1598 title-page, it is evident that the 'Cadiz' leaves were also added separately. This suggests that a number of copies were censored and sold still with the original title-page, perhaps while the new 1599 title-pages were being printed.

29. According to Richard Helgerson, 'The *Principal Navigations* brings merchants into the nation and brings gentry into trade' (*Forms of Nationhood: The Elizabethan Writing of England* (Chicago and London, 1992) p. 176). However, in practical terms, this blurring of the distinction between merchant, gentleman and even nobleman – especially the younger son who had to make his own way in the world – had been going on since at least the 1550s, when the first overseas trading companies became established in England.

# 4

# Sidney's *Arcadia* as Cultural Monument and Proto-Novel

## Peter Lindenbaum

Sir Philip Sidney's *Arcadia* is often reckoned to have been the 'best loved' or 'most admired' work of English prose fiction in the seventeenth century.[1] One hesitates to say 'most popular' because of the manifest difficulty of its complex prose, its often recondite poetical experimentation and because we simply do not know how far down the social scale its readership extended – one assumes not very far. It was, none the less, one of the most frequently reprinted works of prose fiction in the 150-year period before what is generally considered the birth of the English novel, having gone through 13 editions between 1590 and 1674 and two more by 1739.[2] Its importance for the history of the novel is registered in Richardson's appropriation of his title character's name from Sidney's work and perhaps in Fielding's claim to be writing comic epics in prose. The *Arcadia* is definitely part of the *pre*-history of the novel, though and does not present itself as a work in that genre, what with its adherence to the Renaissance rules for epic (as laid down by Minturno), its alternation of prose narrative and poetic interludes, its self-conscious embodiment of aristocratic values and what amounts to its insistence that a reader apprehend its action and characters at some distance from him- or herself. The text presents itself, or rather is presented by its publishers and promoters in the seventeenth century, most of all as a monument to a dead cultural hero. As I shall suggest, however, readers began relatively early on to view the work as something a good deal closer to their own everyday lives.[3]

*The Countess of Pembroke's Arcadia* first appeared in print in 1590, in relatively modest quarto format and form, its modesty signalled in part by a self-deprecating dedicatory letter from Sidney to his sister. On a social level, of course, modesty may not be the right word: the work is dedicated to a titled sister, the title-page bears the family coat of arms and Sidney himself had just three years earlier been sent to his final rest in an extravagant funeral which bankrupted his father-in-law, Sir Francis Walsingham. We understand that Sidney's reference to his work as 'but a trifle and that triflingly handled' was mainly the *sprezzatura* recommended by Castiglione and that Sidney might well have been pleased with and proud of his work. But he did not live in order to write (indeed, he would have preferred not to have had time to do so), or write in order to live. None of his literary works was published in his lifetime and at his death few outside his immediate circle of family or friends knew that he had written anything literary at all. In any case, the 1590 edition is the last for a long while that would have even the slightest pretension to modesty.

The anonymous overseer of the 1590 edition – evidently, Fulke Greville – had, he tells us in a brief note, divided Sidney's text into chapters, 'for the more ease of the Readers'; the overseer of the second edition, the Sidney family secretary Hugh Sanford, seems to have wished to put obstacles in the way of any kind of easy reading. It was Sanford who seems to have been responsible for the elaborate title border, which has a medallion at its base showing a pig or boar backing away from a bush of sweet marjoram, which has entwined in its branches a motto reading '*Spiro non tibi*' (I breathe out, but not for you). The complex emblematic history behind this picture, along with the disagreeable comment in Sanford's Preface to the effect that 'the worthless reader can never worthily esteem of so worthy a writing', suggests that the meaning of the medallion is that only the truly virtuous-minded are capable of enjoying the treasures that follow.[4] However off-putting, Sanford's Preface does at least inform us that it was the Countess of Pembroke herself who was ultimately responsible for 'completing' the unfinished 1590 *Arcadia* with the last three books of the earlier (and very differently designed) manuscript version of the work. And Sanford's own efforts also begin to suggest how the Sidney circle wished the *Arcadia* to be read, as an ethical treasury, a source for examples of virtuous political and moral conduct – just the way, in fact, that Fulke Greville would read it in his own account of the work in the first chapter of his *Dedication to Sir Philip Sidney*, written in the first decade or so of the seventeenth century, but not published until 1652.

The bulk of the *Arcadia* increased by about half from the 1590 to the 1593 edition and the format of the text changed from quarto to folio, the format in which it was to appear throughout the seventeenth century. In an age before advertising, format was anterior to everything else for a potential reader – even to the author's name – and this folio format was through the course of the seventeenth century associated with works of scholarship and learning, with the classics – which was one of several reasons why Ben Jonson's contemporaries were so shocked and amused when he published an edition of his *Workes* (including his plays) in folio and, even worse, while he was still alive.

Subsequent editions of the *Arcadia* grew even larger. In 1598, the rest of Sidney's literary works were included, though following a general title-page announcing only *The Countess of Pembroke's Arcadia*. The volume now numbered 584 folio pages. In 1618, a brief narrative written by Sir William Alexander, designed to serve as a bridge between the point in the action where the 1590 text broke off and the older final three books took up again, was published separately and then added to copies of the 1613 edition that had not yet sold; it reappeared in all subsequent editions through to 1739. Two editions later a sixth book to the *Arcadia* (by Richard Beling) was added and following that, in 1638, James Johnstoun's link or supplement was added to Alexander's and included at the back of the volume.

It is the 1655 edition, however, to whose condition all the earlier sixteenth- and seventeenth-century editions can be said to have aspired and subsequent seventeenth-century editions replicated. Now we have a frontispiece portrait of Sidney, Sidney's Dedicatory Letter to his sister, Hugh Sanford's Preface to the Reader, an 11-page anonymous biographical account of the Life and Death of Sir Philip Sidney, extracts from Camden's *Annals* recording Sidney's death, nine pages of brief commendatory verses and an extract from Peter Heylyn's *Cosmography* providing a brief account of *Arcadia*; then we get the text of Sidney's complete literary works, plus the additions by Alexander, Johnstoun and Beling and an 86-line poem, 'The Remedie of Love', wrongly attributed to Sidney; and finally, the whole volume of 686 pages is capped off with a four-page 'Alphabetical Table, or Clavis, whereby the Reader is let in to view the principal stories contained in the *Arcadia* as they stand in their proper places'. We might consider this last addition a bit odd for a work of fiction, but then Herbert's *The Temple* had a similar 'Alphabetical Table' attached to it in the very next year, in its 1656 edition.

The prefatory Life and Alphabetical Table are of special interest. Annabel Patterson has provided an account of how the pastoral romance as a genre and Sidney's *Arcadia* in particular were appropriated by Charles I and his court and made a coded vehicle for that court's own political and aesthetic vision.[5] The prefatory Life would appear in part to express the bias of such a group. The biographer laments 'the sacrilege of our age wherein tombs of rich materials have tempted fingers no less prophane than covetous to demolish them' and his prose reads like the work of someone supporting Charles' 1633 reissue of *The Book of Sports*, as he defends the *Arcadia* against a Bible-thumping divine who sought to 'batter down the work's esteem, saying it is not only useless but noxious, for youth' to read (sig. C1). The *Arcadia* is, Philophilippos is anxious to assert, 'lawful recreation' and a 'continual Grove of morality, shadowing moral and politic results under the plain and easy emblems of lovers'. But before we accept such sentiments merely as the expression of a displaced Caroline courtier, we need to remember first that the *Arcadia* seems to have enjoyed popularity through the whole of the first three quarters of the seventeenth century and not just in the Caroline period, having been published three times in James' reign (1605, 1613, 1621), three times in Charles' (1627, 1633, 1638) and three times thereafter (1655, 1662, 1674);[6] and secondly, that this particular edition appeared in 1655, during the Interregnum and from the press not of a royalist sympathizer like Humphrey Moseley but from that of William Dugard whose sympathies by 1655 seem to have been firmly with the Interregnum powers.[7]

Dugard was in fact a rather unusual figure in the Stationers' Company. He was not a printer or bookseller by trade and had never had to serve as an apprentice in the Company; rather, as Headmaster of Merchant Taylors' School, he was given special admittance to the Stationers' Company without payment of fees, so that he might help in correcting the Latin schoolbooks that the Company printed. The other particularly distinctive addition to the 1655 edition of the *Arcadia*, the Alphabetical Table or Clavis at the end, would appear to be an outgrowth of Dugard's interests as a pedagogue. For the Table is a slightly odd one, a cross between an outright Index (something which directs a reader's attention to details *within* the text) and the first step towards a Commonplace

Book (a record of what a reader takes *away from* texts for his or her own use). Thus, there are entries which enable a reader to find given incidents, characters or passages in the text (for example, 'Euarchus, his Sentence upon Gynecia and the two princes', '*Arcadia* described'), but almost as frequent are entries which would appear to be devised as starting points for essays or simply directions to memorable expressions which might be used by the reader on future occasions ('Justice – to be preferred before nearest relations', 'Blasphemies against women', 'Gratitude, a notable example of it', 'Hospitality, maintain'd by good husbandry').

The 1655 edition marked the final state of the seventeenth-century *Arcadia*; the 1662 and 1674 editions are page-for-page reprints of the 1655 edition, except that the 1662 edition omitted the frontispiece portrait of Sidney and the 1674 edition contained an altered version of it. It is clear in all of this how those who were responsible for the text wished it to be read. As the anonymous author of the 1655 Life remarked, no monument had been placed over Sidney's grave, but that may not matter because Sidney 'is his own monument, whose memory is eterniz'd in his Writings' (sig. C1). The text and its author are to be reverenced. This is a book for study and for the study, a text one is supposed to derive political, moral and rhetorical lessons from and is not to be read simply for its story or, God forbid, for mere pleasure.

So much, then, for what we can assume the *Arcadia*'s seventeenth-century guardians and publishers intended. Most of what I have discussed thus far can be placed under the rubric of what Gerard Genette has labelled the 'paratext' of a work, that is, all those textual phenomena which may not strictly be part of the text itself, but which in effect reside at the margins, on the threshold of the work and which shape and even control how a reader apprehends the text.[8] I should like now, though, to extend Genette's term and move one step further and in quite a literal manner, into the margins and flyleaves of the text, to see what responses we find there from early readers and hence to try to determine how successful the guardians of the text were in communicating their own designs for and upon it. To do this, I propose to examine a single major collection of Sidney editions, that held at the Folger Library in Washington, DC, one of the three largest collections of early Sidney editions in the world.[9]

The Folger collection is both large enough – it contains 32 copies of editions from 1593 to 1739, plus one of the nine extant manuscripts of the *Old Arcadia* and a manuscript prose redaction of the 1593 version – and random enough to draw legitimate conclusions from. For 22 of the library's 32 printed copies were purchased either by Henry Clay Folger himself or by his agents while Folger was still alive and, as was true of his pursuit of Shakespeare First Folios, the main principle that seems to have governed his collecting was the pursuit of number: that is, Folger does not seem to have sought particularly clean copies, nor copies with particularly fine bindings, nor copies for their annotations.[10] Nor was what we might call completeness or the touching of all bases his aim, that is, a desire simply to own a copy of every one of the editions (or their separate issues) from 1590 to 1739: for after he had purchased a copy of both issues of the 1605 edition, he went on to purchase a third copy; and while possessing a copy of the fourth issue of the 1638 edition, he proceeded to purchase four more of that particular issue. Cognizant as he was from his knowledge of First *Folios* of Shakespeare that no two copies of a seventeenth-century edition were likely to be exactly the same, once Folger learned of *any* decent specimen of a text, he went after it, whether he already had a copy of that edition (or issue) or not and it is the sheer pursuit of number, then, which makes the collection a fair sample.

What we discover when we look at those 32 copies is nicely (and perhaps disappointingly) varied; while there is I think ultimately a pattern or trend in reading practices to be seen in the seventeenth-century readers' annotations, it is not a particularly sharp or striking one. At first view, we have a mix of some early readers plainly following the directions of their paratextual guides and a number of others who in one way or another are resisting such guidance or instruction.

Fifteen of the copies are totally devoid of readers' markings, which could mean either that their early readers viewed the text with such respect that they dared not mark it, or that they simply owned but never read the work. (These could be consonant rather than opposing responses.) Ten copies reveal seventeenth-century readers concerned to establish possession of the text simply by writing their names (but nothing else) on the title-pages, flyleaves or in fact any page in the volume. This category of reader, or rather owner, merges with the next, those showing little or no respect for the text; they often write their names not once but up to four or six times and at various points in the text. The text thereby becomes a volume of paper on which one practises one's penmanship skills.

Thus we see one owner, probably Charles Nollington, practising his large script 'N's some ten times in his copy of the 1638 edition (Folger Copy No. 5) and Elizabeth Pride of North Wotton recording in four different places in the text that this 1621 copy (Folger Copy 2) was her book in 1705, the gift of Laurence Carbon whom she rather ungratefully refers to, in several of her markings, as a very ugly lord or a fool of a lord. One 1627–8 copy (Copy 3) has a laundry list on page 20 and a series of mathematical calculations in the midst of the First Eclogue section and a 1605 copy (Copy 4) has a good deal of what is apparently cipher written across several of the *Astrophil and Stella* pages.

But amidst such disregard or disrespect there is evidence that the efforts of the guardians of the text did not go completely for naught. There is, for instance, a 1593 copy (Copy 1) heavily annotated in a late sixteenth-century hand by an otherwise unknown W. Blount, whose name is written on the title-page. Blount underlined and marked with trefoils passages he thought significant and wrote out in the margins the sources for given passages in Latin and Greek from Lucan, Virgil, Seneca, Martial, Hesiod, Plato and others. The annotations tend to come in spurts or clusters and are to both poetry and prose and the care and seriousness with which the text is being handled are climaxed by a lovingly crafted six-page Index to the work (the index is, significantly, similar to, but different from, the one that appears printed at the back of the 1655 edition, which means that at least two readers responded to the text in the same way)[11] and then an Index to the first lines of the *Arcadia* poems.

Close in spirit to that copy is a 1605 copy (Copy 4) with sporadic underlinings and frequent marginal trefoils and hands pointing to notable speeches or particularly striking turns of phrase, the marginal marks found next to poetry in the *Arcadia* as well as prose and adjacent to the *Defence of Poesy* and *Astrophil and Stella* also. Page 550 even has a brief prose paragraph written in imitation of Sidney's manner. The trefoils suggest that this early seventeenth-century reader too may have been at the point of preparing an index or commonplace book, or at least he or she marked up the text so as to be able to find favourite passages quickly. Both this reader and W. Blount can be said to be preparing for and contributing to the understanding of Sidney that will produce the 1655 paratext.

The other two careful early readers prepare us for something else as well in the later history of the printed *Arcadia*. One of the 1598 copies (Copy 3) has light marginal summary comments and trefoils, again evidently designed to help that reader find particlar passages again quickly. One of the 1627 copies (Copy 1) reveals underlinings, once again, of impressive speeches, aphorisms and turns of phrase. But what differentiates these two copies from the two just described is that it it is only the *prose*, not the poetry, that is underlined and marked. And in both these latter copies there seems, to judge from where the underlinings appear, to be as well a distinct effort not simply to mark the fine phrases and speeches in the romance, but also to follow the story-line.

Now it is of some interest that these four diligently marked copies, whether the markings point to the text as a rhetorical or ethical repository or as the bearer of a good story, should come from among the earlier editions in the Folger collection, in copies printed between 1593 and 1627. Those copies with later imprints tend to have fewer serious, or indeed no, annotations and thus as the seventeenth century wears on there seems to be less and less direct and serious engagement with the text, or at least less evidence of it. This could simply be a sign of the memory of Sidney as a person fading in the consciousness of his potential readers, although the text itself continues to be reprinted. Of course, such a pattern is also in part a function of statistical chance, in that a copy from 1593 or 1605 would probably have gone through more readers' hands than a copy printed in 1674. But such a pattern could point, as well, to a change in reading practices generally in the course of the seventeenth century, that is, readers may be reading just as seriously, but they are not recording their reactions as much in the margins or using books they read as sources for commonplace books. At the least, the consistent reprinting but decreasing overt engagement with the text on the part of readers points to a change in attitude to this text. What I would suggest is happening is that while the appeal of the *Arcadia* continues through the end of the seventeenth century and beginning of the eighteenth, the nature of that appeal is changing: as the *Arcadia* is conceived of less as a compendium or bearer of high Renaissance cultural values, at bottom aristocratic in nature, it is read more and more simply for its story and, in effect, as a novel, a genre more usually associated with the sensibilities of middle-class readers. One reflection of the change is that the 1655 Alphabetical Table is replaced in the two eighteenth-century editions by a List of Characters explaining simply which characters are hidden under which disguises.

There are a number of concatenated bibliographical events in the early eighteenth century which give some support to this suggestion. The *Arcadia* went through what we might call some publishing confusion in its eighteenth-century editions as it moved out of its customary seventeenth-century folio format and appeared first in 1724–5 in a three-volume octavo edition and then in 1739 in a three-volume duodecimo form, this last the format to be identified with the novel from 1740 onwards. I call it publishing confusion – meaningful transition might be a more flattering term – because, while the format moved to that of the emergent novel, the volumes continued to contain all Sidney's works and were given a more accurate title-page, that of *The Works of the Honourable Sir Philip Sidney, Kt.* While it is the 1739 edition that marks the end-point in the progress I am outlining, it is the 1724–5 edition which most clearly highlights the impending change. For we know that Samuel Richardson's firm was one of those engaged in printing the 1724–5 volumes and that edition was published by a group of booksellers, one of whom, the earlier of the two title-pages of the edition informs us, was one Edmund Curll, a figure who more than anyone else in his time catered for a broad public. He was a veritable entrepreneur of popular culture, the very opposite of the William Ponsonby of the 1590s who had been the Sidney family publisher and outlet for the whole Sidney circle and responsible for the first three editions of the *Arcadia*.[12] While Curll and his partners were popularizing the *Arcadia* by making it acessible in a less impressive and expensive format, another figure in 1725 was making the text accessible in another way: a Mrs D. Stanley, who published in that year an edition of Sidney's romance in her own modernized prose. This was a subscription edition and Mrs Stanley was making every effort to please her readers, having in fact decided to omit Sidney's eclogue sections – and in fact all of the poetry – on the advice, she tells us in her Preface, of her subscribers. Her Preface reveals also that her translation was a long time in the making and it thus may very well be that the edition of Curll and his cohorts was put forward in order to compete with Mrs Stanley's.[13]

Sidney's *Arcadia*, having been modernized and appearing in a popularizing publisher's stock, was being drawn, then, in the direction of Richardson's *Pamela*. This process I have been describing, as the romance despite its aristocratic origins is being directed more and more towards a reading public which is to seize upon and cherish the emergent novel, may help to explain, too, why there should have been no more editions after 1739 until 1867 and then only in abridged form and with the eclogue sections removed. When Richardson published his novel in 1740, the year after the last early edition of Sidney and in similar duodecimo format (in which were to appear also *Joseph Andrews, Clarissa, Tom Jones, Amelia* and so on), he plainly had come up with a type of narrative, style and appeal to a new sort of reader that helped to render the *Arcadia* obsolete.

But what an examination of Sidney's text and its paratext on the one hand and its readers' responses over the first 150 years of the printed text's history on the other alerts us to particularly is the *transactional* nature of the relation between a text's guardians, promoters and publishers – those responsible for the paratext, the author himself being dead – and its readers. As Roger Chartier, Natalie Zemon Davis and others have been pointing out for some time, a reader is by no means a merely passive recipient of a text.[14] Readers are drawn to a text by its paratext, even created as readers by it, but they themselves in turn help to shape the future presentation of the text. It is for this reason that I think it is fair to enlarge Genette's conception of the paratext to include marginalia and readers' responses in its definition. For it was from readers like the index-writing W. Blount and the reader of the 1605 edition that the 1655 publisher William Dugard got his lead. And it was from readers as early as the owner of the Clifford manuscript of the *Old Arcadia* who not only underlined impressive figures of speech and turns of phrase, but began in the fifth book to write the names of the speakers in the margins, in an apparent attempt to keep the narrative straight in his or her mind, that we see preparation for reading the *Arcadia* as what I calling a novel rather than as a cultural monument. This trend is continued in those readers who (like the reader of the manuscript) seem to concentrate only on the prose and apparently ignore the poetry. And in this category I would also, cautiously I admit, put even those seventeenth-century readers who scribbled and doodled in the text rather than treat it as an object to be shown off to impressionable acquaintances and paid homage to. When the Dublin publishers of the 1739 edition came out with the *Arcadia* in duodecimo, in what, with the publication of *Pamela* in the next year, was quickly to become the established format of the novel, they were responding to what readers had in one way or another been telling them for quite some time.

## APPENDIX: EARLY EDITIONS OF SIDNEY'S ARCADIA

1. 1590    *The Countess of Pembroke's Arcadia* (the 'New *Arcadia*'). Unfinished: two and a half books. Prefaced by Sidney's Dedicatory Letter to his Sister. *Quarto.*
2. 1593    Combined 1590 *Arcadia* and last three books of manuscript 'Old Arcadia'. Elaborate title-border added, along with Preface by Hugh Sanford. *Folio.*
3. 1598    Adds Sidney's poems, the *Defence of Poesie* and *The Lady of May. Folio.*
4. 1599    Same contents as 1598 ed. Edinburgh piracy. *Folio.*
5. 1605    Same contents. *Folio.*
6. 1613    Same contents. Late copies have inserted William Alexander's Supplement to Book III (published in 1618). *Folio.*
7. 1621–3    Alexander's Supplement in all issues. 1621 issue published in Dublin; later issues in London. *Folio.*
8. 1627–9    Adds Richard Beling's Sixth Book. *Folio.*
9. 1633    Same contents. *Folio.*
10. 1638    Adds James Johnstoun's Supplement to Book III. *Folio.*
11. 1655    Adds Frontispiece Portrait, 'Life and Death of Sir Philip Sidney', extracts from Camden on Sidney's death, commendatory verses, 'The Remedie of Love' and Alphabetical Table. Published by Willam Dugard. *Folio.*
12. 1662    Reprint of 1655 edition, but omits Frontispiece Portrait. Published by Dugard. *Folio.*
13. 1674    Reprint of 1662 edition. Portrait added again. *Folio.*
14. 1725    Three-volume *octavo* published by Edmund Curll et al. Printed in part by Samuel Richardson. Portrait of Sidney by Vertue. New 'Life of Sidney'. 'Criticisms on Pastoral Writings' added and replaces 1655 Alphabetical Table with Explanation of Some Characters in the *Arcadia*. Engravings precede each book.
15. 1739    Three-volume *duodecimo*. Omits portrait and engravings but includes everything else from 1725 edition. Published by T. Moore, Dublin.

## NOTES

1. The phrases are from John Buxton, *Elizabethan Taste* (London, 1963), p. 246 and William A. Ringler, Jr, ed., *The Poems of Sir Philip Sidney* (Oxford, 1962), p. xv. The research for the present paper was originally undertaken while on a grant at the Folger Shakespeare Library. I should like to thank the library both for the grant and the fine working conditions that make study there so enjoyable. I should particularly like to thank Laetitia Yeandle who provided considerable en-

couragement and help in identifying the nature of the script found in the margins of the Sidney texts I examined and on the history of the Folger collection generally. Any study of early Sidney editions is inevitably indebted to the formidable work of Dr Bent Juel-Jensen in his Check-List of Editions of the *Arcadia* to 1739, which first appeared in *The Book Collector* 11 (1962), 468–79 and then in revised and expanded form in *Sir Philip Sidney: An Anthology of Modern Criticism*, ed. Dennis Kay (Oxford, 1987), pp. 289–314.

2. The prize for the most reprinted work of non-overtly didactic prose fiction (that is, excluding works like *Pilgrim's Progress*) in the 150-year period before the rise of the novel would have to go to Greene's *Pandosto*. In '"Social Things": The Production of Popular Culture in the Reception of Robert Greene's *Pandosto'*, *ELH*, 61 (1994), 753–81 (esp. p. 756), Lori Humphrey Newcomb identified 24 different editions of Greene's romance between 1588 and 1700; further research by Prof. Newcomb, who has kindly shared her findings with me, has increased the number to 26 (see below, pp. 95–123). A full determination of the extent of the appeal of the *Arcadia* in the seventeenth century would, however, need to take into account not simply the number of editions but also the various offshoots from Sidney's work, most specifically, Quarles' 5000-line poem *Argalus and Parthenia*, based on a single episode extending from Book I to Book III of the *Arcadia*, which went through 22 editions between its first publication in 1629 and 1700. It was itself reduced to a prose chapbook version which was published five times between 1672 or 1673 and 1700. There was also an abridgement of the whole *Arcadia* which appeared in 1701 (in 158 duodecimo pages) and a longer prose version (that is, longer than the 24-page chapbook version) of the Argalus and Parthenia story, entitled *The Unfortunate Lovers*, which began to appear as early as 1695. There were also continuations of the *Arcadia* that were not absorbed directly into the volume of Sidney's work, for instance, Anna Weamys' *A Continuation of Sir Philip Sidney's Arcadia*, published in 1651 and perhaps again in 1690. Beyond all these are the various plays based on the *Arcadia's* material which were written in the course of the seventeenth century, ranging from *King Lear* and Beaumont and Fletcher's *Cupid's Revenge* (1608) to Shirley's *Arcadia* (1632), Glapthorne's *Argalus and Parthenia* of 1638 (based more on Quarles than Sidney), the anonymous *Andromana* (post-1642) and at least one manuscript play, *Loves Changelinges Change*. For a digest of the early editions of the *Arcadia* itself, see the Appendix.

3. I see the present study as complementing, on the level of the physical or material text, the kind of comparison made by Gillian Beer in her examination of language and class in '*Pamela*: Rethinking *Arcadia'*, in *Samuel Richardson: Tercentenary Essays*, ed. Margaret Anne Doody and Peter Sabar (Cambridge, 1989), pp. 23–39. Viewing Richardson's novel as a 'revisionary reading and rewriting of *Arcadia'*, Beer concentrates on the ways in which Richardson's naming of his heroine 'works to unsteady assumed correspondences between social class and author-

itative writing' (p. 25). I ought perhaps to acknowledge (or confess) that the conception of the novel behind my argument remains close to that put forward in Ian Watt's now often criticized *The Rise of the Novel* (Berkeley and Los Angeles, 1957); while Watt fails to account adequately for a Fielding in the early history of the novel, he does help with his focus on 'formal realism' and the rise of a middle-class reading public to point up the difference between Richardson's *Pamela* and the *Arcadia* (particularly as it is presented in the mid-seventeenth century).

4.		See Margery Corbett and Ronald Lightbown, *The Comely Frontispiece: The Emblematic Title Page in England 1550–1660* (London, 1979), pp. 58–65.

5.		*Censorship and Interpretation: The Conditions of Writing and Reading in Early Modern England* (Madison, WI, 1984), pp. 159–202.

6.		Patterson's claim that the *Arcadia* was appropriated particularly by the Caroline Court for its own aesthetic and political purposes is unfortunately based in part on a misapprehension of the bibliographical evidence. She observes that more editions appeared in Charles I's reign than in any similar period in the history of the text, citing (p. 171) editions of 1627, 1628, 1629, 1633 and 1638. But her editions of 1628 and 1629 are in fact remaining copies of the 1627 edition, with updated title-pages. The title-pages tell us simply that the 1627 edition did not sell-out immediately and are, if anything, evidence perhaps of relatively slow rather than brisk sales.

7.		Dugard had been the first printer of the particular edition of the *Eikon Basilike* which had outraged John Milton in *Eikonoklastes* because it included the prayers Charles I was purported to have uttered while imprisoned before his execution, one of which happens to have been 'stolen word for word' (Milton's phrasing) from the *Arcadia*. Dugard went on to commit the further offence of attempting to print Salmasius's *Defensio Regia* early in 1650, for which act he was imprisoned once again and deprived of his presses. After a month's incarceration, Dugard seems to have emerged from prison a new man and a republican, had his presses restored to him and proceeded to print both Milton's own government-sponsored refutation of Salmasius, *The Defence of the People of England* and get himself appointed Printer to the State. Thus it does not appear that it was as a closet royalist that he published the *Arcadia* in 1655. On Dugard's career as a printer and publisher, see Leona Rostenberg, 'Republican Credo: William Dugard, Pedagogue and Political Apostate', in her *Literary, Political, Scientific, Religious and Legal Publishing, Printing and Bookselling in England, 1551–1700*, 2 vols (New York, 1965), pp. 130–59 and my entry on Dugard in the forthcoming Dictionary of Literary Biography volume, *The British Literary Book Trade 1475–1700*, ed. James K. Bracken and Joel Silver. Several of my comments on Dugard here appear in that entry also.

8.		For Genette's terminology, see his *Seuils* (Paris, 1987), the Introduction to which has been translated by Marie Maclean, in *New Literary*

*History*, 22 (1991), 261–72. Genette's work looks back, in turn, to Phillipe Lejeune's *Le Pacte autobiographique* (Paris, 1975), p. 45.

9.   The Folger collection was until recently one of the *two* largest in the world, surpassed only by the 33 early printed editions in Dr Bent Juel-Jensen's private collection. But with the death of John Buxton in late 1989 and the bequeathing of his 19 early printed editions, the Bodleian with a total of 36 editions (along with one of the complete manuscripts of the *Old Arcadia* and a manuscript of its poems alone) now has the largest single concentration of early Sidney editions held in one place. The Folger collection remains, though, the best one to use as a random sample, because of the way the collection was built up, as I describe in the next paragraph of my text.

10.  There is evidence in Folger's own catalogue that he may have believed that the annotations in one copy of the 1598 edition (Copy 3) were those of Ben Jonson; alas, they are not.

11.  There is yet another such Index, different from the other two, but not directly attached to an edition of the *Arcadia*. It is in a manuscript, formerly in the possession of John Buxton and now in the Bodleian Library (MS Eng.e.2017), apparently dating from the mid-1640s. It seems to have been written in the same hand as a manuscript poem, 'A Draught of Sir Phillip Sidney's *Arcadia*', which can be established with some certainty as from that period; this too was formerly in John Buxton's possession and is now Bodleian MS Eng.e.2016. The index is in two parts: a 26-page Subject Index, which 'may readily lead to the most remarkable passages … in the Book', arranged in page order; and 'A Clavis opening the names and referring to the Characters' arranged in alphabetical order. See Buxton's '"A Draught of Sir Phillip Sidney's *Arcadia*"', in *Historical Essays 1600–1750, Presented to David Ogg*, ed. H. E. Bell and R. L. Ollard (London, 1963), pp. 60–77 (esp. p. 62).

12.  On Curll's career as a publisher, see Ralph Straus, *The Unspeakable Curll: Being Some Account of Edmund Curll, Bookseller* (London, 1927) and particularly the recent work of Alan D. Boehm, 'Edmund Curll and the Politics and Poetics of Popular Bookselling', unpublished paper delivered at the inaugural conference of the Society for the History of Authorship, Reading and Publishing, at CUNY, June 1993, a summary of which appears in *Publishing History*, 35 (1994), 94–5; the paper is based on Chapter III of Boehm's 'The Poetics of Literary Commerce: Popular and Patrician Bookselling and the Rise of Publishing, 1700–1825' (Diss. Indiana University, 1991). On Ponsonby, see Michael Brennan, 'William Ponsonby: Elizabethan Stationer', *Analytical and Enumerative Bibliography*, 7 (1983), 91–110.

13.  The two editions are interlocked in another way, since among Mrs Stanley's listed subscribers are William and John Innys, Booksellers and it is William Innys who evidently bought up the rights and remaining copies of the actual Sidneian *Arcadia* from Curll and his group; the second-state title-page for that edition carries Innys' name alone.

14.  See, for instance, Chartier, *Cultural History: Between Practices and Representations*, trans. Lydia G. Cochrane (Cambridge, 1988), pp. 40ff and Davis, *Society and Culture and Early Modern France* (Stanford, 1975), pp. 191–2.

# 5

# The Triumph of Time: The Fortunate Readers of Robert Greene's *Pandosto*

## Lori Humphrey Newcomb

*Infortunate Fawnia and therefore infortunate because Fawnia!*[1]

Nowadays, we recognize literary evaluations as cultural constructs, as products of particular and contingent histories and we attempt to strip away these accumulations without hoping to restore an originary artifact. But if we wish to trace the evaluative history of an early modern text, what evidence do we have of its earlier fortunes and how can we read that evidence except through our current evaluative conditionings? Unlike historians of modern literature who can draw on rich authorial, critical and publication archives, we are reduced to ingeniously interpreting evidence so thin and contradictory as to seem unreliable. To pick a famous example of these difficulties, Sir Philip Sidney's *Arcadia* was republished steadily through the seventeenth and eighteenth centuries. But that apparently unambiguous publication history is complicated by anecdotal estimations of *Arcadia*'s value, which, as compilers of literary allusions found long ago, rose and fell like 'tennis balls tossed by the racket of the higher powers': late-Elizabethan adulation yielded to Jacobean ambivalence, Caroline nostalgia and Augustan scorn.[2]

Still, despite these vacillating attitudes, the *Arcadia* remained in the literary canon and the forces that put it there have become comprehensible, thanks to recent careful reconstructions. The recent Oxford casebook on Sidney opens with 'a critical heritage' in which Dennis Kay reads those early allusions and the gradual heroicization of the literary Sidney in the context of larger changes in critical practices.[3] In the present volume, Peter Lindenbaum offers a closer

analysis of the reception of the *Arcadia*, depending upon an examination of multiple copies and editions of the romance. By locating
a history of the *Arcadia*'s literary fortunes in the physical evidence
left by its publishers and readers, he is able to demonstrate readers'
power to change the fortunes of the texts they read. We can understand the *Arcadia*'s resilience neither as a fluke nor as a foregone
conclusion once we attend to both the varied judgements of known
critics and the evocative marks of unnamed readers.

In these pages, I want to reconstruct the reception of another
Elizabethan romance, again by juxtaposing scarce and even unflat-
tering anecdotal traces with an edition count that signals great
popularity. Robert Greene's *Pandosto. The Triumph of Time* appeared
only a few years before *The Countess of Pembroke's Arcadia* and was
founded, similarly, on Heliodoran and pastoral romance models.[4]
Its special advantage, the fact that it provided William Shakespeare
with the plot for *The Winter's Tale*, was not recognized by scholars
until the end of the seventeenth century and probably became apparent to a larger theatre-going public only after the revival of the
play in the mid-eighteenth century; for the first century of its life
*Pandosto* established its reputation independently.[5] Like Sidney's
hybrid romance, it enjoyed two centuries of republication and
adaptation for audiences of leisure readers, mostly (after 1635)
under the title used as the running-title in the earliest editions, *The
Pleasant History of Dorastus and Fawnia*. If Greene's romance had the
good fortune to survive well beyond most other Elizabethan works
of fiction, it did so through a series of historical accidents – multiple
decisions to publish, illustrate, edit, cut, update, buy, read, enjoy,
reread and collect. My search for those editions has taken me
through the revised *Short-Title Catalogue*, Wing, the on-line eighteenth-century catalogue and the catalogue of the National Library
of Scotland and I have examined most of the copies they describe.
From these extant copies, I now know that the decision to bring out
an edition of *Pandosto* or *Dorastus and Fawnia* was made more than
40 times. Greene's full text of the romance was published in 1588,
1592, 1595, 1600, 1607, 1609, 1614, 1619, 1629, 1632, 1635?, 1636,
1640?, 1648, 1655, 1664, 1677, 1680?, 1684, 1688, 1690?, 1700? (three
editions assigned to this date), 1703, 1705? and even 1762. Decisions
to publish adaptations, that is, versions with substantially modernized or condensed texts, came later: 1700?, 1705?, 1727/35?, 1760?
(two versions), 1775 (two versions), 1790?, 1795, 1796, 1800?, 1807,
1820?. Most of the editions and adaptations come from familiar

sources of cheap print: the Ballad Partners and their competitors in the later seventeenth century, the London chapbook firms in the eighteenth, but among the last adaptations are imprints from Newcastle, Stirling, Dublin and Boston, Massachusetts. The adaptations vary widely: the first condensation appeared around 1700, but several different lengths were available simultaneously in any period thereafter; a near full-length modernization has been dated to 1727. These adaptations were inventively re-titled to fit prevailing tastes in popular literature ('The Royal Shepherdess', 'The German Princess'), but a common feature is that none claims Greene as its author.[6] By the end of its life as a popular text (as opposed to a scholarly recovery), *Pandosto* had been refocused as the love story of *Dorastus and Fawnia*, had shrunk from 78 quarto pages to 24 or 16 octavo pages and gained woodcuts, chapter divisions and headings making it more widely accessible and appealing. Every indication is that the 40-odd editions represent only a fraction of the many republications of a perennially popular text.

Chapbook adaptation brought *Dorastus and Fawnia* to readers who could not have afforded the full quarto text of *Pandosto*. Such readers could hardly have purchased a folio *Arcadia* but might have known *Argalus and Parthenia*, the chapbook classic derived from it (via Francis Quarles' 1629 verse adaptation in quarto). The fact that these two favourite love stories had similar publishing fortunes is indicated by a confluence of titles. Around 1695 and again in 1716, a prose adaptation of the Argalus and Parthenia story appeared in duodecimo under the name *The Unfortunate Lovers*.[7] William Onley, who printed and published *The Unfortunate Lovers*, simultaneously published *Dorastus and Fawnia* in its full text under its familiar title. Then the 1727 modernization of the love story of Dorastus and Fawnia appeared, together with a retelling of the story of Hero and Leander, under an omnibus title, *The Fortunate and Unfortunate Lovers*, published by the successors of Onley's competitors, who borrowed both his copy and his style in titles.[8] The popularity of the text survived this duplication of effort: it appears that over the seventeenth and eighteenth centuries, *Pandosto* and its variants appeared in more editions than did the *Arcadia* and *Argalus and Parthenia* combined.

While it appears in hindsight that Sidney's work reached a 'high' audience and Greene's a 'lower' popular one, these correlating publication records indicate that the audiences cannot have been mutually exclusive from the start. Nor could the later evaluations of each text have been predicted simply from their original appearances. Sidney's *Arcadia* and Greene's *Pandosto* issued from a common stream of literary influences; as late as 1599, Ben Jonson spoke of works by these two authors as the products of a single romance industry, as I shall show. Records suggest that in their first two decades at least, they reached closely comparable ranges of readers, separated primarily by the price of a folio that set a higher income threshold for ownership of the Sidney text. The reception of the *Arcadia* over the next two centuries includes its rebounding appearances as folio (or multi-volume) masterpiece and its steady popularity as chapbook love-story. Meanwhile, *Pandosto* moved into a position of multiple success at different levels of the chapbook industry. In other words, both texts were pulled into the chapbook market; but only *Pandosto* was also pushed out of the elite market. Greene's work persisted on the popular book market in the face of active denigration in various new literary milieux: only a generation after his death, his romances were mocked, in a prose character, as naive fantasies, fit only for the female servants who were their proper audience; and in the following century, similar mockery attended *Dorastus and Fawnia*, mentioned within fashionable novelistic texts as an authorless popular romance.

Still, the differing trajectories of *Arcadia* and *Pandosto* are reducible neither to the contrasting social positions of the two authors, since both had complex origins and loyalties, nor to their contrasting reputations, which are in large part ideological constructs produced by retroactive historical accidents in the afterlives of authors and their works. One such accident produced the first striking difference between the two texts: Sidney's early death and its political exploitation encouraged far more notice of the *Arcadia* than *Pandosto* ever received. Later republications of the chapbook versions of *Pandosto* appeared in an obscurity which contrasts sharply with the many invocations of Sidney as stellar Elizabethan writer.[9] In other words, the asymmetry of this comparison demands that we understand early modern textual reception as shaped not only by the casual critical judgements we find in the period, but also by the publication and reading practices that we surmise from patterns of republication.

How is it possible to weigh the publication record of *Pandosto*, which is exceptionally steady for a fiction title, against the few contemptuous anecdotes that attributed its survival to the backwardness of popular taste? Although Charles Mish noted in his 1953 article *Pandosto's* exceptional popularity, his estimate of its value was based on the dismissals of the early critics: redaction in chapbook form confirmed the cultural impoverishment of the work's readers and placed *Pandosto* in 'subliterary history'.[10] A contextualized reception study cannot accept such subjective evidence at face value, but even the apparently objective publication record still requires interpretation. Both types of record agree that *Pandosto* was a success on the popular market (the writers of anecdotes clearly assume that their readers know *Pandosto* is much published); they disagree in their estimates of the value of such success and that is where literary history, too, has foundered. Certainly the 40-odd editions tell us to suspect anecdotal suggestions that Greene's romances are devoid of aesthetic value, but the anecdotes cannot be ignored. They demonstrate that early modern criticism had begun to read popularity among 'unfortunate' readers as a crucial marker of aesthetic misfortune – an interpretative assumption that later criticism has tended to share.

In my effort to understand the formation of early modern literary value as something other than arbitrary, I have borrowed the word 'fortune' from Elizabethan fictional discourse, where it was the rubric under which a sense of pattern guiding the accidents of human history was variously asserted and questioned. The multiple associations of the term enabled writers to grapple with competing and even incommensurable measures of human value, much as I have been grappling with competing measures of aesthetic value. In Elizabethan fiction, 'fortune' was used in multiple senses to figure the difficulty of distinguishing the privileges of worth from those of birth. Greene characteristically exploited its ambiguity in the rhetorical figure of antanaclasis, which Puttenham had attempted to explain as 'the *Rebound*, alluding to the tennis ball which being smitten with the racket reboundes backe again', because the figure 'playeth with one word written all alike but carrying diuers sences'.[11] *Pandosto's* heroine, Bellaria, Queen of Bohemia, falsely accused as an adulteress by her husband, King Pandosto, remarks on the difference between her personal torment and her earthly advantages: 'Alas Bellaria, how infortunate art thou because fortunate!'[12] This use of 'fortune' implies that the contradiction between the speaker's socioeconomic status and her claim on happiness is a shocking exception to a norm in which the former predicts the latter, a congruence which is expressed in the antanaclatic speech that I have taken as my epigraph. There the

shepherdess Fawnia bewails the status that makes her unworthy of
the love of Dorastus, whom she knows to be a prince disguised as a
shepherd. As long as she is socially 'infortunate', Fawnia's fortunes
in love seem poor, but she proves instead fortunate enough to
marry Dorastus, because she is identified as the lost princess of
Bohemia. The figure of antanaclasis draws on the multiple ironies
engendered by Fawnia's mistaken identity: it plays on 'fortune' as
both description and prediction, as measure both of birth and
worth.[13] If the ideological force of 'fortune' is to extend descriptions
of social status into evaluations of individual potential, Greene's
use of the term explores the unreliability of that ideology even as
his plot strains to adhere to it. Early modern fiction manipulates the
language of fortune to expose the not quite implacable laws that
derive assessments of individual worth from socioeconomic privilege, much as contemporary criticism questions the language of
value that replicates aesthetic judgements in the form of canonical
status.[14]

Indeed, in this insistence of Elizabethan romance plots to reconcile worth to birth at all costs, contemporary criticism grounded
its judgements against the genre. Critics from Louis Wright to
McKeon have mocked the romances for their magical solutions to
social tensions. But such critical objections also express the other
conflict over ideological fortunes that I have described, that is, the
anxiety about social value; modern criticism reproduces early
modern anecdotes that claim romance's misfortune in being
popular. The anecdotes that mocked *Pandosto* and its readers are
attempts to devalue the work and its readers; both are unfortunate in their attachment to each other. The anecdotes depend
upon the gap between worth and birth which was being exposed
by early modern social changes, particularly the expansion of
leisure reading implied by those 40-odd editions. My effort here
will be to read the history of those editions as a material record of
changes in audience, without assuming, as did the tellers of anecdotes, that such changes confirmed the unworthiness of poorer
readers.

Literary history has too often echoed the prejudices of earlier
anecdotes in condemning the chapbook for its cheapness, which
amounts to condemning its readers for their poverty. Indeed, for
such critics as Mish, the condensed or reduced work became a mere
*sign* of a degraded audience.[15] The relative obscurity of popular
fiction since the work of these bibliographic pioneers has left these

assumptions unexamined for too long. If we think it ill fortune that versons of *Pandosto* managed to circulate for 200 years after its production, we will never avoid thinking of its consumers, too, as unfortunates. On the contrary, I propose here that *Pandosto* was a fortunate text by any measure, not only surviving for over two centuries, but also enjoying adaptation to new purposes. Its readers, even the poorest, were fortunate in finding affordable pleasure-reading, which met specific cultural needs. I also propose that the anecdotes disparaging *Pandosto* were doing the work that Pierre Bourdieu calls distinction. They buttressed the exclusivity of elite tastes by rejecting tastes that were more widely fulfillable; they protected threatened social divisions by creating aesthetic divisions. To characterize the later readers of Elizabethan romance as having reciprocally poor origins and cultural tastes, these anecdotes imagined them as members of two social groups that were notable, during these two centuries, for declining socioeconomic conditions – and, troublingly, increasing literacy. Women's reading for leisure was castigated in terms that drew on the humanist tradition of warnings against female literacy, particularly romance-reading; and servants, particularly female servants, became the scapegoats for consumption, and thus for the materiality of texts denied by elite aesthetics.[16]

Fundamental to our anecdotal evidence, then, is a prejudice against the very materiality represented by publication evidence. The exaggerations of these anecdotes are legible as projections of hostility to commodified print, to the naked marketing of texts. Projection, too, explains the tendency of these anecdotes to accuse readers of popular fiction of indulging in fantasies of class transgression. As I shall show, those who voiced complaints about the popularity of Greene's romance were themselves highly conscious of their own implication in the commodification of literary texts and in the dissemination of fantasies of mobility. All the writers I discuss here – Ben Jonson, Thomas Overbury, Samuel Richardson and Isaac Bickerstaff – were themselves, as their own contemporaries recognized, pursuing social advancement; all did so by deliberate marketing of their carefully authorized textual commodities. In an era that was slow to accept the self-promotion implicit in the act of publication, consigning popular literature to social unfortunates was one way for writers to advance their own fortunes while suppressing doubts about their profession. Today, best way to recover the value of *Pandosto* to its long-lost popular readers is to celebrate the qualities that were most anathematized in anecdotes – the imaginative pleasures of romances and their accessibility in material form. The recovery that follows is a fiction, although it is carefully blended of anecdotal and publishing evidence. It tells a story of the readers of *Pandosto*, who were poor in worldly fortunes but found rich pleasure in their reading.

CHAPTER I. *HOW* PANDOSTO *WAS BORN IN GOOD FORTUNES AND GREW TO BE LOVED BY MANY AND HOW THE CHARACTER-WRITER ACCUSED HIM OF MISLEADING A CHAMBERMAID*[17]

When *Pandosto* was published in 1588, it was recognizably a fashionable book by a well-educated author; indeed, if it is true that a lost edition was published in 1585, the romance must have been written within two years of Greene's taking his master's degree at Cambridge. Though the prefatory material suggests that it was written for publication, with only cursory gestures towards courtly amateurism, Greene's self-presentation here is a far cry from the naked self-promotion of the later cony-catching and repentance pamphlets.[18] In that later self-re-creation, Greene embraced and exploited the conditions of publication that more fashionable writers pretended to eschew and thus may have given all his work, including *Pandosto*, its first impetus toward its degradation by later critics. That degradation is the inverse of the authority given to Sidney's youthful works by his posthumous sanctification, but, like Sidney's fame, Greene's notoriety may have helped to distinguish his works from those of most other Elizabethan fiction writers. Certainly a large number of his titles retained their market value through repeated Jacobean and even Caroline editions, although *Pandosto* would outlast the others. At the end of the sixteenth century, Greene stands prominently in the dubious canon created by Jonson's contempt for romance. In *Every Man Out of His Humour* (1599), a obscure conversation may mark a thin line separating Sidney's quality from Greene's. According to the infatuated Fastidious Brisk, the pretentious court lady, Saviolina, 'does observe as pure a phrase and use as choice figures in her ordinary conferences, as any be i' the *Arcadia*'. Responds the cynical Carlo Buffone, 'Or rather in *Greenes* works, whence she may steale with more security'.[19] Greene's works may be disreputable, prolix or forgotten enough to make it possible to plagiarize their clichés risk-free, but they are like Sidney's *Arcadia* in being condemned by Jonson for licensing affectation.

Yet only 15 years later, claims began to emerge that Greene's readers were not affected court ladies, but naive semi-literates, an accusation that was less often levelled against the *Arcadia*. Greene slipped away from Jonson's notice: now Jonson's strategy of distinction hinged upon the Shakespeare of the late romances, those 'mouldy tales', or on the tragi-comic collaborative team of Shakespeare and Fletcher. In *Bartholomew Fair* (1614; first published 1631), Grace Wellborn asks her two wooers each to choose a word; upon these words will turn her marital choice. They select the names of two romance heroes: Quarlous' 'word is out of the *Arcadia*', Argalus, Sidney's famous tragic lover. Winwife chooses his name 'out of the play', Palemon, one of the two noble kinsmen who themselves figure indistinguishable insipidity.[20] More significantly, in 1615, the sixth impression of Overbury's *Characters* satirized 'a chamber-maide' for qualities that included a taste for Greene: 'She reads *Greenes* works over and over, but is so carried away with the *Myrrour of Knighthood*, she is many times resolv'd to run out of her selfe and become a Ladie Errant.'[21] So Greene's works deserved elite mockery because of their popularity with female, urban domestic servants, but it is more likely that the chambermaid's reading was assigned in order to ridicule Greene. Indeed, when Wye Saltonstall wrote a character which mocked maids' reading of *Amadis* and *Arcadia*, he elicited a response that recognized the character as making an *ad hominem* attack on Sidney: character-writers 'have not spared even Apollo's first-born, incomparable and inimitable Sir Philip Sidney, whose *Arcadia* they confine only to the reading of Chambermaids – a censure that can proceed from none but the sons of kitchenmaids.'[22] This defence recognized Saltonstall's character as an act of inter-generic distinction, elevating the prose character-writer's novelty over the pastoral romance writer's familiarity. Ironically, the character-writers advertised their elitism and their coterie mode of production in a form that was eagerly and profitably published. As in the earlier Jacobean association of chivalric romances with citizen readers and the Elizabethan association of romantic trifles with eroticized female readers, the character-writers blamed imaginary popular readers for ambition and promiscuity, projecting their own implication in social and marketplace competition.[23]

Against this denigration of Greene's Jacobean readership, the material evidence of *Pandosto*'s many editions offers substantial counter-evidence. For nearly a century after 1588, the text of *Pandosto* retained a stability that Shakespearean editors would envy. Over the first 95 years of its reprinting, the editions were so similar – the text set virtually page for page, type for type – that it is difficult to deduce textual evidence for any change in the book's market position. The most obvious change, in a 1635 edition, was the replacement of the original title with the former running title, *The Pleasant History of Dorastus and Fawnia* (later the adjective would be variously replaced by 'delightful' and 'excellent' in competing chapbook adaptations). Some 80 years would pass before the text published by Greene was reduced and then it was only the front matter that was altered. Not a sentence of the romance itself was cut until the great boom in chapbook adaptation in the last decades of the century. Up until then only the verse adaptations had attempted to borrow *Pandosto*'s success.[24] Thus, the falling reputation alleged by the character contrasts with the textual integrity of *Pandosto* during the same period, a stability that almost exceeds what D. F. McKenzie has famously called 'the non-uniformity of uniformity' in early modern printing.[25] The Overbury Character portrayed its coterie author's social inferior reading a degraded book, but the price of a Greene text, based on its unchanged length, would have remained the same from 1588 to 1615 and beyond.[26] Even as late as midcentury, one library inventory offers evidence that Greene's place was not yet at the cultural margins. A mid-century collector whom we know to have owned a Greene romance was, significantly, gentle – but female. Fraunces Wolfreston, the matron of a Staffordshire family of minor country gentry, owned an early edition of Greene's *Mamillia*.[27] None of this material evidence can speak alone, but it can contradict prejudicial anecdotes such as that of the character. On the other hand, the readership patterns of early anecdotes, while recognizably exaggerated, none the less predict the directions in which degraded cultural commodities would be pushed.

The single greatest change in *Pandosto*'s first century of publication was in the kind of publisher. By the 1630s, Greene's work was in the hands of the cartel that would become known as the Ballad Partners, since they sold ballads and popular literature to provincial booksellers and peddlars. While this transfer suggests that the work was increasingly marketed to the provinces, not just in London, it was hardly consignment to the bargain bins. *Dorastus and Fawnia* remained a 56-page quarto, a more expensive book than a provincial servant woman was likely to buy.

Only between 1680 and 1700 did the publishing of *Dorastus and Fawnia* enter a new and more volatile phase. In that 20-year period, it appeared in several different formats, with undated title-pages, in joint binding with another story and even in a 16-page chapbook redaction which dropped Greene's name. Some of the variations may be understood as efforts to justify publishing a work whose copy was legitimately held by another publisher. But since the holders of the original copy apparently never challenged their competitors, they seem to have shared the assumption that demand was sufficient to permit multiple versions, especially at varied price points. The publishers of popular texts collectively diversified the market for secular popular print, as Tessa Watt has argued publishers had done almost a century earlier, when they adapted devotional texts into short adaptations, popular ballads and pictorial broadsides.[28] This tiered publication strategy depended upon *Dorastus and Fawnia* appealing not to a single bottom rung, but to multiple audiences on different rungs of the social ladder. The continued production of full-length editions into the mid-eighteenth century argued that the romance could still interest more experienced and affluent readers. The material record suggests, then, that interest in Greene among the gentle remained steadier than the anecdotes suggest, but confirms that the more noticeable phenomenon in the period was production of texts specifically designed for the humbler readers newly come to literacy. Chapbook adaptations probably reified and marketed new uses of the text that readers had previously discovered by adapting their reading practices to their books; but no evidence for that claim can exist.

CHAPTER 2. *HOW* PANDOSTO *WAS READ BY SERVANT WOMEN AND RAISED SOCIAL ALARMS*

In the mid-eighteenth century, elite writers again began to differentiate their audiences from the readers of such fictional forms as the cheaper chapbook redactions of *Dorastus and Fawnia*, finding new ways to call those non-elite readers unfortunate. A new set of anecdotes about servant women consuming works like *Dorastus and Fawnia* endorsed the commentators' cultural preferences as superior to those of foolish domestics. For male observers, such references to private pleasure-reading were mildly salacious, as they had been since Lyly's time or before. They also enabled male writers to excuse their own impulse towards fiction-reading by blaming women for its excesses; by extension, ridicule of fiction-reading as feminine devalued one of the few areas in which women of the leisure classes retained any cultural or economic influence. Indeed, the remoteness of women of the working classes from the arenas of privilege made them, in mid-eighteenth-century representations, convenient scapegoats for the culture of consumption that obsessed the prosperous.[29]

Mockery of popular romance was a by-product of the emergent novel and the criticism that endorsed it. The Restoration debate between the long-winded French romance and the shorter novella (including Behn's 'unfortunate' titles) had not emphasized social tensions, since the outmoded multi-volume French romances were not very suitable for poorer audiences. But the emergent theory of the novel, or of the 'moral' romance, tended to degrade the novella by associating it with more popular 'small' romance forms. As authors and critics worked to raise the novel, they debased older forms of the romance, identifying it as the repository of the tendencies of fiction towards the incredible and inferior and as reading material fit for the uneducated and credulous.[30] Indeed, the vehemence of the attack on popular romance forms in early novels and novel criticism is startling and is not explained by the traditional argument that Restoration efforts to segregate genders and social classes further separated elite and popular cultural spheres as well. Even on Bourdieu's model, a deepening of social divisions would have made class distinction through cultural preference a less urgent necessity. It is more productive to recognize cultural spheres as places where the tensions produced by social change can find indirect expression and to conclude that the hardening of social categories heightened both the pleasures and the risks inherent in crossing cultural boundaries. During this era, *Dorastus and Fawnia* represented a type of text that was increasingly superfluous to the needs of gentle readers, for whom many new genres and forms of publication emerged. The segregation of cultures by class, gender and income enabled elite men to scorn some cheap romances, but they were not unaware of such forms or of the spread of literacy among women, artisans and servants, who now could take part in the consumption of cultural and material goods to an extent that discomforted their superiors.

Elite anecdotes about the impropriety of consumption among women and servants do not reveal, as they seem to, that readers in these groups were so pampered as to abnegate their roles. Rather, the appropriate roles for women and servants were being redefined to centre on consumption and to bear the burden of men's ambivalence about the culture of consumption which rose from their own economic activities. Women's power in the sphere of consumption was, in large part, a measure of their economic marginalization: the 'undermining of the family economy' meant that 'women lost certain roles in economic production; they took on new and subordinated roles in economic consumption.'[31] The same axiologies that classed women as consumers rather than producers also classed domestic servants as agents of consumption, not production. Female servants, who devoted their human capital to displaying the status of their masters and mistresses, were castigated routinely as 'idle' spenders; it was servants, not their masters and mistresses, who were blamed for 'consum[ing] without mercy the produce of the state, with very little return of advantageous labour'.[32]

Male property-owners and their female family members, heavy investors in commodity culture, were especially worried by the prospect of servants who could buy fashionable clothes, drink fashionable beverages or read fashionable romances, seeing such actions as 'mimetic venture[s]' emulating tastes that were the prerogative of servants' betters.[33] Despite complaints about servants' efforts at gentrification (efforts which might have enhanced the reputations of the refined servants' employers), the danger was not that the adoption of fashionable artifacts could costume the bearer for ill-deserved social mobility, as had been claimed in the Jacobean period. Lower-class consumption of fiction, lace or tea, without either extensive capital or a pedigree, could not deceive the public about the fortunes of the consumer. But servants' keeping up with fashion did at least lay bare the ideologies that associated moral and social worth with commodity consumption. More effectively than lace or tea, fiction demonstrated that ladders of worth and birth were themselves 'mimetic', a means for representing individuals through their preferences in cultural consumption. McKeon quotes one of Samuel Richardson's readers, who predicted that *Pamela*, 'by teaching Maids, to deserve to be Mistresses', would 'stir up Mistresses to support their Distinction'. This reader acknowledges the cycle of distinction, only to claim that it furthers moral development (McKeon, p. 365).

Ian Watt has called Pamela the 'culture-heroine' of conspicuous literacy, but it should be clear that she is a culture-heroine of conspicuous consumption, too, demonstrating the one possible avenue for parleying tasteful consumption into a substantial alteration in one's fortunes: the attractive young servant's marriage to a gentleman, which exposes the gentry's marriage market as yet another game of social distinction. After all, if *Pamela, or Virtue Rewarded* (1740–2) was proferred by Richardson as offering instruction in the acquisition and display of virtue, it did not limit those who could aspire to such worth and its rewards. In this context, Pamela's famous self-description as a 'tennis-ball of fortune' seems to admit the continued identification of fiction with social aspiration, even as Pamela (and Richardson) attempt to deny it – especially since the full statement constructs 'fortune' as parallel to the social rank of 'the Great': 'said I, here I am again! a pure Sporting-piece for the Great! a mere Tennis-ball of Fortune!'[34]

A few years later, Richardson denied that *Clarissa* (1747–8) was either 'a light Novel, or transitory Romance', but in a crucial scene he demonstrated his awareness of the class distinction between the two forms.[35] The romance he chose as his example was *Dorastus and Fawnia*, and it is invoked in a passage that has, as I shall show, a further intertextual affiliation. In a letter to his friend Belford, Lovelace is recounting the midnight events that have brought Clarissa, in negligée, into his arms:

> At a little after two ... I was alarmed by a confused buzz of mixed voices... . Downstairs ran Dorcas and at my door ... cried out: Fire! Fire! ... I cried out, Where? Where? almost as much terrified as the wench: while she, more than half undressed ... pointed upstairs. I was there in a moment and found all owing to the carelessness of Mrs. Sinclair's cook-maid, who, having set up to read the simple history of Dorastus and Faunia when she should have been in bed, had set fire to an old pair of calico window-curtains. (pp. 261–2)

Lovelace makes sure the kitchen maid has doused the fire, while Dorcas rouses 'the charmingest creature in the world', but he fails to press his advantage on the frightened but suspicious Clarissa (p. 262). Every detail sets the romance in a context of light-hearted denigration: the overheated atmosphere of sexual desire, the snide reference to the servant's unproductive 'carelessness', and the

phrase 'simple history', a parody of the various titles that appeared
in chapbook versions of *Dorastus and Fawnia*.

The passage implies that the pleasures of lower-class romance-
readers are somehow less conscious than those of Richardson's
middle-class readers, but in fact careful readers will realize that this
appearance of *Dorastus and Fawnia* in Lovelace's stirring tale is as
suspect as Lovelace's sexual intentions. The first clue that the reference is part of a game is that it echoes a similar mention in
*Gulliver's Travels* (1726), which Richardson knew and admired. This
is how Gulliver described the fire in Lilliput:

> I was alarmed at midnight with the cries of many hundred
> people at my door ... [S]everal of the emperor's court ... in-
> treated me to come immediately to the palace, where her
> Imperial Majesty's apartment was on fire, by the carelessness of a
> maid of honour who fell asleep while she was reading a
> romance.[36]

Swift and Richardson alike set the destructive 'carelessness' of the
reading maid in contrast to the urgent loyalty of those who raise
the alarm (courtiers, Dorcas) and to the prompt, 'heroic' action of
the narrators (Lovelace, Gulliver). Of course, Richardson's echo of
Swift serves to sharpen the attack on the romance. The unnamed
romance in Swift's tall tale simply underlines the small-mindedness
of court society, for the late-night reader is a maid of honor. In
*Clarissa*, she is a kitchen maid who serves a housekeeper and her
careless immersion in fiction distinguishes her from the conscientious audience addressed by Richardson. Plainly, he knew his chapbook titles, having been a bookseller and some of his readers could
have recognized *Dorastus and Fawnia* from drolls or chapbooks
(why else mention this particular name?).[37] Still, the social dynamics of this little story imply that those who undertook *Clarissa*
would recognize the sensation of being lost in a book, but would
not be satisfied by any 'simple history'.

There is another reason to suspect this anecdotal reference to
*Dorastus and Fawnia*: epistemologically, the events of this little story
*cannot* have taken place. The vividness of Lovelace's description of
the alarm encourages readers to forget what they, like Clarissa,
know, that the fire is Lovelace's 'plot'.[38] While Lovelace swears that
'Upon my soul, madam, the fire was real. (*And so it was, Jack!*)',
its setting was planned in advance: 'all agreed upon between

the women and me' (pp. 265, 261), since the maid, Dorcas and Mrs Sinclair all serve him in his plot. In his story about the romance-reading servant, Lovelace momentarily deceives Belford as he did Clarissa – and Richardson momentarily does the same to his readers. Lovelace's pleasure in fiction-making exceeds the demands of his plot against Clarissa; but to indulge that pleasure, Lovelace engages the services of women of lower class, implying that they, not he, are obsessed with elaborate fantasies. Richardson's anecdote about servants' taste for fiction must be recognized as a fiction developed expressly to differentiate his novel from popular romance, the two respectively bourgeois and humble, modern and dated, virtuous and self-indulgent, productive and idle.

But why did Richardson portray his servant readers so unsympathetically? That more middle-class readers than servants read books of the length and ambition of Richardson's and that more servant readers than fashionable readers would have chosen to buy chapbooks, remains unarguable, though unprovable. However, recent research by Naomi Tadmor and Jan Fergus supports my claim that the boundary between these two fictional fields was more permeable than Richardson wished to admit (although they do not support James Lackington's claims that even his poorest library patrons rushed to read *Pamela*). Tadmor has reconstructed the reading practices of a modest Sussex couple during the 1750s. Peggy, a farmer's daughter and former household servant, married Thomas Turner, the keeper of a small drapery-shop in East Hoathly, Sussex. The Turners enjoyed reading aloud to one another, alternating Tillotson's sermons with *Clarissa Harlowe*.[39] Fergus has studied the records of the Clays, a provincial bookselling family and particularly the patterns of special orders, purchases and borrowings by servants (although customers' ranks were not noted systematically). She has found that servants were far from being idle and oblivious to self-improvement, as implied by the structure of opposition in Richardson's anecdote between his instructional works and the spell-binding *Dorastus and Fawnia*. Among the Clays' customers, servants were especially interested in buying conduct books; otherwise, their selections fell into about the same balance of leisure and informational reading as those of more middling customers. Fergus has found only one reference to a servant purchasing a novel, the seventh volume of *Clarissa*.[40]

There is another way to test Richardson's vertical categorization of taste, however and that is to look at eighteenth-century adaptations of Greene's Elizabethan romance. By this date, *Dorastus and Fawnia* could be bought in several different forms. There were still reprints of the full text available in the 1750s; the one that survives runs to 116 pages in duodecimo. There were octavo chapbooks of about 18 pages at the other end of the market. And there was *The Fortunate Lovers*, the modernization by Hugh Stanhope from about 1727–35, which dressed the story up with the moralizing language of the novellas of the period. In other words, it was deemed profitable to bring the chapbook into line with both stylistic and ethical patterns of the fiction form preferred by the fashionable. Comparison with Sidney enables the point to be specified. It was around 1695 that the adaptation of Quarles' version of Sidney's Argalus and Parthenia story was published as *The Unfortunate Lovers*, well before the first 'novella-ization' of *Dorastus and Fawnia*. The two are similar in format, although not produced by the same firms. A better-known modernization, *Sir Philip Sidney's Arcadia, Moderniz'd by Mrs. Stanley,* appeared in 1725. It is understandable that *Argalus and Parthenia*, a shorter text dissociated from Sidney's name, should have been more subject to adaptation than the monumental *Arcadia* itself; but it is striking that the movement towards modernization appears first in the popularized form, generally deemed impervious to fashion. Furthermore, Mrs Stanley's adaptation has generally been regarded as the last gasp of *Arcadia* as a non-scholarly text; but *The Unfortunate Lovers* and *The Fortunate Lovers* were much reprinted, even in competition with other versions of the stories.

*The Fortunate Lovers* was the first version of *Pandosto* explicitly to voice disapproval of social mobility. Its 'translator', a self-styled 'gentleman' (identified by Wing as the minor dramatist William Bond), offers a prefatory summary of the story's 'Rules of Morality' that disapproves of Porrus's improvised social rise: 'was it fair or honest in him to conceal the Riches of Fawnia and convert part of them to his own use?' By this logic, social mobility appears to be achieved only by those who are unfair and dishonest. Despite Stanhope's stand against ambition, he indulges Fawnia in her pursuit of the prince, even revising her euphuistic sighings about the hopelessness of love across classes. Greene's Fawnia considered the 'impossibility' of her love, but Stanhope's considers 'the Improbability, if not Impossibility of obtaining her Desire'.

Stanhope also adds a peroration emphasizing Fawnia's recognition that her status must be overcome: '"O the Gods! Why did you give me a Soul capable of the most noble Passion and not a Fortune to answer my desire[?]"' (p. 24).

Stanhope makes Fawnia a proto-Pamela, showing how the fortunes of a mid-eighteenth-century female domestic servant might quickly run from remote dreams to immediate risks. As Lawrence Stone once put it, maids were 'the most exploited and most defenceless' women of the period: their defenselessness was underwritten by the paternalistic ideologies that still portrayed the master's relationship to his servant as one of parental guardianship, while the lapse from paternalism in practice left servants without economic promise or legal protection.[41] As though in response to this increase in risk, Stanhope expands and politicizes the scenes in which Fawnia defends her vulnerable social position and her threatened sexual honour. Near the end of the romance, she has fled (with Dorastus and Porrus) to the court of Pandosto. Pandosto lusts after her, unaware either of her humble upbringing or his own relationship to her. The defence of Stanhope's Fawnia is longer than that of Greene's and newly 'stinging and resolute' (47): she recognizes that the king has 'Power', but charges that he has 'exercised it, in an arbitrary manner upon the Innocent', likening his attempted seduction to an army's massacre of 'a small Village, that is weak and defenceless' (50–1). She repels his advances in terms assuming the sovereignty of the individual: 'I have a Monarch's Soul, though the Gods have been pleased to cover it with Plebean Clay.'[42] Despite his conservatism, Stanhope re-situates the romance within the period's emergent discourse of the dominion of the individual, making that discourse applicable to women and available to a humble readership.

*The Fortunate Lovers* is not, of course, political theory. Nor is it in length a proto-*Clarissa* or even a proto-*Pamela*. In following the plot line of *Dorastus and Fawnia*, it is by McKeon's measure more bound up in 'conservative ideology' than is Pamela. But political conservatism should not be confused with old-fashionedness: this text was reshaped in response to the same cultural changes that produced the novella and pressed toward the novel. Furthermore, while the novel moved away from conservative ideology in the period, the drama moved back towards it, a development in which, again, *Dorastus and Fawnia* would play a role.

## CHAPTER 3. *HOW* DORASTUS AND FAWNIA *CAME TO THE COTTAGE WALL AND THE LONDON STAGE*

In her study of servant readership in the mid-eighteenth century, Fergus remarks that by far the favourite leisure reading among the Clays' servant customers is *Love in a Village*, the comic opera by Bickerstaff. This was the Irish dramatist's first and most successful comic opera, first performed at Covent Garden in 1762 and produced there 183 times, a solid one-third of the number of performances of *The Beggar's Opera* (1747). Fergus notes that the play might have 'a particular appeal for servants' and 'with such a plot ... the young'; and she quotes a line from the opera which compares its improbabilities to 'the loves of Dorastus and Faunia'.[43] Material and anecdotal evidence meet, then, face-to-face over a chapbook edition of *Pandosto*.

The opera opens at the country estate of Justice Woodcock, where his daughter Lucinda is sheltering her friend Rossetta, who has run away from her father's house in dread of a marriage he has arranged with the son of an affable stranger. Lucinda expresses her dismay at seeing Rossetta 'in the character of a chambermaid' although she treats her as an equal throughout the opera. Rossetta reminds Lucinda that 'It is the only character, my dear, in which I could hope to lie concealed', the final phrase explicitly connecting the pleasures of country torpor, role-playing, deceit and seduction.[44] Luckily, Rossetta finds her disguise an asset: 'I have had so many admirers since I commenced Abigail, that I am quite charmed with my situation' (5). The admirer she cares for, however, is Thomas, the Woodcocks' new gardener. In the next scene, Thomas obligingly explains to the audience that he, too, has adopted the garb of a servant to evade an arranged marriage. He says that marrying the Woodcocks' chambermaid is 'impossible', although he sings a pastoral air about that forbidden fantasy, an air that turns 'infortunate Fawnia' on its head:

> Oh! had I been by fate decreed
> Some humble cottage swain;
> In fair Rossetta's sight to feed,
> My sheep upon the plain.
> What bliss had I been born to taste,
> Which now I ne'er must know:

> To envious pow'rs! why have ye plac'd
> My fair one's lot so low? (7)

'Prudence' prevents his marrying, 'honour' his 'making a mistress of her if I could' (p. 9).[45] His honour turns out to be superior (to modern eyes), to that of Rossetta's father, Hawthorne, who has come to visit Woodcock. Hawthorne sings of Woodcock's right 'to toy and to kiss' with his chambermaid, not recognizing his daughter (p. 41). By III.i, the all too indulgent Hawthorne and Sir William Meadows (father of 'Thomas') realize that the disguised lovers are in fact the children they intended to pair off:

> Why Sir William it is romance, a novel, a pleasanter history by half, than the loves of *Dorastus* and *Faunia*; we shall have ballads made of it within these two months, setting forth, how a young 'squire became a serving man of low degree: and it will be stuck up with *Margret*'s ghost and the Spanish lady, against the walls of every cottage in the country. (52)

They ask Rossetta whether she had loved the gardener. She too places class prudence before passion: 'had I not look'd upon him as person so much below me, I should have had no objection to receiving his courtship.' She then changes her claim, perhaps taking courage to confront codes, perhaps relieved of the necessity of doing so:

> I love to speak my sentiments and I assure you Sir *William*, in my own opinion, I should prefer a gardener, with your son's good qualities, to a knight of the shire without them.
>
> > 'Tis not wealth, it is not birth,
> > Can value to the soul convey;
> > Minds possess superior worth,
> > Which chance nor gives, nor takes away. (55)

That protest seems insincere, given the knowledge that she need make no such choice and the tendency of 'superior worth' to collapse back to birth, or as Bourdieu would put it, of cultural capital effortlessly to generate economic capital.

This opera seems conservative indeed. It is a truism that by the mid-eighteenth century, drama had lost its critical perspective towards the marriage market, devising elaborate plots which justify the arranged marriages that the youth of Restoration drama had successfully plotted to evade. In Bickerstaff's opera, those magical resolutions call attention to themselves in their artifice. Rossetta says to Hodge, the servant, besotted with her, who has hard-heartedly sacrificed to the London streets Margery, the *real* serving maid he has got in trouble, 'Oh lord *Hodge*! I beg your pardon; I protest I forgot; but I must reconcile you and *Madge* I think; and give you a wedding dinner to make you amends' (p. 73). The very heedlessness of fortune that Greene's heroines (and heroes) had be-wailed is now sited within the heroine's actions and lapses, so that the workings of the plot all serve to enhance her charms, rather than the reverse. The fortunes of a Rossetta are always already happy.

Such attitudes may reflect the literacy of the gentle characters, the sign of their superior cultural capital. So in Rossetta's supposedly democratic aria, the emphasis on 'minds' endorses the rationality and the bookishness of this pair. In Act I, Lucinda says that 'Thomas' has written verses about Rossetta and then 'Thomas' sees Rossetta as she 'sat reading' in the garden as he is making notes in his 'pocket book' (5–7). A superiority based on bookishness is con-trasted with the view of Woodcock's maiden sister that Lucinda's love is

> mighty pretty romantick stuff! but you learn it out of your play books and novels. Girls in my time, had other employments, we work'd at our needles and kept ourselves from idle thoughts: ... I never looked into a book, but when I said my prayers, except it was the compleat housewife, or the great family receipt book: whereas you are always at your studies: Ah! I never knew a woman come to good, that was fond of reading. (p. 60)

But if the contrast in material culture can be understood as a mockery of the illiteracy of the provincial past, the contrast in moral codes of the two generations is less clear. The older woman's faith has a dignity that the younger worshippers of Cupid seem to lack.

All this may reveal the ambivalence of Bickerstaff (a young man recently arrived from Dublin) towards the literacy of fashion that he was exploiting. The full burden of cultural commodification falls upon the ballads conjured up by Hawthorne's whimsical remark. These ballads are to be 'stuck up against the walls of every cottage

in the country'. In the 1763 edition of the opera, a brief 'advertisement' disingenuously underestimates the extent of its debt to
Charles Johnson's *The Village Opera* (1729), which was the whole
plot, not the stated 'incident or two' ([A4]). Although his collabora-
tor's music won the day in this case, Bickerstaff was thereafter
under a constant cloud, continually getting caught in the grey area
between adaptation and plagiarism. The impact of that difficulty
was doubly registered in the front matter of his next comic effort,
*The Maid of the Mill*, in which a two-page preface carefully explained its indebtedness to Richardson's *Pamela*. And on leaf A4,
without any heading, was a new advertisement: 'This Opera is
entered at STATIONERS HALL and whoever presumes to Print the
Songs, or any Part of them, will be prosecuted by the Proprietors.'
In other words, the notice issues a threat to those who would do
exactly what Hawthorne had promised ballad publishers would do
with the plot of *Love in a Village*.

Indeed, the possibility emerges that the reference to *Dorastus and
Fawnia*, unlike the other anecdotes I have discussed, may have
opened up boundaries between fields of cultural consumption,
rather than seeking to close them. It may be a subtle joke about the
broad cultural diffusion of romances of service and fabulous entertainment. The claim that the play's events resemble a story is itself
reminiscent of *The Winter's Tale*, which Bickerstaff had probably
read. So, too, is the rural labourer's fair in Act I.[46] The opera and
particularly the hero's pastoral songs, may have emulated the soft-
ened pastoral elements of new adaptations of Shakespeare's play.
Bickerstaff could have seen both the Macnamara Morgan adaptation, *The Sheep-Shearing*, a success in London and Dublin in 1754–5
and David Garrick's *Florizel and Perdita, a Dramatic Pastoral*,
presented at Drury Lane from 1756–62.[47]

The actor playing Justice Woodcock, father of Lucinda and
straight man to Hawthorne the humorist, was Ned Shuter, whom
Arthur Scouten calls 'the famous low comedian'.[48] From 1754
Shuter had also taken the role of Autolycus in Morgan's adaptation
of *The Winter's Tale* at Covent Garden. Miss Brent, who played
Rossetta in 1762, had played Perdita in 1760–2. Meanwhile, Richard
Yates originated the role of Autolycus in David Garrick's adaptation (1756, revived at Drury Lane, 1762). But in earlier summer
months, another Richard Yates mounted drolls (short playlets) at
fairs, as an alternative to the patent theatres; at Bartholomew Fair,
Yates' company had performed *Dorastus and Fawnia* in May 1749

(no cast list survives). The coincidence is striking because, as Stanley Wells has pointed out, the one surviving advertisement listing the cast of a droll *Dorastus and Fawnia* freely intermixes names from Shakespeare's plays.[49] A 1729 performance of the droll *Dorastus and Fawnia* (its first recorded performance is 1703) appropriately cast a Thomas Chapman as Autolycus, a role he went on to play in the 1741 Goodman's Fields production of *The Winter's Tale* that ended the play's hundred years of absence from the stage.[50] *Dorastus and Fawnia* may have been named in *Love in a Village* as a famous love story sold as a ballad, but it was also remembered as a famous love story to be viewed in a context of cultural mixing: at the Fair, where all classes recreated themselves; and in a droll whose *dramatis personae* mixed in names from Shakespeare.

On the other hand, if such speculation seems too ingenious to be 'material', it may seem fortunate that history has preserved a ballad version of *Dorastus and Fawnia*. Its title, *The Royal Courtly Garland*, links it to a miscellany tradition dating back to Elizabethan examples and Restoration revivals; a Thomas Deloney collection was published as *The Royal Garland of Love and Delight* in 1674. This edition of the *Garland*, which tells the story of Dorastus and Fawnia in six parts over eight small pages, has been dated to around 1800 on the basis of its appearance – and filed in the Folger Shakespeare Library's card catalog under 'Shakespeare – *Winter's Tale* – Adaptations'.

This essay suggests that despite the caution with which it must be read, anecdotal evidence continues to reward critical attention, for the very patterns of its exaggerations bring out social dynamics that could not emerge from a study of the extant editions alone. But recent research on eighteenth-century readership patterns suggests a range of reading preferences that does not match the lines drawn in contemporary anecdotes. In negotiating between anecdotal evidence and material evidence, then, we must be cautious of the prejudice against the very materiality of chapbook romances; we must recognize that those anecdotes should not dictate the generic and social frameworks we use to categorize these texts. In the end, the fact that we have different kinds of evidence for reconstructing the history of a supposedly forgotten Elizabethan romance is, of course, reason for gratitude. For the modern literary historian as for early modern readers, the trajectory of *Pandosto* can truly be called fortunate. In the game of distinction played between the backhanded testimonies of defensive elite writers to its popularity and the aggressive press of popular publishers on their market, *Pandosto* long continued to serve and be served.

## NOTES

1. Robert Greene, *Pandosto. The Triumph of Time*, in Paul Salzman, ed., *An Anthology of Elizabethan Prose Fiction* (Oxford, 1987), p. 182 (hereafter cited as *Elizabethan*).
2. The phrase is Sidney's own and surely self-reflexive. See *The Countess of Pembroke's Arcadia*, ed. Maurice Evans (Harmondsworth, 1977), p. 817.
3. Kay notes that the tennis-ball image was echoed by both John Webster's Bosola and Samuel Richardson's Pamela. See Dennis Kay, ed., *Sir Philip Sidney: An Anthology of Modern Criticism* (Oxford, 1987), pp. 18, 32, hereafter cited as Kay.
4. Salzman's edition assumes the existence of a lost first edition of the text from *c.* 1585 (Salzman, *Elizabethan*, xvii, xxvii), a theory first advanced by Alexander Rodger in 'Roger Ward's Shrewsbury Stock: An Inventory of 1585', *The Library*, 5th ser., 13 (1958): 247–68. If this is true, Greene wrote *Pandosto* around the time of his other more courtly romances and when Sidney was revising the *Arcadia* – and before Thomas Underdowne's 1587 Englishing of Heliodorus' *Aethiopica*. If Sidney's *Old Arcadia* was the innovator in prose imitations of Heliodorus, the Hellenistic author had apparently already been naturalized to the stage: in a 1582 polemic, *Plays Confuted in Five Actions*, Stephen Gosson lists 'the Oethiopian historie' among the foreign works 'thoroughly ransackt to furnish the Playe houses in London'.
5. Gerard Langbaine's *Momus Triumphans* (1697) first connects Greene's romance and Shakespeare's play.
6. This list refers to editions, not to copies of those editions (most survive in unique copies). It excludes the verse adaptations mentioned below and Charlotte Lennox's retelling of most of *Pandosto* as the source of *The Winter's Tale in Shakespear Illustrated* (1753) (reprint edn, New York, 1973). My search for editions was aided by a generous grant from the Bibliographical Society of America. For speculations about readership in light of the patterns discussed in this article, see my article, 'The Romance of Service: The Simple History of *Pandosto's* Servant Readers', in *Framing Elizabethan Fictions: Contemporary Approaches to Early Modern Narrative Prose*, edited by Constance C. Relihan (Kent, OH, 1996), pp. 117–39.
7. Wing U57A. The entry does not mention Quarles or Sidney, although anonymous adaptations of *Pandosto* are listed under Greene's name.
8. It is, of course, Hero and Leander who are unfortunate and Dorastus and Fawnia who are fortunate. I thank Peter Lindenbaum for calling my attention to this conjunction and many others. The new titles affiliate these familiar texts with more fashionable high-keyed works

ranging from William Davenant's tragedy, *The Unfortunate Lovers* (1638) to Aphra Behn's novellas, *The Unfortunate Happy Lady* and *The Fortunate Bride* (1696).

9.   Greene's later works became infamous after his ignominious death in 1592, but there was nothing like Sidney's posthumous canonization. For Sidney's author-function in seventeenth-century culture, see Arthur F. Marotti, *Manuscript, Print and the English Renaissance Lyric* (Ithaca, NY, 1995) and Wendy Wall, *The Imprint of Gender: Authorship and Publication in Early Modern English Renaissance* (Ithaca, NY, 1993).

10.  Charles Mish, 'Best Sellers in Seventeenth-Century Fiction', *PBSA* 47 (1953), p. 373. The number of editions of *Pandosto* published during the century was exceeded only by Aesop's *Fables*, Bunyan's *Pilgrim's Progress* and Bernard's *Isle of Man*, three didactic works whose audiences were broader than the market for fiction more specifically written for entertainment. Mish supported the view that the popular fictions of the seventeenth century were antiquated fairy tales, foisted by cheap publishers on a captive audience of naive citizens who deserved their marginal status. He spoke of the chivalric romance circulating to 'ever more culturally immature readers' ('English Short Fiction in the Seventeenth Century', *Studies in Short Fiction* 6 [1969], p. 323). Similarly, even Louis B. Wright, the champion of 'middle-class culture', accepted the view that the popularization of romance amounted to descent: see *Middle-Class Culture in Elizabethan England* (1935; reprint edn, Ithaca, NY, 1958), p. 376.

11.  George Puttenham, *The Arte of English Poesie* (1589; reprint edn, Kent, OH: Kent State University Press, 1970 [reissue of Edward Arber's 1906 edition], p. 216). Puttenham's examples seem to recognize antanaclasis only in homonymic puns, but most classical and modern definitions of antanaclasis would seem to include the kinds of repetition I have cited here.

12.  Salzman, *Elizabethan*, p. 164.

13.  Michael McKeon names such tensions 'questions of virtue'. McKeon hails the novel for its investigation of these questions and accuses Elizabethan romances of hiding them under a cloak of 'romance ideology': see *The Origins of the English Novel 1600–1740* (Baltimore, 1987), pp. 131–3. Further references cited parenthetically.

14.  In a further twist, *Pandosto* and other early modern narratives (following the example of Greek romance) also give the name of fortune to the threatened failure of such systems of prediction. As the title puts it: 'although by the means of sinister fortune truth may be concealed, yet by time in spite of fortune it is most manifestly revealed' (Salzman, *Elizabethan*, p. 153).

15.  For one response to criticism's hostility to textual reduction, see John Osburn, 'The Dramaturgy of the Tabloid: Climax and Novelty in a Theory of Condensed Forms', *Theatre Journal* 46:2 (1994): 507–22.

16.  On the denial of materiality, see Roger Chartier, *The Order of Books* (Stanford, CA, 1994). I discuss servant readers in 'The Romance of Service' (see note 6).

17.  The argument of this section is adapted from "Social Things': The Production of Popular Culture in the Reception of Robert Greene's *Pandosto*', *ELH* 61 (1994): 753–81.

18.  See John Clark Jordan's classic biography, *Robert Greene* (New York, 1915) and Richard Helgerson, *Elizabethan Prodigals* (Berkeley, 1976).

19.  Ben Jonson, *Every Man out of his Humour*, II.iii.224–8, in *Ben Jonson*, ed. C. H. Herford and Percy and Evelyn Simpson (Oxford, 1927–52), Vol. III. I have modernized u's and v's. The word 'ordinary' may allude to Greene's famous recollection in the 1592 *Repentance* that in his fame as playwright and romance-writer, there were none 'for that trade growne so ordinary about London as *Robert Greene*'.

20.  Jonson, *Bartholomew Fair*, ed. G. R. Hibbard (London, 1977), IV.iii.65–6.

21.  W. J. Paylor, ed., *The Overburian Characters* (1936; reprint edn, New York, 1977), p. 43. Overbury's remark and others like it, have been accepted by literary historians as testimony that romances were read almost exclusively by lower-class women. See Louis B. Wright,'The Reading of Renaissance English Women', *Studies in Philology* 28:3 (1931): 147–50; Henry Thomas, *Spanish and Portuguese Romances of Chivalry* (1920, reprint edn, New York, 1969), pp. 292–4; Caroline Lucas, *Writing for Women: The Example of Woman as Reader in Elizabethan Romance* (Milton Keynes, 1989). Relatively few of the characters involve women, although Overbury's literary game of 'newes' apparently included Lady Southwell and Anne Clifford (Sackville): see *The 'Conceited Newes' of Sir Thomas Overbury and His Friends*, ed. James E. Savage (Gainesville, FL, 1968), p. xl.

22.  Quoted in Kay, p. 28.

23.  My argument here is indebted to recent work on the voyeuristic Elizabethan text, including Wall; Juliet Fleming, 'The Ladies' Man and the Age of Elizabeth', in *Sexuality and Gender in Early Modern Europe*, ed. James Grantham Turner (Cambridge, 1993), pp. 158–81; and Constance C. Relihan, *Fashioning Authority: The Development of Elizabethan Novelistic Discourse* (Kent, OH, 1994).

24.  In 1595, Francis Sabie published a verse adaptation in two parts, *The Fisshermans Tale* and *Flora's Fortune*; and in 1672 (reprinted 1688) the story was 'rendered in delightful English verse' by the versatile Samuel Sheppard under the startling title: '*Fortunes tennis-ball, or the most excellent history of Dorastus and Fawnia*. The Sidneian echo, together with the publication dates, could hint at political overtones to this tale of royal reversals. In 1664, similarly, a ballad summarizing *The Winter's Tale* appeared in *The Royal Arbor of Loyal Poesie*.

25.  This phrase, from D. F. McKenzie, 'Printers of the Mind: Some Notes on Bibliographical Theories and Printing-House Practices', *Studies in Bibliography* 22 (1969): 1–75, is quoted in Margreta De Grazia and Peter Stallybrass, 'The Materiality of the Shakespeare Text', *Shakespeare Quarterly* 44 (1993): 255–83.

26.  The Stationers' Company ordinance of 1598 fixed the maximum retail price of printed books, based on the number of signatures and the typeface chosen, with exceptions allowed for dense or complicated work (Francis Johnson, 'Notes on English Retail Book-prices,

1550–1640', *The Library* 5th ser., 5 [1950], p. 84). These variables corresponded to the capital costs (paper) and the labour costs (presswork and composition). The price for most works of about 1/2 d per sheet remained stable until about 1635, while prices for most other goods doubled over that period (p. 93). As long as *Pandosto* remained a straightforward quarto fitted neatly into seven signatures, its unbound cost could not vary much. Although Johnson postulates that English booksellers sometimes charged lower prices for reprints, his own examples of prices for Greene titles do not bear out that theory (pp. 94, 103). The various options for binding, always at extra charge, would have offered buyers scope for distinguishing themselves by income, but few editions of *Pandosto* retain original bindings.

27. Paul Morgan, 'Fraunces Wolfreston and "Hor Bouks": A Seventeenth-Century Woman Book-Collector', *The Library*, 6th ser., 11 (1989), p. 214.

28. Tessa Watt, *Cheap Print and Popular Piety, 1550–1640* (Cambridge, 1991).

29. On the culture of consumption, see Neil McKendrick, John Brewer and J. H. Plumb, *The Birth of a Consumer Society: The Commercialization of Eighteenth-Century England* (Bloomington, IN, 1982), especially McKendrick's chapter on the commercialization of fashion; Colin Campbell, *The Romantic Ethic and the Spirit of Modern Consumerism* (Oxford, 1987); and Lorna Weatherill, *Consumer Behaviour and Material Culture in Britain, 1660–1760* (London, 1988).

30. This struggle is currently being reconstructed by Nancy Armstrong, John Richetti and William B. Warner, among others. These studies tend to focus on the relationship between relatively fashionable romance forms and the now-canonical novels that challenged them, not mentioning the older popular romances still available during the period.

31. The first phrase is the title of Chapter 4 in Bridget Hill, *Women and Work in Eighteenth-Century England* (Oxford, 1989), pp. 47–68; the second is from Susan Cahn, *Industry of Devotion: The Transformation of Woman's Work in England, 1500–1660* (New York, 1987), p. 4.

32. This 1767 remark is quoted in J. Jean Hecht, *The Domestic Servant Class in Eighteenth-Century England* (London, 1956), p. 178; also see pp. 4–5 and passim. Changes in agricultural service from a life-cycle interval to a permanent class are detailed in Ann Kussmaul, *Servants in Husbandry in Early Modern England* (Cambridge, 1981), pp. 3, 16–18.

33. Hecht, p. 219.

34. Kay, p. 32, cites Pamela's words to the second edition, 1742, Vol. ii, p. 36. Richardson had published, in 1724, the first illustrated edition of the *Arcadia*, as a triple-decker (Kay, p. 31).

35. Samuel Richardson, *Clarissa, or The History of a Young Lady*, abr. and ed. George Sherburn (Boston, 1962), xxi. Subsequent references cited parenthetically.

36. Jonathan Swift, *Gulliver's Travels and Other Writings*, ed. Louis A. Landa (Boston, 1960), p. 44. Subsequent references cited parenthetically.

37.  An exhaustive survey of Richardson's printing career may be found
     in T. C. Duncan Eaves and Ben D. Kimpel, *Samuel Richardson: A
     Biography* (Oxford, 1971).
38.  Richardson, *Clarissa*, p. 261. Clarissa uses the same word, highly
     significant in this metafictional context, writing that Lovelace, 'I have
     too much reason to believe, formed a plot to fire the house, to frighten
     me, almost naked, into his arms' (p. 278). Those commentators on
     Greene who have noted this late reference have completely missed its
     ironies (René Pruvost, *Robert Greene et ses romans* [Paris, 1938], p. 284;
     Caroline Lucas, *Writing for Women: The Example of Woman as Reader in
     Elizabethan Romance* [Milton Keynes, 1989], p. 51).
39.  Naomi Tadmor, '"In the even my wife read to me": Women, Reading
     and Household Life in the Eighteenth Century', in *The Practice and
     Representation of Reading in England*, ed. James Raven, Helen Small and
     Naomi Tadmor (Cambridge, 1996), pp. 168–70.
40.  Jan Fergus, 'Provincial Servants' Reading in the Eighteenth Century',
     in Raven, *et al.*, pp. 216, 225, 217. Of course, if we could be sure that
     this record meant the servant took only this seventh volume, we
     might surmise that he was bringing it to another reader who had
     already made some headway through the previous volumes, presum-
     ably a mistress or master.
41.  On self-advertisement, see Amussen, 159. On exploitation, see
     Lawrence Stone, *The Family, Sex and Marriage in England, 1500–1800*
     (abr. edn, New York, 1979), p. 381; and Ilana Krausman Ben-Amos,
     *Adolescence and Youth in Early Modern England* (New Haven, CT, 1994),
     p. 202. Bridget Hill comments that 'What has been called "the erotic-
     ism of inequality" may in part explain the frequency with which
     masters are found seducing their dependent menials'; she excerpts
     conduct books for female servants advising 'circumspection' in deal-
     ings with male employers and fellow employees (*Women and Work*,
     pp. 146, 137, 234–5).
42.  Stanhope, p. 47. Of course, readers know that Fawnia's royal birth
     ironizes this claim, but Fawnia herself does not.
43.  Fergus, p. 221.
44.  Reproduction of the 1763 edition of *Love in a Village; a Comic Opera* in
     *The Plays of Isaac Bickerstaff*, ed. Peter A. Tasch (New York, 1981),
     Vol. I, p. 4. Further references cited parenthetically.
45.  In Bickerstaff's underacknowledged source, Charles Johnson's *The
     Village Opera* (1729), the analogous character alludes to 'Reason and
     Honour.' See Peter A. Tasch, *The Dramatic Cobbler: The Life and Works
     of Isaac Bickerstaff* (Lewisburg, PN, 1971), p. 48.
46.  Presumably the main buyers of the ballad of Rossetta and 'Thomas'
     would be the villagers, represented to the opera's audience mainly as
     the young working women whom Woodcock and Hawthorne had
     'chuck[ed] ... under the chin' at the statute (hiring fair for servants
     and labourers) (p. 21).
47.  See Dennis Bartholomeusz, *'The Winter's Tale' in Performance in
     England and America, 1611–1976* (Cambridge, 1982), pp. 28–41. For
     careful discussion of the nature of eighteenth-century adaptation of

Shakespeare's play, particularly in its shifting of gender ideologies, see Jean I. Marsden, *The Re-Imagined Text: Shakespeare, Adaptation and Eighteenth-Century Literary Theory* (Lexington, KY, 1995), pp. 77–86.

48. Arthur H. Scouten, *The London Stage, 1660–1800, Part 3: 1729–1747* (Carbondale, IL, 1962), Vol. I, p. cxxxi.

49. Stanley Wells, ed., *'Perymedes the Blacksmith' and 'Pandosto' by Robert Greene: A Critical Edition* (1961. Repr. edn, New York, 1988), p. 187.

50. Scouten, Vol. I, pp. 457, 471. Such links can be extended endlessly, given the smallness of the theatrical community. Macnamara Morgan mounted another play at Covent Garden in 1754, with most of the actors from *The Sheep-Shearing*; called *Philoclea*, it was based on *Arcadia* and was crushingly reviewed. See George Winchester Stone, Jr., *The London Stage, 1660–1800, Part IV: 1747–1776* (Carbondale, IL, 1962), Vol. I, pp. 404–5.

# 6

# Editing Sexuality, Narrative and Authorship: The Altered Texts of Shakespeare's *Lucrece*

## Sasha Roberts

How far does the format of a book shape the interpretation of the text within? In this essay I want to explore an intriguing history of textual transformation and transmission surrounding the publication of one of Shakespeare's most popular reading texts in the early seventeenth century, *Lucrece*. First published in 1594, *Lucrece* went through nine editions by 1655 and in this 50-year period the text and structure of the poem were reshaped for the reader: textual variants increasingly offered a more 'polite' reading of the poem; the poem was divided into chapters, with the editorial apparatus of chapter and marginal headings working to render unambiguous the 'chaste' interpretation of the poem; and Shakespeare, whose name was not mentioned on the title-page of Q1, became a central point of reference on the title-page of Q9 of 1655. The history of the later quartos of *Lucrece* raises the role of the editor, the representation of sexuality, the presentation of narrative and the canonization of both Shakespeare and English poetry for the seventeenth-century reading public.[1]

## LUCRECE'S HIDDEN SHAME

Despite Lucrece's iconic status as an exemplary, chaste wife, her innocence as a raped woman was not universally acknowledged. The dominant view of her chastity and devotion as a wife was countered by dissenting voices, which saw her as dissembling, seductive and ultimately selfish. This tradition centred on two perceived difficulties raised by St Augustine: her submission to rape and her act of suicide. In John Healey's 1610 translation of *The City of God*, Augustine asks,

> if it were no unchasteness in her to suffer the rape unwillingly, it was no justice in her being chaste to make away herself willingly ... This deed did Lucretia, that so famous Lucretia: this Lucretia being innocent, chaste and forcibly wronged, even by Lucretia's self was murdered: now give your sentence.[2]

For Augustine, Lucrece's act of suicide casts doubt upon her sexual integrity: 'not dying guiltless', Lucrece was 'privy to her own sin'. Lucrece's guilt is that of her 'lustful consent' to adultery: Tarquin and Lucrece were both guilty, 'the one by a violent enforcement, the other by a secret consent ... she died not innocent [but] only discovered the infirmity of her own shame'. Augustine concludes, 'nor is there any way out of this argument: If she be an adulteress, why is she commended? If she be chaste, why did she kill herself?' (p. 24) *The City of God* will admit the violated but not those like Lucrece who take their own lives in order to mask their shame, or are 'covetous of glory'; as William Tyndale put it, Lucrece 'sought her own glory in her chastity and not God's'.[3] Laura Bromley and Ian Donaldson have noted how Augustine's comments raise differences between 'Roman' and 'Christian' value systems in the interpretation of suicide: while suicide could be read as an act of Stoicism in classical texts, in a Christian context it was more problematically defined as an act against God (consider the doubts about whether Ophelia merits a Christian burial in sanctified ground in *Hamlet*).[4] Augustine in fact addresses the disjunction between these value systems, explaining that while Lucrece acted as 'a Roman', Christian women 'live still, howsoever violated ... they have the glory of their chastity still within them, it being the testimony of their conscience' (p. 24).

Augustine's reservations about Lucrece's integrity fuelled lively debate in the seventeenth century; indeed, Don Cameron Allen has argued that Shakespeare was drawn to Lucrece in part because she was at 'the centre of a Christian controversy'.[5] In the first decade of the seventeenth century, for instance, the faculty of the University of Altdorf broke into a heated argument over her virtue following the performance of a play about her at the university; the

Vice-Chancellor responded by reciting a poem doubting her integrity, thus translated by Robert Carew in 1607:

> Were that unchast mate welcome to thy bed,
> *Lucrece*, thy lust was justly punished.
> Why seek'st thou fame that di'dst deservedly?
> But if foule force defil'd thine honest bed,
> His onely rage should have bene punished:
> Why diest thou for anothers villanie?
> Both wayes thy thirst of fame is too unjust,
> Dying, or for fond rage, or guiltie lust.[6]

Lucrece's 'thirst of fame' continued to be questioned by English commentators in the seventeenth century. Thus even in a text on female heroism dedicated to a woman, Lady Dorothy Sidney, *The Heroinae: or the Lives of Arria, Pauline, Lucrecia, Dido, Theutila, Cyprianan, Aretaphila* (London, 1639), George Rivers presents arguments against Lucrece's sexual innocence and suppression of adulterous sexual pleasure during the actual rape: 'This revenge may argue chastitie before and after: but not in the nick of the act, which yeelding to some secret enticement, might staine her thought; then loathing her selfe ... held death a more satisfactory revenge then repentance' (p. 67). For Rivers, 'she was dishonoured' both through 'carnall delight' and 'her insatiable thirst of glory' (pp. 68–9).[7]

N. N.'s translation of Jacques de Bosc's *The Compleat Woman*, published in the same year (1639), goes one step further:

> I am almost of the opinion of a great Authour, who accuseth her for having been not alwayes so chast, as she would make us beleeve. And that if she had not been guilty, without doubt she had found more remedie in her Conscience, then in her death. They say, she resisted rather of a humour, then of vertue and that having spent her time with other Gallants of lesse qualitie, then the Tyrant, she feared least all her other faults would be discovered in this and that this feare made her resolve to go forth of the world, by her own hand, rather then to remaine there any long time, to see her reputation lost. (p. 52)

Here Lucrece's suicide represents not an exemplum of marital chastity, but an exercise in damage limitation.

It is *Lucrece's* sexual duplicity, too, that becomes the central point of interest for Robert Burton. He owned a copy of Shakespeare's *Lucrece* (he listed the volume in his will), but in *The Anatomy of Melancholy* (1621) he turned to Aretino's ironic portrayal of 'Lucrezia Porzia, patrizia romana' as the prostitute Madam-don't-want ('Madremo-non-vuole') in his dialogue between two women about the arts of prostitution:

> Peter Aretine's Lucretia telleth as much and more of herself: 'I counterfeited honesty, as if I had been *Virgo virginissima*, more than a vestal virgin, I looked like a wife, I was so demure and chaste, I did add such gestures, tunes, speeches, signs and motions upon all occasions, that my spectators and auditors were stupefied, enchanted, fastened all to their places, like so many stocks and stones'.[8]

For Burton, Lucretia's manipulation of the 'gestures' of chastity for erotic purposes only demonstrates how desire 'is immoderate, inordinate and not to be comprehended in any bounds. It will not contain itself within the union of marriage, or apply to one object, but is a wandering, extravagant, a domineering, a boundless, an irrefragable, a destructive passion ... Aretine's Lucretia sold her maidenhead a thousand times before she was twenty-four years old' (p. 54). Thus even the icon of Lucretia's chastity can be reversed to show the darker, anarchic presence of female desire.

Lucrece was thus a potentially ambivalent figure of femininity for some late sixteenth- and seventeenth-century readers – even as she was adopted in the same period as a model of marital chastity for early modern women – and this raises the prospect of a sceptical response to, or ironical reading of, Lucrece as an exemplary figure in Shakespeare's poem. In fact this is precisely what we witness in one reader's marginalia upon a Q1 copy of Shakespeare's *Lucrece* now in the British Library. Early in the poem we learn that on Tarquin's arrival 'Well was he welcom'd by the Roman dame' and given some supper (51–122). Later, after trying to seduce her, Tarquin threatens to defame Lucrece with 'thy trespass' of adultery if she does not consent to his desires: 'For thy husband and thy children's sake, / Tender my suit' (524–33). At these lines, written in an anonymous seventeenth-century hand, is the remark, 'who euer made a feast for a single guest?' – implying that the 'supper' Lucrece prepared for Tarquin went beyond the bounds of dutiful hospitality and tells instead of Lucrece's desire for her 'single guest'.[9] For this reader, the provision of food becomes equated with the provision of sexual favours; Lucrece's innocence does not stand up to scrutiny.

A contemporary reader of Thomas Heywood's play *The Rape of Lucrece* (1608) was also suspicious of Lucrece's integrity, but on the grounds of her dubious faith. At the conclusion of a 1608 copy of the play in the British Library the following annotation in a seventeenth-century hand appears:

Thus ended is the rape of fayre Lucrece
Rebuke and shame hath Tarkin, Rome hath peace;
But though some men commend this Act Lucretian [of suicide]
She shewd her self in't (for all that) no good Christian
Nay eu'n those men yt seeme to make ye best ont
Call her a Papish good, no good Protestant.
Of this opinion Grendon John was the
Nine and fiftyeth of June one thousand hundred thirty and three.[10]

Heywood's play labours her exemplary huswifery modesty and marital fidelity, yet John Grendon remained unconvinced about her integrity: there are no extenuating circumstances for suicide and in taking her own life Lucrece acts as 'no good Protestant'. Moreover, Grendon implies that many 'men' share such a view: even those who seek to defend her and 'make the best ont' have to admit that she behaves no better than a Papist. Grendon's annotation shares the scepticism and co-opts her as a target for anti-Catholicism.

Richard Levin has, however, questioned the validity of a sceptical or 'ironical' reading of Shakespeare's Lucrece. He points out that Shakespeare's references to her in his other works present 'an entirely favourable view'; that other reworkings of the Lucrece legend that followed Shakespeare's poem – Thomas Middleton's *The Ghost of Lucrece* (1600) and Heywood's *The Rape of Lucrece* – present Lucrece as 'wholly innocent and wholly admirable'; and that contemporary allusions to the poem (collected in *The Shakespeare Allusion Book*) assume Lucrece's exemplary chastity: 'they all indicate very clearly that she was accepted "at face value" as a praiseworthy character'.[11] He concludes that 'the overwhelming majority, if not all, of the people for whom Shakespeare was writing found his Lucrece entirely sympathetic and admirable'.[12] I do not deny that this may have been the dominant reading in the period: my interest is more in the disjunction between dominant and dissident readings and the ways in which the material artefact of the book may be fashioned with a view to intervening in, or pre-empting, that disjunction. John Grendon and the anonymous reader of Shakespeare's Q1 *Lucrece* show how contemporary readers could bring a sceptical response to Lucrece's rape and act of suicide. Q1 of *Lucrece* (1594), which has the minimum of editorial apparatus, allows the reader to draw their own interpretations without the guiding hand of commentary; indeed, Ian Donaldson argues that Shakespeare's *Lucrece* (Q1) is open-ended, for 'the central moral complexities of the story are in some ways curiously evaded ... where Shakespeare's poem stands in relation to the familiar "disputation" about the classical Lucretia ... are matters which are far from clear'.[13] Later quartos of the poem, however, reshape Shakespeare's text precisely at the points of critical contention – Lucrece's 'consent' to the rape and her decision to commit suicide – and in so doing they suggest an attempt to direct the reader towards particular readings, to 'make clear' the proper interpretation of the poem.

## 'SUBTLE SHINING SECRECIES / WRIT IN THE GLASSY MARGENTS': DIRECTING THE READER

Print situates words in space more relentlessly than writing ever did. Writing moves words from the sound world to the world of visual space, but print locks words into position in this space. Control of position is everything in print.
Walter J. Ong, *Orality and Literacy: the Technologizing of the Word*[14]

Without access to multiple texts, a reader's experience is shaped by the specificities of the edition in which they read it. As Roger Chartier has argued, 'readers, in fact, never confront abstract, idealized texts detached from any materiality. They hold in their hands or perceive objects and forms whose structures and modalities govern their reading or hearing and consequently the possible comprehension of the text read or heard.'[15] While Shakespeare's dramatic texts have long been scrutinized for textual variants and their significance, the textual history of his narrative poems has rarely been examined, despite their considerable popularity until the mid-seventeenth century. As H. R. Woudhuysen argued in 1994, the 'casual treatment of later editions is a curious aspect of how Shakespeare's poems are usually edited: play editors will give detailed accounts of productions ... up to modern times, but the poems' editors rarely have much to say about their later histories.'[16] This is perhaps because *Venus and Adonis* (1593) and *Lucrece* (1594) appear to present few textual difficulties: it is argued that Shakespeare presented these texts with more care than any of his other works (both poems, for instance, are prefaced with signed dedications) and the extant first quartos of both poems are agreed to be the 'authoritative' texts upon which to base modern editions.[17] But the privileged status accorded to the 'authoritative' text of *Lucrece* (Q1) has entailed dismissing the later quartos and in so doing ignores not only the transformation and transmission of Shakespeare's poem, but what the history of that transmission may reveal for relations between print culture and cultural change in early modern England.

The editorial apparatus of Q1 of Shakespeare's *Lucrece* (printed in 1594 by Richard Field for John Harrison) is kept to a bare minimum. Following the title-page, dedication and argument, it is printed as a continuous long poem without breaks or divisions, using roman type throughout. But in 1616 a new edition of the poem appeared (Q6): *The Rape of Lucrece. By Mr. William Shakespeare. Newly Revised*, printed by Thomas Snodham for Roger Jackson (who had gained the rights to *Lucrece* a couple of years earlier).[18] As promised by its title-page, this edition had been altered considerably from Q1: not only does it contain numerous variant readings, newly italicized words and an expanded title, The *Rape* of Lucrece (my emphasis), but the poem had been divided into twelve 'chapters' or sections. Section headings were listed in a table of contents, while in the main text they were inserted into the margins of the text (sometimes in expanded form). This editorial apparatus was maintained in subsequent editions until Q9 of 1655, where the main text was divided into discrete sections, separated by a line of printer's ornaments (and sometimes a complete page break) and marked with the appropriate section heading.[19] The section and marginal headings re-present the development of the poem: in restructuring the narrative, Q6–Q9 provided a new interpretative framework through which the poem could be read.

Marginal headings were used across a very wide range of books in early modern England and for a number of purposes. William

Slights argues, however, that extended poems, collections of lyrics and stage plays 'have almost no marginalia' with a few important exceptions (*The Shepheardes Calender, Sejanus*, Jonson's folio *Workes*).[20] He characterizes the use of printed marginalia as an exercise in 'reader management', taking the reader 'through what the marginalist ... deemed appropriate doorways', which could 'relocate an author's emphasis' (pp. 683 and 697–8). Similarly, Evelyn Tribble has drawn attention to the interpretative status of editorial apparatus, arguing that the margins of texts and the 'text proper' 'were in shifting relationships of authority; the margin might affirm, summarize, underwrite the main text block and thus tend to stabilize meaning, but it might equally assume a contestatory or parodic relation to the text ... . Nor is the margin consistently the site of the secondary, for the margins of texts were often central in their importance.'[21]

In my view the marginal and section headings of Q6–Q9 of Shakespeare's poem are integral to the 'text proper' and its presentation. Moreover, the editorial apparatus works 'to stabilize meaning' – to reiterate the conventional, mainstream interpretation of Lucrece as an icon of marital chastity and coerce a moralistic reading of the poem. Tribble's focus is upon early modern texts with more elaborate editorial apparatus than *Lucrece*, but the 'potential slippage' she observes between 'explanation and coercion; the opposition of public and private realms of meaning, of consensual and individual reading' (p. 17) can also make sense of the presentation and reception of Shakespeare's poem. The 'consensual', mainstream reading of Lucrece did not preclude the existence of 'individual', dissident readings. As John Kerrigan has argued, an awareness of reader diversity was 'widespread' in the period and

almost a condition of authorship in the expanding market for print. In the addresses 'To the Reader' printed with early modern literary texts there is a recurrent stress on division. Authors set 'fond curious, or rather currish backbiters' against 'courteous Readers', separate the 'captious' from the 'vertuous', the 'Pretender' from the 'Vnderstander'.[22]

Against the context of reader diversity and dissident readings, literature could be 'rendered "profitable" by the editorial reading-interventions' of writers, annotators, publishers and printers – such as the "marginal summaries" added to Q6 of *The Rape of Lucrece*'

(p. 117). The marginal heading, in other words, could be used to control readings in the context of reader diversity.

If the section and marginal headings of Q6 *The Rape of Lucrece* emphasize Lucrece's innocence in her rape and validate her suicide, these values become more explicit in the section headings of the 1655 edition of the poem, suggesting the consolidation of an increasingly 'moralistic' presentation of the text. Consider, for instance, the headings of sections six and seven in Q6 and Q9, which describe the critical moment of Lucrece's rape. In Q1 Tarquin enters Lucrece's chamber and invites her to entertain him as 'thy secret friend: the fault unknown is as a thought unacted'. When she refuses, he threatens to 'destroy' her reputation by killing her and placing in her dead arms the body of 'some worthless slave', 'swearing I slew him, seeing thee embrace him' (515–27). Lucrece then tries to dissuade him: 'She conjures him by high almighty Jove, / By knighthood, gentry and sweet friendship's oath ... That to his borrowed bed he make retire, / And stop to honour, not to foul desire' (568–75). At this point an apparently innocuous marginal heading is inserted in Q6 (and reproduced in the contents page):

She pleads in defence of Chastity.

The capitalisation stresses chastity as a concept rather than a localized act. Also, the heading describes Lucrece's plea as a 'defence of Chastity' – a familiar topos to the contemporary reader against which to read her words.

A similar effect is created in the heading of section eight, '*Lucrece* complaines on her abuse', evoking the tradition of the female complaint. The equivalent heading of section six in Q9 goes one step further –

*Lucrece* pleadeth in defence of Chastity and exprobateth his unciuill lust – highlighting the contrast between Chastity and lust, civility and uncivility and emphasizing Lucrece's active defence (exprobation) of herself rather than her passive submission to Tarquin's will.

Lucrece's innocence in the rape is then confirmed by the Q6 heading of section seven, inserted at the point where Tarquin

finally interrupts Lucrece's pleas for restraint ('"No more", quoth
he, "by heavens I will not hear thee"', l.666):

> *Tarquin* all impatient interrupts her and rauisheth her by force.[23]

Any doubt about Lucrece's 'secret' satisfaction 'in the nick of the
act' is ruled out: the section heading denies the possibility of her
adulterous duplicity. Q9 of 1655 phrases the section heading rather
differently, ruling out seduction and stressing the violation of her
body:

> *Tarquin* all impatient, interrupts her; and denyed of consent,
> breaketh the enclosure of her Chastity (p. 26)

The headings of sections six and seven in both Q6 and Q9 (followed
by the heading of section eight in which Lucrece 'complaines on
her *abuse*'; my emphasis) direct the reader towards the 'mainstream' interpretation of Lucrece as an innocent woman abused
and a worthy icon of marital chastity.

Turning to Lucrece's debate about whether to kill herself following her rape, we witness once again the interpretative hand of the
section heading. The final section heading of the Q6 *Rape of Lucrece*
listed on the contents page explains the motive of Lucrece's suicide
thus:

> *Lucrece* relateth the mischiefe: they swear reuenge and she to
> exasperate the matter killeth her selfe.

The verb 'to exasperate' carried a range of meanings in the early
seventeenth century: to make more fierce or violent (1611), to em-
bitter or intensify (1548) and to irritate or incense (1534; *OED*). The
heading confirms that Lucrece did not kill herself out of her 'thirst
of fame', nor to preserve her honour, but rather to intensify
Collatine's revenge. This is made more explicit in the expanded
marginal heading of the Q6 text (used as the section heading in Q9):

> Upon the relation of *Lucrece* her rape, *Collatine* and the rest
> swear to reuenge; but this seems not full satisfaction to her losses.
> She killeth herself to exasperate them the more to punish the
> delinquent.

By invoking justice, or punishment, the heading arguably renders her suicide less problematic.

To attend to 'the subtle shining secrecies / Writ in the glassy margents' (*Lucrece*, 101–2) of later quartos of *The Rape of Lucrece* is to reveal the ideological (or, less emphatically, the interpretative) work of editorial apparatus. Within this 'newly revised' editorial apparatus, variant readings and italicization were adopted. Both F. T. Prince, the Arden 2 editor of *Lucrece*, and John Roe, the New Cambridge editor, argue that the variant readings of later quartos of the poem were performed with the serious intention of 'improving' the poem – F. T. Prince points out that most of the new readings in Q6 were adopted by seventeenth- and eighteenth-century editors 'precisely because they had been introduced for their "correctness". A conscious ideal can be seen at work' (p. xix). Prince and Roe discuss these variant readings largely in terms of regularising metre and diction (Prince, p. xix; Roe, p. 292); my interest, however, is in the ways in which variant readings and the use of the italic typeface alter the possible senses of a line.

In the description of Lucrece's rape, for instance, Q1's line 'O that prone lust should stain so pure a bed!' (684) is emended in Q6 to 'O that fowle *lust* should stain so pure a bed!'. Q6's 'fowle' both eliminates sexual innuendo from the line and introduces a value judgement, while the italicization of '*lust*' helps draw attention to Tarquin's depravity. In the following stanza, Q1's 'Pure chastitie is rifled of her store' (692) becomes in Q6 'Pure *Chastity* is rifled of her store'. Here the italicized and capitalised '*Chastity*' evokes chastity as a concept in keeping with the section headings of the edition. A similar example of the use of italics to emphasize specific concepts or meanings comes in Q1's line 'That for his pray to pray he doth begin, / As if the Heavens should countenance his sin', emended in Q6 to 'That for his *Prey* to pray he doth begin, / As if the *heavens* should countenance his *sinne*'. Here the capitalization and italicization of '*Prey*' confirm Lucrece's status as victim to Tarquin, while the italicization of '*heavens*' and '*sinne*' calls attention to the contrast between good and evil, a contrast which through the use of italics Q6 repeatedly animates in the poem. Likewise at the point where Lucrece crucially questions her innocence – 'May my pure mind with the foul act dispense' (1704) – the use of italics in Q6 emphasises the contrast between action and intent, body and mind: 'May my pure *mind* with the foule *act* dispence'. The cumulative effect of these local alterations, embedded within a new editorial apparatus, is to construct a more polite and moralistic poem than originally appeared in 1594.

Such a construction in fact appears to be the project of John Stafford's 1655 inter-textual volume of Shakespeare's poem: *The Rape of / Lucrece, / Committed by / Tarquin the Sixt; / and / The Remarkable Judgments that befell him for it. / By / The incomparable Master of our English Poetry, / WILL: SHAKESPEARE Gent. / Whereunto is annexed, / The Banishment of Tarquin: / Or, the Reward of Lust. / By J. Quarles.* (London: J. G. for John Stafford, 1655). Q1's simple title *Lucrece* is now replaced with a title that signals a rape, a crime 'committed' by a perpetrator and the retribution he undergoes – although in fact, Shakespeare's text barely dwells upon 'the Remarkable Judgments that befell' Tarquin (his fate is summarily only hinted at in the final four lines of the poem, 1852–5). The task of outlining Tarquin's retribution falls instead to John Quarles, who in his preface 'To the Reader' seeks to vindicate Lucrece from any hint of blame, although he still registers some doubt about her culpability in the act of suicide: 'so died poor *Lucretia*, blameable in nothing but that she was the Author of her own death' (sig. Av). Quarles' poem opens by demonizing Tarquin as 'this Master-piece of Hell' and includes a protracted defence of Lucrece's submission to rape:

Had chast *Lucretia* follow'd the advice
Of lustfull *Tarquin*, what a lavish price
Had she layd out for sin and yet the shame
Had been far greater and her death the same
  If not much worse, for had she not reveal'd it,
  T' had prov'd her death to think she had conceal'd it.

(pp. 1–2)

'Virtue was opprest by violence,' Quarles concludes  The poem then describes Tarquin's spiritual 'fall' and growing burden of guilt in his banishment ('He soon deplor'd his miserable state'). Finally he is pursued by Philomel and a flock of nightingales who harrass him; he 'reels into an extasie' and dies and they pick out his eyes (p. 9). The union of the two texts in a single volume didacticizes *Lucrece*: Quarles' text responds to the poem as a defence of Chastity, the moral of which is clarified with 'the Remarkable Judgments that befell' Tarquin. Here inter-textuality serves to emphasize particular readings over others: the chaste over the ironic, the moralistic over the sceptical.


## PRINT CULTURE AND CULTURAL CHANGE

Who are the agents of change in early modern print culture? In the case of later quartos of *Lucrece*, it is hard to specify: it is not known who was responsible for making the alterations to Shakepeare's text in 1616. John Roe and John Kerrigan speculate that it was the printer Thomas Snodham, while F. T. Prince suggests that it was the publisher Roger Jackson, a London bookseller active in 1601–25 who 'presented the poem with various improvements and embellishments' (p. xvii).[24] It is perhaps worth noting that precisely the same format was used for Q7 (1624), also published by Roger Jackson but printed this time by John Beale, a volume which McKerrow describes as one of 'many notable and interesting books' that Jackson published (*Dictionary of Printers and Booksellers*, p. 151). Roger Jackson was, according to Harry Farr, 'one of the most notable stationers of the early seventeenth century'; his output included the work of Gervase Markham, Robert Greene and Ludovico Ariosto, extended to lavishly illustrated folio productions, and included jest-books, news and current affairs, non-fiction, a few literary texts and numerous religious texts.[25]

Many of these works employed the same editorial apparatus as *The Rape of Lucrece* – the section or chapter heading and contents page (or table), chapter summaries and marginal headings or notes – while Jackson's personal involvement in publication is apparent from his reference to his role as a publisher, such as in the initialled note to the reader he supplied to Gervase Markham's *The English Hus-wife* (John Beale for Roger Jackson, 1615).[26] In this context, however, it is Jackson's publication of *Ariosto's Satyres* – one of only a few volumes of poetry he published – that is most suggestive as a possible precedent for his treatment of *Lucrece*. Ariosto's satires had previously appeared in Italian with the minimum of editorial apparatus; in 1608, Jackson published an English translation (printed by Nicholas Okes) reputedly by Gervase Markham (in fact by Robert Tofte), with a substantially altered editorial apparatus. The volume opened with an 'argument of the whole work and the reasons why *Ludouico Ariosto* writ these Seauen Satyres' providing a historical and biographical background to the poems. Each satire was prefaced by an 'Argument' set out in printer's ornaments summarising the satire, while marginal notes provided explanatory and sometimes extensive commentary to the text. In the Fourth Satire 'shewing how hard a matter it is for a man to keep his wife honest and chast', for instance, the lines 'Let her well loved selfe, her selfe preserue, / And from all goatish sents he[r] skinne conserue', appears with the following marginal note: 'Sluttishness in women was so much detested with the antient Romans, that one of the cheefe noble men of the citie put his wife from him by diuorce, as if she had been incontinent & vnchaste of her bodie, yea only for that fault' (pp. 48 and 58). Jackson's edition of Ariosto's *Satyres* enacts a similar (though not identical) transformation upon the format of extended poetry as takes place in his edition of Q6 *The Rape of Lucrece*. Although we cannot conclude from this that Jackson was responsible for the editorial apparatus of Q6, we can at least note that the volume was concordant with the output of his publishing house in Fleet Street.

But texts were also subject to the agency and 'editorial reading-interventions' of individual readers. Arthur Marotti points out that 'in the system of manuscript transmission, it was normal for lyrics to elicit revisions, corrections, supplements and answers'. Similarly John Kerrigan argues that 'the level of textual variation in seventeenth-century manuscripts is too high for us not to conclude that what was transcribed was often corrected in the sense of "improved"' (p. 118).[27] He cites the example of Sir John Suckling's 'A Supplement of an imperfect Copy of Verses of Mr. Will. Shakespeares, By the Author' as an 'instance of rewriting growing out of editorial activity by a reader' (p. 117).

Suckling's 'Verses', which appear in the posthumous volume published by Humphrey Moseley, *Fragmenta Aurea. A Collection of all the Incomparable Peeces, written by Sir John Suckling* (1646), describe the moment when Tarquin discovers the sleeping Lucrece in bed (386 96) and substantially alter the text of Shakespeare's poem. For instance, Suckling seems to reject the sexual undertones of Shakespeare's description of Lucrece's pillow 'Swelling on either side to want his bliss' (389), emending the line to the less erotically evocative 'Which therefore swell'd, & seem'd to part assunder'. He also rejects Shakespeare's image of Lucrece lying 'like a virtuous monument' leered at by 'lewd unhallowed eyes' (391–2), while in the final stanzas of his 'Verses' he omits altogether to 'copy' the description of her breasts (407–13). In the second stanza of his poem, he rejects the bodily detail of the 'pearly sweat' upon Lucrece's hand and adopts a more sterile image of her hand as 'perfect white' as 'unmelt snow', leading into a somewhat sentimental description of the hand as a 'pretty purdue'.[28] Suckling's 'Verses' demonstrate his agency as a reader and he directs that agency towards producing a more sanitized version of Shakespeare's text.

This raises the question of casual treatment of authorial authority in the period. In *Fragmenta Aurea* the opening two stanzas of Suckling's 'Verses' (neither of which correspond to the regular seven-line structure of Shakespeare's poem), are nevertheless attributed to Shakespeare: a marginal note at the end of the second stanza confusingly reads 'Thus far *Shakspear*' (p. 30). However, Suckling may not have been working from the 'authoritative' quarto of *Lucrece*: Thomas Clayton points out that he might have used the extract of the poem published without stanza-division in *England's Parnassus* (1600), where it revealingly appears under the heading 'Descriptions of Beautie & personage'.[29] As Kerrigan says, the fact that the opening might derive from the miscellany 'is a reminder of how user-inflected the reception of Shakespeare's poetry was' (p. 118).

In his *Account of the English Dramatick Poets* (Oxford, 1691), Gerard Langbaine confirms the currency of the 'corrected' edition among late seventeenth-century readers by noting of Shakespeare that 'our Author has writ two small Poems, *viz. Venus and Adonis*, printed 8o. *Lond.* 1602. and *The Rape of Lucrece*, printed 8o. Lond. 1655, published by Mr. *Quarles*, with a little Poem annext of his own production' (p. 467).[30] What is more, Suckling is mentioned for his respect for, not casual treatment of, Shakespeare's text. Langbaine went on to explain, 'Sr. *John Sucklin* [sic] had so great a Value for our Author, that (as Mr. *Dryden* observes in his *Dramatick Essay*) he preferred him to *Johnson*: and what value he had for this small Piece of *Lucrece*, may appear from his supplement which he writ' (vol. II, p. 467). Printed poetic texts were regarded as much as resources for the reader as vehicles for the author.

Trying to account for the editorial emendations to *Lucrece* in the context of cultural change in the mid-seventeenth century presents considerable difficulties. We might speculate that the increasingly 'chaste' presentation of the text from 1616 to 1655 (continued in the variant readings and marginal headings in the 1707 edition of the poem in *Poems on Affairs of State*) corresponds to changing sensibilities towards sexuality and its representation and locate the 'newly revised' *Lucrece* in the context of an increasingly 'polite' society. Perhaps this participates in what Norbert Elias describes as 'the civilising process'.[31] We might observe that in his 1640 edition of Shakespeare's *Sonnets, Poems: Written by Wil. Shake-speare*, John Benson altered the sensibilities of the collection by emending the pronouns of poems addressed to the young man so as to construct a heterosexual love affair, whilst providing titles to the sonnets which establish them as typical renditions of amorous experience: 'True admiration', 'Loves crueltie', 'Happiness in content', 'In prayse of his Love'.[32] Benson chastens the Shakespearean text, rather as Q6–Q9 *The Rape of Lucrece* focus attention upon Chastity in the reading of the poem.

On the other hand, we might read the editorial apparatus and textual emendations in *Lucrece* in the context of changes in the perception of women. The publication of Q6 *The Rape of Lucrece* with its emphasis upon Lucrece's heroic chastity coincides with the vigorous debate upon the virtues and vices of women in the second decade of the century, the Querelles des Femmes (Joseph Swetnam's *Arraignment of Lewd, idle, forward and unconstant women* appeared in 1615; and Rachel Speight, Ester Sowernam and Constantia Munda published their responses to Swetnam in 1617). Thus, in *The Women's Sharp Revenge* (1640) 'performed by Mary Tattle-well and Joan-Hit-home, spinsters', Lucrece is cited 'for the defence of us women': 'One swallow makes not a summer: nor for the delinquency of one are all to be delivered up to censure. As there was a Lais, so there was a Lucrece; and a wise Cornelia as there was a wanton Corinna. And the same sex that hath bred malefactors hath brought forth martyrs.'[33]

Alternatively, we could interpret the 'chaste' presentation of the text as an intervention against an increasingly sceptical reading public; certainly the doubts cast upon Lucrece's suicide continued to be voiced throughout the seventeenth century. In 1664, for instance, Margaret Cavendish included a discussion of its dubious merits in her *Sociable Letters*: 'The Lady G. B. said, that though she did believe *Lucretia* was a very chast Woman and a Virtuous and Loving Wife, yet whether she Kill'd her self to save her Husbands Honour or her Own, she could not Judge…'[34] Lady G. B. claims that Lucrece would have 'been a Fool to have Kill'd her self' if she was unmarried, and the argument between the two ladies over Lucrece's suicide disintegrates into a farcical fight – 'in such a Fury they were, as they were ready to Beat one another, nay, I was afraid they would have Kill'd each other' (p. 110). 'Truth might Rationally be questioned,' Margaret Cavendish goes on to argue, 'if not of the Person, yet of the Manner of the Action, for perchance the clear Truth was never Recorded' (p. 110). Cavendish also questions the integrity of the legend: 'you never knew or heard of' Lucrece, she reminds her friends, 'but as in an old Wife's Tale' (pp. 110–11).

Similarly, in *Seneca Unmasqued* (1685), Aphra Behn remarked in her opening letter to the reader that 'the Actions of the greatest part of Mankind [are] esteemed Virtuous, when most commonly they have but the Image and bare resemblance of it ... Who applauded the Chastity of *Lucretia* (whom all the World now celebrates for a Vertuous Woman) till they made it a subject of private Revenge and the occasion of the Liberty of *Rome*?'[35] While acknowledging the dominant iconology of Lucrece as a heroine of Chastity, Behn's comment points to the changing status accorded to and thus the provisionality of, her 'Glorious Actions'. She writes in her opening letter that with 'unbiassed judgment' one may 'find self-love enough [to] debauch your nicest Virtue; at least to find there is an allay of self-love that renders it not so pure as it ought' (p. 6), while her opening 'moral reflection' explains that Virtue 'is most commonly but a mixture of divers Actions and of several Interests... 'tis not Courage that makes a Man Brave, nor Chastity that makes a Woman Honest' (p. 11).

More emphatically, we might see the increasingly chastened text of *Lucrece* as an intervention that betrays anxiety about declining standards of sexual morality and the growth of a libertine culture. In the decade following the first publication in 1594, commentators tended to stress pity and seriousness: '*Shake-speare*, paints poore *Lucrece* rape', reads a manuscript annotation to *Willobie his Avisa* (1594); in an epigram to 'Honie-tong'd *Shakespeare* of 1595, John Weever refers to 'Chaste *Lucretia* virgine-like her dresses'; in 'A Remembrance of some English Poets' (1598) Richard Barnfield writes of Shakespeare's Lucrece as 'sweete and chaste'; while in his marginalia Gabriel Harvey commented that 'the younger sort take much delight in Shakespeare's Venus and Adonis; but his Lucrece and his tragedy of Hamlet, Prince of Denmarke, have it in them to please the wiser sort'.[36] But by the time of the Restoration, Lucrece's iconic status was frequently countered with her portrayal as a dissembling woman open to seduction and we get a sense of this scepticism in the ambivalent tone of *The History of Tarquin and Lucretia* (1669), appropriately written under the pseudonym of 'Philander'.[37]

The poem begins by adopting an ironical stance: 'what dull Sports are all the Exercises of Hawks, Hounds, Horses and Drinking, to this of adoring your Sex' (dedication, sig. A3v). On Lucrece's rape, 'Philander' observes that 'such Accidents may inevitably fall out some times' and that from the example of her 'flood of Tears' and suicide 'the ladies of our times may learn to be fore-witted' (sig. A2v). The poem itself is largely taken up with an almost good-humoured debate between Tarquin and Lucretia about marriage and sex and although Lucretia 'Conjur'd him not to touch her more, / Yet like a Supliant did him there implore' (p. 15). She later describes herself not as a victim of abuse, but as a 'Fool' that has 'done amiss' (p. 17). 'Philander' trivialises the rape as an accident that speaks more of female 'fore-wit' than honour. In his *Poems chiefly consisting of Satyrs and Satyrical Epistles* (1688), Robert Gould also characterizes the Lucrece legend in terms of a woman stooping to folly. In 'Instructions to a Young Lady' (which follows a mock-panegyric to Shakespeare and other 'Immortal, tuneful Men'), Gould advises young women to 'Think of *Lucretia*, then of *Tarquin's* lust. / If Barefac't Violence does not prevail / To work your Ruin, Flatt'ry will not fail', insinuating that Lucrece was a fallen woman and the victim of her own vanity.[38] In my view, however, specula-tions about the cultural context of the chastened text of Shakespeare's *Lucrece* cannot be determined without much more precise information about relations between text, publisher, reader-ship and cultural change.

Seeking to analyse the editorial apparatus of Q6–Q9 *The Rape of Lucrece* in terms of the characteristic treatment of different literary genres in the period raises further problems of interpretation. On one hand, we might argue that the construction of Shakespeare's poem marks a 'novelistic' treatment of the poetic text. Q6 *The Rape of Lucrece* arguably resembles the format of prose fiction divided into chapters with explanatory headings, such as editions of Thomas Deloney's *The Pleasant History of John Winchcome [Jack of Newbury]* (London, 1633) and *Thomas of Reading, Or, The Sixe Worthy Yeoman of the West* (London, 1612), Emanuel Forde's *The First Part of Parismus, the renowned Prince of Bohemia* (London, 1615) and *The Most Pleasant Historie of Ornatus and Artesia* (London, 1634). We might argue for a transition in the boundaries of literary genres in the period, whereby the format of prose fiction increasingly intercedes in the genre of narrative poetry (and ultimately super-sedes it as the dominant form of narrative fiction). But again, such speculations need to be more precisely located. While we can question the 'novelisation' of Shakespeare's *The Rape of Lucrece*, there are counter-examples of prose fiction that are not structured as a series of chapters – such as Robert Greene's *The Pleasant Historie of Dorastus and Fawnia* (London, 1636) or Henry Robarts' *The Mayden Knight* (London, 1595) – and prose fiction that is published in chapter form also tends to be printed in the typeface associated with popular and ephemeral literature, black letter gothic, while Shakespeare's poem is consistently printed in the roman (and/or italic) typefaces traditionally used for prestigious, classical texts.[39]

More to the point, there are many examples of narrative poems which do not undergo the structural transformation of *Lucrece*, including Shakespeare's own *Venus and Adonis* (1593). Published even more frequently in the first half of the seventeenth-century than *Lucrece*, *Venus and Adonis* is subject to variant readings and the increasing use of italicisation between editions, but not re-structuring: the continuous and unadorned format of Q1 is maintained and the title-pages make no reference to a 'newly revised' edition or even, interestingly, to Shakespeare as the author of the poem.[40] The publishing histories of Shakespeare's two narrative poems thus have different stories to tell. Similarly, other 1590s narrative poems reprinted in the seventeenth century do not share the editorial apparatus of Q6–Q9 *The Rape of Lucrece*: Marlowe's *Hero and Leander*, for instance, maintains the format of the second quarto of 1598 in editions to 1637 (except that after 1606 editions intriguingly do not distinguish between Marlowe's opening sestiads and Chapman's continuation of the poem), as does *Salmacis and Hermaphroditus*, ascribed to Beaumont, in editions to 1660. (Other epyllia from the 1590s do not seem to have enjoyed the popularity of Shakespeare's narrative poems or Marlowe's *Hero and Leander* in the seventeenth century and were rarely republished.)[41] Indeed, there are apparently few instances of narrative poetry published in quarto that share the editorial apparatus of Q6 *The Rape of Lucrece*: of the few examples I have found, Samuel Daniel's *Poeticall Essayes... Newly corrected and augmented* (P. Short for Simon Waterson, 1599) includes marginal notes to *The Civill Wars*, but they indicate only historical individuals mentioned in the text, while *Poems: By Michael Drayton, Esquire, Newly Corrected by the Author* (London: W. Stansby for John Smethwicke, 1613) makes no alteration to the editorial apparatus of the poems' previous publication by Nicholas Ling in 1605.[42]

John Benson's edition of Shakespeare's *Sonnets* (1640), already mentioned, is a more compelling case of the interpretative hand of editorial apparatus, which I have already mentioned: the sonnets of the 1609 quarto are reordered, titled and conflated so as to produce 'a new literary artifact' (Marotti, 'Shakespeare's Sonnets', p. 161).[43] Contemporary writers remark on such practice (as well as on straightforward misprints). In 1656 Abraham Cowley protested against the 'mangled and imperfect' publication of his work: 'I began to reflect upon the fortune of almost all *Writers* and especially *Poets*, whose *Works* (commonly printed after their deaths) we finde stuffed out'.[44] He was referring to the practice of augmenting editions of poets' works with 'counterfeit pieces' or poems previously rejected by the poet for publication, but he sees his complaint as relevant to the publication of Shakespeare's poetry. Stationers, he complains, are

> like *Vintners* with sophisticate mixtures, [who] spoil the whole vessel of wine, to make it yield more *profit*. This has been the case with *Shakespear*, *Fletcher*, *Johnson* and many others; part of whose *Poems* I should take the boldness to prune and lop away, if the care of replanting them in print did belong to me.[45]

The later quartos of *The Rape of Lucrece* participate in this profitable 'mixing' of the authentic and the counterfeit, the authoritative and unauthoritative; in this sense, we can view the altered texts of *Lucrece* in terms of the casual treatment of English poetry, especially the work of dead poets, by seventeenth-century publishers.

The many examples and counter-examples of the use of editorial apparatus across different genres make it difficult to describe general patterns in the presentation of narrative poetry in the seventeenth century: different authors, printers and publishers adopt different formats for different publications. But the altered texts of *Lucrece* can indicate and arguably participated in, developments in the print culture of poetry at large in the period. The prestige of the English poet was by no means guaranteed in the late-sixteenth century: the publication of poetry still carried, to a greater or lesser extent, the 'stigma of print'; H. S. Bennett notes that vernacular poetry constituted only a fraction of English books published from 1475 to 1640 and J. W. Saunders describes 'poetry and works of imagination' as 'the poor orphans of the printed book market'.[46] As Arthur Marotti notes, 'English literature, like English nationhood, was a developing entity in the sixteenth century and it took the achievements of a series of extraordinary writers as well as the growth of some sense of English literary history to put English vernacular literature on an equal footing both with other European traditions and with classical literature'.[47] The publication of poetry in new forms and dimensions in the late sixteenth and seventeenth centuries helped to establish that literary history. Poetry anthologies became increasingly popular, while the publication of 'landmark' poetic texts – such as Speght's folio *Chaucer* (1598 and 1602), Ponsonby's folio of Sidney's *Workes* (1598, 1599 and 1604), Jonson's folio *Workes* (1616), the folios of Spenser's collected poetry (1611 and 1617), the 1623 edition of Daniel's collected works, the 1633 editions of the poems of John Donne and George Herbert and Benson's 1640 edition of Shakespeare's poems – developed the prestige of English poetry and validated works of English printed verse 'as serious cultural artifacts' (p. 253).[48]

As Paulina Kewes has argued, the later seventeenth century saw a growing concern with the integrity of an author's *oeuvre*, while the increase of non-commercial compilations listing writers and their works – such as Langbaine's *Account of the English Dramatick Poets* (1691) – attest to a growing interest in the identification of a native literary and dramatic tradition.[49] By the time of the Civil War and Interregnum, the publication of single-authored editions of English poets had proliferated; in particular, the work of publisher Humphrey Moseley in the 1640s and 1650s helped to promote the canonization of English poetry. Moseley published the work of a considerable number of poets, including Suckling's *Fragmenta Aurea* (1646, 1648 and 1658), Quarles (1642), Milton (1645), Shirley (1646), Carew (1651) and Vaughan (1651 and 1654); he also printed a series of playtexts and the 1647 folio of Beaumont and Fletcher.[50] The altered texts of Q6–Q9 *The Rape of Lucrece* can be viewed in this context, as a new literary artefact that participates in the emerging canonization of both vernacular poetry and the English poet in the seventeenth century. Consider the changes made to the title-page in the period 1594–1655: in Q1 of 1594 Shakespeare's name does not appear (his authorship is indicated only by his signature to the dedication). In Q6 Shakespeare is acknowledged as the poem's author in the title-page – *The Rape of Lucrece. By Mr. William Shakespeare. Newly Revised* – while Q9 of 1655 goes one step further by praising Shakespeare's skill: *The Rape of Lucrece... By the incomparable Master of our English Poetry, WILL:*

*SHAKESPEARE Gent.* Shakespeare, a gentleman, is now memorial-
ized as an 'incomparable Master' of a national tradition, 'our
English Poetry'. We are seeing a transition in the fashioning of
authorship and, by implication, in the anticipated interests of
contemporary readers.

Stafford's 1655 edition also makes a significant addition with the
inclusion of a frontispiece portrait, which as Marotti notes was 'a
common means in print culture for elevating the sociocultural
status of authorship'.[51] Opposite the title-page is an engraving of
Lucrece in a quasi-classical setting about to stab herself while
Collatine raises his hand as though seeking to prevent the act;
above both characters is a medallion, marked off by a bold white
border, depicting Shakespeare's portrait. Although not centrally
placed, Shakespeare dominates the frontispiece: he is portrayed on
a much larger scale than Lucrece or Collatine and looks above the
characters towards the reader. In her examination of Moseley's
serial publication of play collections during the Civil War and
Interregnum, Paulina Kewes notes that he deliberately sought out
portraits: in his 1647 folio edition of Beaumont and Fletcher's
works, for instance, Moseley was 'very ambitious to get
Mr. Beaumonts picture; but could not possibly, though I spared no
enquirie'.[52] She concludes for Moseley's output that

> the prominence of the author's name on the title-page, the ap-
> pearance of his engraved likeness at the frontispiece and the
> wealth of author-centred paratextual material... show that each
> volume is organized around the figure of the author. The author,
> immortalized in each booklet's engraved frontispiece, emerges as
> a central, unifying presence. (pp. 10–11)

Thus the title-pages of Q6–Q9 *Lucrece* and the 1655 frontispiece are
sites which register the developing canonization of the poet and the
canonization of English poetry in the seventeenth century.

The form and structure, errors and emendations of the
Shakespearean text – whether 'good', 'bad', corrupt or unauthoritative – play a significant role in terms of their use as reading texts, as
objects which once had a place and value in men and women's li-
braries. Consider, for instance, the example of Frances Wolfreston
(1607–77), a gentlewoman who built up her own library of some
hundred volumes at her home in Staffordshire and who possibly
obtained her books from local booksellers in the Midlands or on

occasional trips to London. Her copy of Shakespeare's *Lucrece* (one of ten Shakespeare quartos Wolfreston owned) was Q6 of 1616. From the vantage-point of an early modern reader like Wolfreston, without access to multiple texts, the later quarto could play a decisive role in the reception of Shakespeare.[53] Although the later quartos – poetic texts in particular – are seldom the subject of critical analysis, they can yield fascinating insights into the treatment and transmission of the Shakespearean text in early modern England. By turning to their histories we can more fully understand relations between texts, print culture and cultural change in early modern England.

## NOTES

1. I wish to thank Ann Thompson and Jim Rigney for commenting on earlier drafts of this chapter and Cedric Brown and Arthur Marotti for supporting the project.
2. Augustine, *The City of God*, Book I, ch. 18; trans. John Healey (1610), ed. Ernest Barker (London, 1957), p. 23. 'The sanctity of the body is no more lost', argued Augustine, 'if the sanctity of mind remain (though the body be ravished), than it is kept, if the mind's holiness be polluted, though the body itself be untouched' (p. 22). Roland Mushat Frye argues that 'Shakespeare would have had as easy access to [Augustine's] writings as to those of any of the sixteenth-century writers ...' (*Shakespeare and Christian Doctrine* [London: Oxford University Press, 1963], p. 11). On Augustine's criticism of Lucrece and the problematic definition of her rape and suicide, see Ian Donaldson, *The Rapes of Lucretia: A Myth and its Transformations* (Oxford, 1982), pp. 21–39; Stephanie Jed, *Chaste Thinking: The Rape of Lucretia and the Birth of Humanism* (Bloomington and Indianapolis, 1989), pp. 3–4, 13, 39–47; Carolyn D. Williams, '"Silence, like a Lucrece knife": Shakespeare and the Meanings of Rape', *Yearbook of English Studies*, 23 (1993): 93–110; A. Robin Bowers, 'Iconography and Rhetoric in *Lucrece*', *Shakespeare Survey* 14 (1981): 1–21, esp. pp. 1–2; Laura Bromley, 'Lucrece's Re-creation', *Shakespeare Quarterly*, 34:2 (Summer, 1983): 200–11, esp. pp. 200–1; Don Cameron Allen, 'Some Observations on *The Rape of Lucrece*', *Shakespeare Survey* 15 (1962): 89–98; Roy Battenhouse, *Shakespearean Tragedy: Its Art and its Christian Premises* (Bloomington, 1969), pp. 3–41; and Annabel Patterson, *Reading between the Lines* (London, 1993), pp. 299 and 304.
3. *City of God*, p. 30; Tyndale cited by Donaldson, *The Rapes of Lucretia* p. 45.
4. *The Rapes of Lucretia*, pp. 21–39 and 45–6; Bromley, 'Lucrece's Re-Creation', pp. 200–4; see also Bowers, 'Iconography and Rhetoric in *Lucrece*', p. 2; and Heather Dubrow, *Captive Victors: Shakespeare's*

*Narrative Poems* (London, 1987), p. 90. Augustine argues that Lucrece acted 'as a Roman woman, excessively eager for honour... Such has not been the behaviour of Christian women' (p. 30).

5. 'Some Observations on "The Rape of Lucrece"', p. 90.
6. Robert Carew, trans., *A World of Wonders* (London, 1607), p. 101; cited by Allen, 'Some Observations on "The Rape of Lucrece"', p. 90.
7. Rivers presents these arguments against Lucrece's virtue in the form of an argument 'Pro Lucrecia' and 'Contra Lucrecia'. Although he articulates standard defences of Lucrece when writing 'Pro Lucrecia' ('there were two in the act, one in the sinne', p. 64), what interests me about his arguments 'Contra Lucrecia' is his strategy of *debating* the case against Lucrece as a model of feminine virtue and encouraging his woman reader, Lady Dorothy Sydney, to consider that debate.
8. *The Anatomy of Melancholy* (London, 1964), vol. III, p. 108. For Aretino see 'La ultima giornata del Capriccio Aretino nella quale la nanna narra alla antonia la vita delled puttane', *Ragionamento della Nonna e della Antonia*, in *Opere di Pietro Aretino e di Anton Francesco Doni*, ed. Carlo Cordie (Milan, 1976), vol. III, pp. 185–7. For Burton's copy of Shakespeare's *Lucrece* see Nichola K. Kiessling, *The Library of Robert Burton* (Oxford, 1988), pp. 278 and 398.
9. *Lucrece* (1594), E1v (British Library: G.11178).
10. British Library, C.34.h.44. The date Grendon assigns to his annotation is puzzling.
11. 'The ironic reading of "The Rape of Lucrece" and the problem of external evidence', *Shakespeare Survey*, 85–92, esp. pp. 89 and 91. As Levin notes, Shakespeare's nine references to Lucrece in his plays tend to stress her chastity and innocence – perhaps above all in *Titus Andronicus*, where Demetrius claims 'Lucrece was not more chaste / Than this Lavinia' (2.1.108–9) and *Cymbeline*, where Iachimo is reminded of the 'chastity' Tarquin 'wounded' when he intrudes into Imogen's bedchamber (2.2.12–14).
12. 'The ironic reading of "The Rape of Lucrece"', p. 90. I have some reservations with Levin's otherwise persuasive argument: first, he assumes that references to Lucrece collected in the *Shakespeare Allusion Book* necessarily refer to Shakespeare's poem (the collators of the *Shakespeare Allusion Book* are more circumspect); secondly, he assumes that these references 'constitute a representative sample' of contemporary responses to Shakespeare's poem (p. 90); thirdly, his strategy of privileging the 'meaning' or 'attitude' of a text leads him to downplay the disjunction between a 'chaste' text and an ironical, contemporary reader. This is precisely the case of Grendon's comment upon Heywood's *Rape of Lucrece*, which Levin addresses only summarily in a footnote (p. 89, n.8).
13. *The Rapes of Lucretia*, pp. 40–1. A. Robin Bowers takes the opposite view, that 'Shakespeare develops his legend to demonstrate Lucrece's virtue which is forcibly and unwillingly violated by Tarquin' (p. 3); Philippa Berry argues that the poem articulates 'a new, feminine model of *virtu*', in 'Woman, Language and History in *The Rape of Lucrece*', *Shakespeare Survey* 44 (1991): 33–9, esp. p. 38; Carolyn D.

Williams concludes that Shakespeare's Lucrece 'is probably best understood as his representation of the archetypal rape victim, strug-
gling to state her case in a way that will get her the fair hearing she
desperately needs, but fears she never will obtain', 'Shakespeare and
the meanings of rape', p. 109. For other critical discussions of
Shakespeare's *Lucrece*, see Nancy Vickers, '"The blazon of sweet
beauty's best": Shakespeare's *Lucrece*', in *Shakespeare and the Question
of Theory*, eds Patricia Parker and Geoffrey Hartman (London, 1985),
95–115; Coppelia Kahn, 'The Rape in Shakespeare's *Lucrece*',
*Shakespeare Studies* 9 (1976): 53–7; Annabel Patterson, *Reading between
the Lines* (London, 1993), pp. 297–312.

14. *Orality and Literacy: The Technologizing of the Word* (1982; London,
1993), p. 121.

15. Roger Chartier, 'Laborers and Voyagers: From the Text to the Reader',
in *Diacritics*, 22 (summer 1992): 49–61, p. 50. See also Jerome J.
McGann, *The Textual Condition* (Princeton, 1991), p. 11: 'Literary works
do not know themselves and cannot *be* known, apart from their
specific material modes of existence/resistance.'

16. 'The Year's Contributions to Textual Studies: 'Editions and Textual
Studies', in *Shakespeare Survey* 46 (1994): 241–58, p. 248.

17. See, for instance, F. T. Prince (ed.), Shakespeare, *The Poems* (1960;
London and New York, 1988), p. xiii. As Arthur Marotti points out,
however, there is little evidence that Shakespeare took extensive care
over the publication of his poems: 'he failed to take the opportunity
usually afforded to authors to check proofs at the printer's'
('Shakespeare's Sonnets as Literary Property', in *Soliciting
Interpretation: Literary Theory and Seventeenth-Century English Poetry*
eds. Elizabeth D. Harvey and Katharine Eisaman Maus [Chicago and
London, 1990], pp. 143–73, esp. p. 144).

18. Edward Arber, *Transcript of the Stationer's Company*, vol. III, p. 542.

19. The chapter headings as listed on the contents page of Q6 *The Rape of
Lucrece* are as follows: 1. LUCRECE praises for chaste, vertuous and
beautifull, enamoreth *Tarquin*. 2. *Tarquin* welcomed by *Lucrece*. 3.
*Tarquin* overthrowes all disputing with wilfulnesse. 4. He puts his resolution in practice. 5. *Lucrece* awakes and is amazed to be so sur-
prised. 6. She pleads in defence of Chastity. 7. *Tarquin* all impatient
interrupteth her and ravisheth her by force. 8. *Lucrece* complaines on
her abuse. 9. She disputeth whether she should kill her selfe or no. 10.
She is resolved on her selfe-murder, yet sendeth first for her Husband.
11. *Colatinus* with his friends returne home. 12. *Lucrece* relateth the
mischiefe: they sweare revenge and she to exasperate the matter
killeth her selfe (sig.A3v).

20. 'The Edifying Margins of Renaissance English Books', *Renaissance
Quarterly*, XLII: 4 (Winter 1989): 682–716, p. 687.

21. Evelyn B. Tribble, *Margins and Marginality: The Printed Page in Early
Modern England* (Charlottesville and London, 1993), p. 2. See also
Lawrence Lipking, 'The Marginal Gloss', *Critical Inquiry* 3 (1977):
609–55; William W. E. Slights, '"Marginall notes that spoile the text":
Scriptural annotation in the English Renaissance', *Huntington Library*

*Quarterly* 55:2 (1992): 255–78; Robert Darnton, *The Kiss of Lamourette. Reflections in Cultural History* (London, 1990), pp. 177–9 and 182–5.

22. 'The Editor as Reader', in *The Practice and Representation of Reading in England*, eds. James Raven, Helen Small and Naomi Tadmor (Cambridge, 1995), p. 112. See also Eugene R. Kintgen, 'Reconstructing Elizabethan Reading', *Studies in English Literature*, 30:1 (winter 1990), 1–18, esp. p. 13; and Debra Belt, 'The Poetics of Hostile Response, 1575–1610', *Criticism*, 33 (1991): 419–59, esp. pp. 422–32.

23. Shakespeare's sources for *Lucrece* are arguably ambivalent about the nature of Lucrece's submission to Tarquin: William Painter's translation of Livy's *Historia*, *The Pallace of Pleasure* (1566) tells that Tarquin's 'fleshlye and licentious enterprice *overcame* the puritie of her chaste and honest hart', while in the *Fasti*, Ovid relates that '*overcome* by fear of infamy, *the dame gave way*' (Prince, ed., *The Poems*, pp. 194 and 200; my emphasis).

24. Decisions about the size and format of printed books were generally the responsibility of the publisher, bookseller and/or the master-printer who had to cost the book, order the paper and fit the book's production into the work pattern of the printing house; see for instance Philip Gaskell, *A New Introduction to Bibliography* (Oxford, 1974), p. 40; and George Walton Williams, *The Craft of Printing and the Publication of Shakespeare's Works* (London and Toronto, 1985), p. 53. Simon Caughi examines negotiations between printer and author in 'The "setting foorth" of Harington's Ariosto', *Studies in Bibliography*, XXXVI (1983): 137–68; Adrian Weiss examines the process of textual production in 'Shared printing, printer's copy and the text(s) of Gascoigne's *A Hundreth Sundrie Flowres*' in *Studies in Bibliography*, XLV (1992): 71–104. Thomas Snodham was a printer in London active from 1603 to 1625 at St Botolph without Aldersgate. His extensive output was apparently dominated by religious texts, particularly sermons; among the few literary texts he printed were Seneca's *Tragedies* in Latin (1624) and George Chapman's *The Revenge of Bussy D'Ambois* (1613); other works from his printing house include Thomas Elyot's *Book of the Governor* and Serlio's *Five Books of Architecture* (a prestigious folio production), current affairs and the songs of William Byrd and John Dowland; see McKerrow, *Dictionary of Printers and Booksellers*, 250–1; and E. Arber, *A Transcript of the registers of the Company of Stationers of London, 1554–1640* (London: privately printed), vol. III, pp. 413 and 465.

25. Harry Farr, 'Notes on Shakespeare's Printers and Publishers', *The Library*, 4th series, III:4 (March 1923): 225–60, p. 248; McKerrow, *Dictionary*, p. 151; see also Arber, *Transcript of the Stationer's Records*, II. p. 648, III, p. 542, IV. 111–12 and 149. Jackson's literary output included Ariosto's *A president for Satirists* (1608), Greene's *Ghost Haunting Cunny Catchers* (1602), Francis Davison's *Poemes or a Poeticall Rapsodye* (1623), Arthur Saul's *The Famous Game of Chesse-play* (1614) and Nicholas Breton's *Fantastiques* (1626); non-fiction included Gervase Markham's *A Way to get Wealth* (1623), F. N.'s *The*

*Husbandman's Fruitfull Orchard* (1608) and Robert Record's *The Ground of Arts: teaching the perfect worke and practise of arithmeticke... augmented by Mr John Dee* (1623); religious texts included Dod and Clever's *A plaine and familiar expositione of the thirteenth and fourteenth chapters of Proverbs* (1608), Stephen Jerome's *Origen's Repentance* (1619) and Johann Gerhard's *A Christian mans weekes worke* (1611); see also Arber, *Transcript,* III., p. 542 and IV, p. 149.

26.  To the Reader, *The English Hus-wife.* This may well be the marketing strategy of an astute publisher; my point is simply that Jackson publicly involves himself in the publication of his volumes, addressing the reader directly. For other examples of the use of editorial apparatus in Jackson's publications see Gervase Markham's *Cheape and Good Husbandry* (Thomas Snodham for Roger Jackson, 1614), *The English Hus-wife* (John Beale for Roger Jackson, 1615), *Markham's Methode or Epitome* (Thomas Snodham for Roger Jackson, 1616); Dodd and Cleaver's *A Plaine and familiar exposition of the thirteenth and fourteenth chapters of the Proverbs of Solomon* (R. B. for Roger Jackson, 1609) includes marginal headings and notes, but no contents page. Robert Greene's *Ghost Hunting Conie-Catchers* (I. North for Roger Jackson, 1602) is rare among Jackson's publications in employing the bare minimum of editorial apparatus.

27.  Arthur Marotti, *Manuscript, Print and the English Renaissance Lyric* (Ithaca, NY and London, 1995), p. 135. For Kerrigan see 'The Editor as Reader', p. 118.

28.  *Fragmenta Aurea* (London, 1646), pp. 29–30. The verses are also quoted by Gerard Langbaine, *An Account of the English Dramatick Poets* (Oxford, 1691), vol. II, p. 468.

29.  Clayton (ed.), *Sir John Suckling: The Non-Dramatic Works* (Oxford, 1971), p. 228. The extract from *Lucrece* as it appears in *Englands Parnassus* (pp. 396–7) has no stanza divisions, but otherwise remains fairly close to the text of Q1, ll.386–413.

30.  Charles Gildon's continuation of Langbaine's *Account, The Lives and Characters of the English Dramatick Poets... First begun by Mr. Langbain, improv'd and continued down to the Time, by a Careful Hand* (1698) confirms the currency of the 1655 quarto of *The Rape of Lucrece*: after listing Shakespeare's plays, Gildon writes 'our Author writ little else, we find in print only two small pieces of Poetry published by Mr. Quarles, viz. *Venus and Adonis, 8vo.* 1602. and *The Rape of Lucrece, 8vo.* 1655' (cited in *The Shakespeare Allusion Book* (Oxford, 1932), vol. II, p. 422).

31.  See Elias, *The History of Manners. The Civilizing Process: Volume 1* (New York, 1978), esp pp. 164, 167–9, 182 and 189–90.

32.  See Marotti, 'Shakespeare's Sonnets as Literary Property', p. 161; Kerrigan, 'The Editor as Reader', pp. 118–19.

33.  Reprinted in *The Women's Sharp Revenge. Five Women's Pamphlets from the Renaissance*, ed. Simon Shepherd (London, 1985), p. 170.

34.  *CCXI Sociable Letters, wiritten by the Thrice Noble, Illustrious and Excellent Princess, the Lady Marchioness of Newcastle* (London, William Wilson, 1664), letter LIV, p. 109.

35. 'Astrea to Lysander', prefixed to *Seneca Unmasqued, or, More Reflections*, trans. Aphra Behn (London, 1685), reprinted in Janet Todd, ed., *The Pickering Masters: Works of Aphra Behn* (London, 1993), vol. 4, pp. 5–6.

36. Cited in *The Shakespeare Allusion Book*, vol. I, pp. 8, 24, 51 and 56; see also pp. 23 and 40. On Shakespeare's own later references to the legend (for instance, in *Cymbeline*) see note 9.

37. In 1651 Edward Sherburne sought to counter contemporary scepticism about the 'Rape of Helen' which, he notes, is 'diversly reported': 'There be those yet who think her not worth the Honour of so famous a Contention... *Homer* might be ashamed to make that the Argument of his Work, nor will beleeve that any man could be such a Wittall, as to seek by force to regain one to his Bed, that had so notoriously wronged it' (*Salmacis, Lyriam, Sylvia, Forsaken Lydia, The Rape of Helen, A Comment thereon, with severall other poems and translations* [London, W. Hunt for Thomas Drink, 1651], sigs. C7–C7v).

38. Cited in *The Shakespeare Allusion Book*, vol. II, p. 295.

39. On the social currency of typefaces, see Marotti, *Manuscript, Print and the English Renaissance Lyric*, pp. 283–5, and D. F. McKenzie, 'Typography and Meaning: The Case of Congreve', in *Wolfenbutteler Schriften zur Geschichte des Buchwessens*, eds. G. Barber and B. Fabian (Hamburg, 1981): 81–125.

40. Italicization appears for proper names by Q2 of 1596 and only the 1627 edition drops the use of italics; after Q1 all volumes of *Venus and Adonis* were published in octavo. I discuss the multiple texts of *Venus and Adonis* and their implications for notions of textual authority in 'Reading the Shakespearean Text in Early Modern England', *Critical Survey* 7:3 (Winter 1995), 299–306.

41. I have compared the 1598 (Q2), 1606, 1613, 1629 and 1637 editions of Marlowe's *Hero and Leander*, and the 1640, 1653 and 1660 editions of Francis Beaumont's *Poems*; the first quarto of *Hero and Leander* (1598) was not divided into sestiads – this structure was introduced, together with Chapman's prefatory summaries and continuation, in Q2 of 1598. Michael Drayton's epyllion, *Endimion and Phoebe*, was not reprinted in seventeenth-century editions of his *Poems* to 1655.

42. In Drayton's volume corrections centre upon emendations to capitalization, italicization and spelling: for instance, 'Bloud-thirsting Warre' is amended in 1613 to 'Blood-thirsting warre' (*The Barons Warres*, from *Poems*, 1605, sig. B2 and 1613, sig. B2). On Nicholas Ling's publication of Drayton, see Gerald D. Johnson, 'Nicholas Ling, Publisher 1580–1607', *Studies in Bibliography*, XXXVIII (1985), 203–16, pp. 204–5.

43. See also *Manuscript, Print and the English Renaissance Lyric*, p. 285.

44. Cited by Marotti, *Manuscript, Print and the English Renaissance Lyric*, pp. 263–4; see also William A. Ringler, Jr., 'The 1640 and 1653 *Poems: By Francis Beaumont, Gent.* and the canon of Beaumont's nondramatic verse', *Studies in Bibliography* 45 (1992): 120–40, p. 139.

45. Cited by Marotti, *Manuscript, Print and the English Renaissance Lyric*, p. 264.

46. Cited by Marotti, *Manuscript, Print and the English Renaissance Lyric*, p. 211, notes 6 and 7.
47. *Manuscript, Print and the English Renaissance Lyric*, p. 210. Harington's edition of Ariosto's *Orlando Furioso* marks another case in point of the prestigious folio format being used for poetry. See Caughi, p. 138.
48. My discussion is indebted to Marotti's examination of print and the lyric in *Manuscript, Print and the English Renaissance Lyric*; see esp. pp. 211, 252–3 and 257.
49. See Paulina Kewes, 'Between the "triumvirate of wit" and the Bard: The English Dramatic Canon, 1660–1720' (this volume), pp. 200–24.
50. See Marotti, pp. 259–62; and Paulina Kewes, '"Give me the social pocket-books...": Humphrey Moseley's Serial Publication of Octavo Play Collections', *Publishing History* 38 (1995): 5–21, p. 6. See also Peter Lindenbaum, 'Milton's Contract', *Cardozo Arts and Entertainment Law Journal*, Vol. X, no. 2 (1992), p. 451; and Warren Chernaik, 'Books as Memorials: The Politics of Consolation', *The Yearbook of English Studies: Politics and Literature in England, 1558–1658*, Vol. XXI (1991): 207–16.
51. *Manuscript, Print and the English Renaissance Lyric*, p. 240; see also D. F. McKenzie, 'Typography and Meaning', p. 93. The 'augmented' edition of Daniel's *Delia and Rosamund* (London: Simon Waterson, 1594) is an early example of the frontispiece being used for a quarto volume of English poetry; for other examples of frontispieces attached to poetry, see Harington's *Orlando Furioso* (1591), Speght's *Chaucer* (1598) and Suckling's *Fragmenta Aurea* (1646).
52. Cited by Kewes, '"Give me the social pocket-books...", p. 16, n.20.
53. I discuss the example of Frances Wolfreston as a woman reader of Shakespeare in 'Reading the Shakespearean text in early modern England', *Critical Survey* 7:3 (Winter 1995): 299–306, and '"Shakespeare creepes into the womens closets about bedtime": Women Reading in a Room of their Own', in *Renaissance Configurations: Voices, Bodies, Spaces*, ed. Gordon McMullen (forthcoming from Macmillan); see also Paul Morgan, 'Frances Wolfreston and "Hor Bouks": A Seventeenth-century Woman Book-Collector', *The Library*, 6th series, XI:3 (September 1989), pp. 207 and 217.

# 7

# The Birth of the Author

## Richard Dutton

Why did Shakespeare not print his own plays? There is a fair consensus that he did not, though 13 of them were printed in his own lifetime, in texts that editors have generally agreed are based on the author's papers or a good playhouse copy.[1] Yet hardly anyone has supposed that Shakespeare actively saw them into print. This is one of those 'facts' about Shakespeare's career usually taken quietly for granted. In the course of this paper I shall review a number of these, arguing that they need to be re-assessed in the light of recent thinking about early modern culture and the place of Shakespeare's career within it. In particular, I shall be considering: the copyright of play-texts and how it related to their licensing; the relationship between acting companies and their retained playwrights; and the practice of circulating play-texts in manuscript.

Shakespeare clearly was responsible for the publication of *Venus and Adonis* (1593) and *Lucrece* (1594), both of which carried signed dedications to the Earl of Southampton and were printed by his fellow Stratfordian, Richard Field. Yet Field had no hand in the printing of any of the plays; none of the play texts until *Love's Labour's Lost* (1598) even had an indication of authorship; and none in Shakespeare's lifetime carried an author's preface or commendations from friends, the usual marks of the writer's personal involvement. Shakespeare was not shy of print, it seems, only of printing plays (and perhaps sonnets).[2] Why this should be so is still a subject for conjecture. For some scholars, only staging mattered to Shakespeare; Leeds Barroll, for instance, argues that Shakespeare wrote plays only when he could anticipate immediate performance: 'Denied the visual and auditory realization of his plays on stage, Shakespeare's creative drive for drama seems to have faltered.'[3] For others, legal and practical restraints also deflected Shakespeare from print,[4] with most of the evidence revolving around three commonly agreed facts: copyright belonged to the acting companies, not to the author; and though the companies condoned the printing of many of their plays,[5] others they were clearly reluctant to have published.[6]

## COPYRIGHT

Bentley seeks to order this evidence by suggesting that the actors had different contractual arrangements with writers who were retained as 'ordinary poets' and those who wrote for them only on an occasional basis. Shakespeare's understanding with the King's Men, he argues, is likely to have concurred with the stipulation in the one contract for an 'ordinary poet' of which we have documentary evidence (Richard Brome's with Salisbury Court), which states that the author 'should not suffer any play made or to be made or composed by him' for the company to be printed with his consent or knowledge, 'without the license from the said company or the major part of them'.[7] Other writers, who had no such contractual relationships, seem to have suffered few restrictions on their rights to sell their scripts to a printer (though it is not impossible that they had to agree to a lower fee in return); and though they may have been expected to observe some delay between first performance and publication, even this is doubtful in many instances. The obvious question, therefore, is why the actors should expect some of their writers to observe this restraint and others not. A play was just a play and its commercial value was never more than marginally related to the person who actually wrote it.

We may deduce that freelance authors had permission to print from the fact that they frequently wrote again for companies whose plays they had published. Jonson, for example, printed *Every Man Out of His Humour* in 1600 and *Every Man In His Humour* in 1601, but was employed again by the King's Men for *Sejanus*, *The Alchemist* and *Catiline*, all published within two years of their performance, then re-published in Jonson's 1616 *Works*. While *Sejanus* and *Catiline* were failures in the theatre and so might not have been regarded as 'viable' stage-pieces, this is not true of the majority. Both *Every Man* plays were in the King's Men repertoire in 1605 and performed at court, with *Every Man In* revived as late as 1631. This suggests that the companies thought them valuable stage properties and calls into question the common explanation that

actors were reluctant to have plays printed which were still successful on stage.

This view was championed by E. K. Chambers, citing the Epistle
to *The English Traveller* (1633), where Heywood observes that some
of his plays 'are still retained in the hands of some actors, who
think it against their peculiar profit to have them come in print'.[8]
Heywood's wording here suggest that only some and not all, actors
took this view of the matter, which may reflect his different contractual experiences as a freelance and 'ordinary poet'. Chambers,
however, goes on to speculate that 'Presumably the danger was not
so much that readers would not become spectators, as that other
companies might buy the plays and act them', a supposition which
is commonly accepted as fact. To take an example almost at
random, J. R. Mulryne seeks to explain the 30-year delay in the
publication of Middleton's *Women Beware Women* in these terms: 'It
is tempting to guess that the players were unwilling to allow into
print one of their best properties', adding in a note, '[a]s was often
the case, they may not have wished to have the play published and
thus made available to rival companies'.[9]

Yet our (admittedly limited) knowledge of performance histories
down to the closing of the theatres suggests that this supposed
threat was minimal. To pursue the case of Jonson, for example:
with one exception (a Dublin performance of *The Alchemist* between
1637 and 1640) there is no evidence that any acting company other
than the King's Men attempted to stage the plays mentioned above,
even though they were in print and no commercial rival exploited
their availability in London where it really mattered. The same is
true of plays by Shakespeare, which were all in print by 1623. There
are records of amateur and provincial performances of *Richard II*
and *Hamlet* in 1607/8 by the company of the Dragon of Sierra
Leone and of *Pericles* and *King Lear* by Sir Richard Cholmeley's
players in Yorkshire in 1610 and possibly of *Hamlet* by Queen
Anne's Men in Oxford in 1607 and by a group at Newcastle in the
same year. But none challenges the King's Men's exclusive right to
profitable London performances.

Such challenges were rare, I would argue, because the danger
Chambers presumed did not exist. When the Master of the Revels
granted a licence to perform a play it was specific to the companies
which acquired it and could only be passed on to others with their
consent. In granting a licence Sir Henry Herbert always records the

name of the company or, occasionally, of the theatre where that company performed (e.g. '1623, August. For the Company at the Curtain; a Tragedy of *the Plantation of Virginia*').[10] Herbert was not issuing a general licence for the play: he was conferring on a known company, with a known playhouse, the exclusive right of performance – at least in the London region – and any deviation from this understanding would be an affront to his authority. The few surviving office-book entries by Herbert's predecessor, Sir John Astley, are less consistent in format but at times even more conclusive in wording.[11]

Herbert's papers also demonstrate how the passing on of performance rights was regulated. Several circumstances required further clearance from the Master of the Revels, as when a company wished to adopt a play formerly licensed to someone else.[12] An office-book entry for 21 August 1623 records: 'For the Lady Elizabeth's Servants of the Cockpit; An Old Play, called, *Match me in London*, which had been formerly allowed by Sir George Bucke'.[13] This records a transfer of performing rights, since the play, written by Dekker *c.* 1611–3 for Queen Anne's Men (defunct by 1623), was not printed until 1631. A similar process presumably governed boy company plays which passed into the adult repertoire, though no records have survived. Fletcher's *The Scornful Lady* and Jonson's *The Silent Woman* were both first printed in 1616. The former had passed to the King's Men by 1625, when a reprint announced them on the title-page as the acting company. *The Silent Woman* had probably passed to the King's Men when it was considered for performance at court in 1619/20; and certainly had done so when it was performed there twice in 1636.[14] Both works demonstrate that a play was not liable to unlicensed appropriation simply because it was in print, even when the original licensees were defunct: they both passed in an orderly way to a new licence-holder. They also demonstrate that publication need not diminish commercial viability in the theatre.

One notorious instance of a company appearing not to respect licensed performing rights and to take advantage of the fact that a rival company's plays was in print, is the King's Men's performance of Marston's *The Malcontent*. This apparently occurred after the first of its three printings in 1604, since Webster's 'additions acted by the King's Majesty's Servants' were not available to the press until the third edition. Webster's dialogue for the actors 'playing' themselves is quite unabashed about what had happened:

*Sly.* ... I would know how you came by this play.
*Condell.* Faith, sir, the book was lost; and, because 'twas pity
so good a play should be lost, we found it and play it.
*Sly.* I wonder you would play it, another company having
interest in it.
*Condell.* Why not Malevole in folio with us, as Jeronimo in
decimo-sexto with them? They taught us a name for our play: we
call it *One for another.*

(Induction, 72–80)[15]

As Sly points out, the performing rights to the play still reside
with the Blackfriars company, the Children of the Queen's Revels.
Condell makes light of this, implying that it is a quid-pro-quo for
that troupe having played 'Jeronimo', presumably a lost King's
Men's play on a theme related to *The Spanish Tragedy* (since the
company did not themselves own that play). What the Induction
does not settle categorically is whether these appropriations were
by mutual consent, or forms of piracy: Condell implies the latter,
but this could very easily be an in-joke.

If the former, my case about the protection of performing right is
not affected: there are known instances of adult and boys companies sharing in a play and apparently both performing it, most
notably the collaboration of the Lord Chamberlain's Men and
Paul's Boys over Dekker's *Satiromastix*. If the latter (piracy), it is the
dating which provides the likeliest explanation for the irregularity.
The Children of the Chapel Royal were re-incorporated in February
1604 as the Children of the Queen's Revels, at which point they left
the control of the Master of the Revels and were given their own
licenser. Their patent specifies 'that noe such playes or Shewes
shalbee presented ... or by them any where publiqelie acted but by
the approbacion and allowaunce of Samuell Danyell'.[16] As I have
argued elsewhere, this division of the authority for dramatic licensing in part explains the controversial theatrical activity early in the
reign of James I, so much of it centring upon the Blackfriars
company in its various guises.[17] So the circumstances in which the
King's Men appropriated *The Malcontent* were so unusual as to be
exceptional, with a real possibility of friction between the licensing
authorities themselves, which the actors may have exploited. The
case is an exception that proves the rule, significant in its rarity, not
as evidence of what was commonly likely to befall plays appearing
in print.

'ORDINARY POETS'

Given the evidence that printing plays did not make them more liable to piracy by rival companies and did not necessarily reduce their audience appeal, we can understand E. M. Albright's conclusion that 'the probability is, that there was no such widespread and constant objection to publication as has been supposed'.[18] Yet Heywood did observe that 'some actors ... think it against their peculiar profit to have them come in print'. It is possible that those who had paid good money for a play were less certain that I can now be that publication would not reduce its value. After all, the late revivals of the Jonson plays I have mentioned may represent an after-life created *specifically* by their earlier circulation in print – but no one could have predicted such an outcome when they first released the copyright. More compelling, however, is G. E. Bentley's evidence that it was the works of contracted 'ordinary poets' that companies were particularly anxious to keep out of print. It is clear that this was due to the companies, rather than to the writers themselves, since men like Fletcher, Heywood and Brome were quite willing to help plays into print (as we see from their signed prefaces) which were *not* the product of their work as contracted 'ordinary poets', in those instances behaving exactly like freelancers such as Jonson.[19] Shakespeare, however – always the exception – never seems to have been other than a retained author in the period from 1594, when we can really trace his career.

Reviewing the total picture of which plays got into print and when, one is almost drawn to the conclusion – contrary to the received wisdom – that the plays of such authors were the only ones to which the companies held a copyright respected by the Stationers' Company and the licensers for the press, since there is no apparent consistency to the way in which plays by other authors were or were not allowed into print. (Actually, this could never be gauged accurately, since there is no telling how many plays would never have been printed simply because there was no demand for them.) The evidence, however, will not sustain so categorical a conclusion, though it does seem that the works of 'ordinary poets' were more rigorously denied the press than those of other authors. In 1600 the almost systematic piracy of play-books by unscrupulous printers was a possibility and the principal companies of the day, the Lord Admiral's and Lord Chamberlain's Men, took steps to forestall it. On 28 March Henslowe put up for the former the not inconsiderable sum of £2 for the 'stayinge of printinge' of *Patient Grissell*, while the Lord Chamberlain's Men had 'staying' entries in the Stationers' Register on 27 May and 4 August.[20] There is no evidence that the companies were resisting print *per se*; it seems likely that they were trying to preclude unauthorized publication by establishing prior copyright. My point is that the Lord Chamberlain's Men acted to protect plays written by Jonson (*Every Man In His Humour*) and two anonymous authors, as well as recent work by their 'ordinary poet', Shakespeare (*Much Ado About Nothing* and *Henry V*). Henslowe's papers reveal no individual enjoying the special position reflected in the Brome contract and apparently enjoyed by Shakespeare, but he was still prepared to protect copyrights.[21]

The fact that the Henslowe papers, our fullest information about the business of play-writing in the period, contain no example of anyone employed on this exclusive basis doubtless colours our sense of what was normal. Part of the continuing success of the Lord Chamberlain's/King's Men, however – answerable to no entrepreneur like Henslowe – must be ascribed to their shrewd retention of one popular and proficient 'ordinary poet' after another, a practice which must subtly have coloured their corporate ethos. Though a more convenient and assured way of acquiring suitable plays than *ad hoc* commissioning, it perhaps led to payments above the market rate. It is difficult to be sure of this, since our knowledge of the going-rate for plays throughout the period is patchy and the relativities of the figures we do have must be heavily distorted by inflation.[22] Moreover, retained authors were not paid by the play but mainly by a weekly wage, for which they undertook to produce a specified number of plays annually (in Brome's case three, in Shakespeare's probably two). This makes real comparisons all but impossible.

But it must be significant (a point overlooked by Bentley) that the injunction against Brome printing his plays without the permission of the company, noted above, was not part of his first contract with the Salisbury Court, negotiated in July 1635; it was part of the renegotiation of the contract in August 1638, when his salary was also raised from 15 to 20 shillings a week. This may suggest that such injunctions were not always a feature of the contracts of 'ordinary poets', but perhaps became so when such contracts involved a salary above the market rate. In Brome's case this seems to have followed what amounts to an initial trial period with the company

– one, as it happens, not without mutal recriminations at law, which in some respects the new contract was intended to resolve. In 1594 Shakespeare was already a very well-established dramatist, by some way the most successful of those who continued to write for the theatres after the plague of 1593/4, following the deaths of Greene, Marlowe and Kyd and various other defections. It would have been shrewd sense for the Lord Chamberlain's Men to retain his services on the most attractive terms they could muster. Even so, in such a context, it might have seemed reasonable to put some restrictions on the right to print plays, in return for secure and relatively handsome remuneration.

Perhaps more important than the financial implications of a copyright was how it related to the co-operative structure of the acting company. 'The London companies after about 1580 consisted of a core of between eight and twelve co-owning players, "sharers" in both profits and costs'.[23] Verbal agreements became more formalized, carrying stipulations such as those agreed to by the actor Robert Dawes and Henslowe: penalties for turning up late, or missing rehearsals or performances, or being drunk when he should be performing. Penalties were measured in pence or shillings, rising to a maximum of a pound, save for a £40 penalty for absconding with costumes or props.[24] This particular agreement says nothing about play-books and their copyright, though these may have been classed as 'propertie'. The contract for the sharers in the King's Revels company (10 March 1608) is more explicit. The specific prohibition against putting the company's plays into print without permission is part of a much wider set of understandings about its property.[25] The swingeing penalties – £40 or loss of the entire share – were clearly not ways of dealing with minor infringements such as turning up drunk. They were part of a wider attempt to define the company and its standards, exercises in corporate bonding.

It is important to bear in mind that these agreements cited relate to sharers in an acting and/or theatre company, often, though not always, actors themselves: not specifically to the writers of their plays, who would not normally be members of the company in anything like the same sense. Brome, for example, was never a sharer in Salisbury Court only an employee. The most he stood to lose, if he broke his agreement, was employment – unless (as actually happened) he was sued for breach of contract, where the issue was putative loss of earnings to the company through dereliction and bad faith, not a penalty for breaching the company's own code of conduct.[26] This was presumably also true of other 'ordinary poets' like Fletcher and Massinger. But Shakespeare was significantly different, since from the inception of the Lord Chamberlain's Men in 1594 he was a shareholder – and sufficiently senior to be, along with Richard Burbage and Will Kempe, trusted to receive payment from court on the company's behalf. In due course he was also a shareholder in the Globe and Blackfriars theatres, companies whose membership significantly overlapped with that of the acting company which performed in them. Of those who signed the syndicate agreement for the Globe of 21 February 1599, five besides Shakespeare were actors.

We do no know precisely what constraints any 'sharing' agreements placed on Shakespeare. But if we compare the Whitefriars theatre contract, Henslowe's agreement with Dawes and the Brome contract, we conclude that he was bound by constraints of corporate bonding virtually unparalleled in the period. Since these constraints commonly seem to have put an embargo on the printing of corporately-owned playbooks for both shareholders and 'ordinary poets', Shakespeare must have felt massively restricted. As I have argued, there is little evidence that the printing of plays did actually reduce their value as theatre pieces. But we see in the Whitefriars contract concerns that run deeper. Draconian penalties awaiting anyone who, without common consent, removed company property 'exceeding the value of two shillings' bespeak a need to put corporate interests above individual desires. In such a context the inviolability of the 'ordinary poet's' plays might take on an almost fetishistic significance, disproportionate to their strict commercial value. They were, so to speak, the company's family silver, not to be traded in by any of the sharers, even the author. Works commissioned from freelancers such as Jonson would never have the same value to the corporate psyche, even though it would be prudent (as in 1600) to guard such properties against outright piracy.

The short answer, then, to why Shakespeare never published his own plays is quite likely to be that he was a company man, too identified with an ethos in which any removal of company property warranted expulsion from its ranks, too bound to a small group by ties that went beyond a mere contractual framework, if the bequests in his will to Burbage, Heminge and Condell of money to buy rings denote real friendship. Perhaps the strongest corroboration we can find for the strength of company affiliations comes from the only other man in the period to occupy anything like the same position, Thomas Heywood. The Queen's Men copied the Globe arrangements; some of the actor-shareholders also became sharers in 'the house', the Red Bull (*ES*, I 357). Heywood was one of these and also their 'ordinary poet'. Throughout a long career, in which he famously claimed to have written or 'had a main finger' in 220 plays (address to the reader in *The English Traveller*), barely 20 found their way into print.

The 1608 quarto of *The Rape of Lucrece* stands out because, as Heywood was aware, it is the one instance where publication cut across his contractual status at the time as an 'ordinary poet':

> Though some have used a double sale of their labors, first to the stage and after to the press, for my own part I here proclaim myself ever faithful to the first [i.e. Queen Anne's company] and never guilty of the last.

Yet because of the threatened illicit publication of a mangled version of this play Heywood was willing to print it correctly, with the permission of the rightful owners, Queen Anne's company.[27] There is an element of disingenuousness about this disclaimer. If Heywood truly discovered that it was 'accidentally' coming into the hands of the printers (along, apparently, with others not contractually bound) he could, with the rest of the company, assert their true copyright with the Stationers' Company. None the less, Heywood felt it necessary to assert publicly that his decision to supply an accurate copy has the full 'consent' of other members of the company, to which he himself has been 'ever faithful'.

Since Shakespeare never even condescended to supply prefaces of this nature, we cannot be certain that he did not actually co-operate with the printers in this way, only that he never advertised the fact. Yet the history of Shakespeare editing is littered with suggestions that some of the quartos (e.g. *2 Henry IV*, *Much Ado About Nothing*, the 1599 *Romeo and Juliet*) are based on the author's 'foul papers', though no one has squared this with the orthodox view that he played no part in their publication. If Shakespeare's 'foul papers' found their way to the print-shops, the supposition seems to be, it must be from the playhouse, not from his study and not by his hands. The fact that 'foul papers' or prompt-copies of so many reputable texts reached the printers probably challenges the assumption that the Lord Chamberlain's Men were *implacably* opposed to their 'ordinary poet's' work appearing in print. There have been numerous explanations for certain specific 'breaches'. Andrew Gurr has argued persuasively that the shareholders might have released *Richard III, Love's Labour's Lost* and *1 Henry IV* for print in 1597/8 only because they faced a financial crisis when unable to use either the Burbages' new Blackfriars venue or the Theatre.[28] And it had been suggested more than once that the appearance of a 'good' quarto in the wake of a 'bad' one (the 1599 *Romeo and Juliet* and the 1604/5 *Hamlet* are examples) may reflect the company's preference, once the issue had been forced, to sanction respectable texts rather than let their own and their poet's reputation be sullied by the travesties already in print. (If so, we have to ask why they did not also do so in the case of, say, *Henry V* and *The Merry Wives of Windsor*. Or did not do so until the 1623 folio.)

## MANUSCRIPT CIRCULATION

All in all, however, too many reputable Shakespeare texts found their way into print for it to be entirely credible that they did so as a result of *ad hoc* company decisions, contravening their apparent general policy. Even if we accept that there were compelling corporate pressures against Shakespeare as an individual going into print (whatever the company as a whole may, from time to time, have decided) that is not evidence that he was indifferent to his plays as works to be read. I am thinking here of the circulation of plays in manuscript. This, again, is supposed not to have happened. As Leeds Barroll puts it: 'Before Shakespeare's death, public stage plays were seldom composed to be circulated in manuscripts or in printed books as was, say Sir Philip Sidney's *Arcadia* or Edmund Spenser's *Faerie Queene*.'[29] But if much of the evidence for this practice applies to plays dating from after Shakespeare's death, it is only because theatrical documentation is much fuller for the later period and more manuscripts of all sorts found their way into collections where they were respected and preserved. There is no real reason to suppose that the circulation of commercial playscripts changed significantly between, say, 1590 and 1642.

We know, of course, that it happened with *A Game at Chess*. No fewer than six manuscripts of that play have survived, none of them the licensed play house copy. The existence of so many copies of the play may, of course, be ascribed to the phenomenal interest it aroused, something which Middleton perhaps anticipated and made arrangements to cash in on.[30] Yet if the scandal over the play prompted manuscripts in unusual numbers (how many were lost if six actually survive?), it does not follow that it was unusual *per se* for transcripts to be made in this way. Beaumont and Fletcher's *A King and No King*, dating from 1611 when Shakespeare was still active, was printed in 1619, apparently from a manuscript copy supplied by Sir Thomas Neville. Similarly, Ralph Crane copied both Middleton's *The Witch* (c. 1609–16) and Fletcher's popular *Demetrius and Enanthe* as presentation copies. As F. P. Wilson observed, 'it is curious that so notable a get-penny as *Demetrius and Enanthe* should have been allowed to stray outside the playhouse and should have existed in a private transcript twenty-two years before it got into print.'[31]

But is it really so curious? Humphrey Moseley's preface to his monumental first folio of Beaumont and Fletcher (1647) contains two remarkable admissions: that *The Wilde-goose Chase* was lost when 'a Person of Quality borrowed it from the *Actours*' and that the actors commonly omitted passages of plays for performance – but that when 'private friends desir'd a Copy, they then (and justly too) transcribed what they *Acted*'.[32] This suggest practices that were relatively commonplace and of long-standing and implies an altogether more relaxed attitude than is commonly supposed to the distribution of manuscript copies of even the most popular plays, though they were still barred from print. More importantly, it also suggests that there was an understanding that the text supplied by the author and that performed by the actors (which would be the one licensed by the Master of the Revels) enjoyed a different status. Moseley actually makes a selling-point of his care to print complete texts, perhaps implying that these always enjoyed more cachet with discerning readers: 'the Care & Pains was wholly mine, which I find to be than you'd easily imagine, unless you knew into how many hands the Originalls were dispersed' (p. xiv). The actors, then, were quite careless about preserving the texts as they were originally written (though these had some cachet among readers), but fairly ready to supply copies of what they actually performed (which was commonly different). Six Beaumont and Fletcher manuscripts seem to have survived only because copies were made in this way. Moseley's defensive 'and justly too' even suggests that it would have been improper of the actors deliberately to circulate more than the acting text, that the originals still belong in some way (presumably) to their authors.

Might such practices have gone on during Shakespeares lifetime? It will be objected that all this was years after his death, when stage-plays supposedly enjoyed a social cachet unimaginable earlier. Besides, no texts by Shakespeare or his immediate contemporaries have survived by anything like these practices. But the survival of any theatrical manuscript from the late sixteenth or early seventeenth century, as I have already argued, is rare and fortuitous. Of the 280 plays mentioned in Henslowe's diary, only 30 have survived in print and perhaps one in manuscript.[33] In the case of Shakespeare, the 1623 folio must have made the manuscripts of his plays seem redundant. His daughter, Susanna Hall, still had some 'play-writings' by her father at the time Queen Henrietta Maria stayed at New Place during the Civil War, but there is no evidence that she appreciated their possible value.[34] Probably no one did until it was too late. Apart from the Fletcher examples I mentioned earlier, none of the apparently numerous copies to which Moseley refers seems to have survived either.

But it will still be objected that in Shakespeare's day play-scripts simply did not have the cachet with readers that Moseley seems to reflect, so that there would not have been a demand for copies. This seems to me, to say the least, questionable. We know from Francis Meres' *Palladis Tamia* (1598) that Shakespeare circulated his 'sugared sonnets among his private friends'. Why might he not have done the same with his plays, as the actors were to do later with those of Beaumont and Fletcher? One of the strongest arguments for at least taking this possibility seriously is the sheer length of so many of the surviving texts. I quote here from Philip Edwards on this point, though to draw very different conclusions: 'Why is it that nearly all [Shakespeare's] tragedies were far too long to be performed in full on his stage? The average length of Elizabethan plays was under 2,500 words, allowing two to two-and-a-half hours' playing time ... Only three or four of Shakespeare's plays are within that limit' and five are over 3,500 lines each.[35]

But Edwards goes on to say: 'I can see only one solution to this problem [of texts too long to be acted]. Everything that Shakespeare wrote, he wrote in terms of the stage ... At the same time, those long, brilliant, unwieldy texts which have come down to us witness to an ideal theatre in Shakespeare's imagination. He wrote for himself perhaps' (p. 22). There is indeed 'only one solution' if one starts convinced that Shakespeare never wrote with a readership in mind. But Edwards' perplexities disappear if we entertain the possibility that Shakespeare's plays have survived in versions that reflect his expectation that they would be read as well as acted. We know from Moseley that this is what happened to the plays of Beaumont and Fletcher, apparently with the consent of the authors. Edwards argues: 'The only other dramatist who persistently wrote overlength plays was Ben Jonson. Jonson most certainly regarded his plays as literature to be read and pondered and he carefully published the full texts as literary texts' (p. 21). *Every Man Out of His Humour* (1600) was published 'As It Was First Composed by the Author B. J. / Containing more than hath been Publicly Spoken or Acted', something we may suspect of many if not all of his printed plays. It may be, however, that Edwards is too categorical in describing Jonson as 'the only other dramatist' to *write* overlength plays. Jonson, it is true, was the author who made the most persistent point of seeing the fullest, most 'readerly' versions of his plays into print. Yet Webster advertised the same of *The Duchess of Malfi* (1623), declaring it to be 'The perfect and exact Copy, with diverse things Printed, that the length of the play would not beare in the Presentment'. And, again, we know that the writers of the Beaumont and Fletcher canon regularly wrote more than the actors could use – and moreover that there was a demand from readers for that fuller version. How many other plays of the period may similarly have been written over-length, but only survive (like those of the Beaumont and Fletcher works for which Moseley could not recover the originals) in the cut-down acting versions?

Jonson, Webster and Beaumont and Fletcher – all wrote overlength plays, either with the expectation of a print readership, or knowing that they would be circulated in manuscript. There is no reason in principle to suppose that Shakespeare should not have done the same, though – for the reasons we have reviewed (and others I shall suggest later) – print was not for him an option. Indeed, there is every reason to suppose that, like Jonson, he had a sense of them as 'literary texts', albeit not the same sense that Jonson had and not one that envisaged the same (print) readership. Many features of Shakespeare's work (including 'authorial revision') appear in a new light once such a possibility is entertained, but I shall confine myself to one broad and one specific observation. First, it would help to explain just how so many quartos based on 'foul papers' (not playhouse versions) found their way into print, if there were multiple copies of his unadapted manuscripts and those not under the control of the actors. Secondly, it would provide an intelligible explanation for the notorious conundrum of the two states of the 1609 quarto of *Troilus and Cressida* (third longest of all Shakespeare's plays). The first of these announces the play as 'The Historie of Troylus and Cresseida. As it was acted by the Kings Majesties servants at the Globe. Written by William Shakespeare'. The second omits all mention of performance, describing it as 'a new play, never staled with the stage, never clapper-clawed with the palms of the vulgar' and, concludes with an apparent side-swipe at the King's Men as the jealous copyright holders. The text has been conjectured to be 'printed from a private transcript of Shakespeare's own draft made by himself or a scribe', with little or no evidence of playhouse adaption.[36]

Explanations for these discrepancies range from publishers' hype to suggestions that the play had been performed only at some private venue and in that sense was never demeaned by 'the smoky breath of the multitude'. Special performances were not unknown, but plays written by a professional dramatist *exclusively* for private performance are. There is a more logical explanation and Sam Schoenbaum grasps half the nettle: 'The play could have been "new" only to readers ... Had the publishers got hold of a transcript in private hands?'[37] But he still rehearses the private performance theory to explain references to 'the multitude'. Surely the point of the epistle is that it is announcing a reading version of the play, new to a print readership and superior to what had doubtless been performed in a cut text by the King's Men at the Globe. Indeed, the difference may well have been what got the publishers their licence.

As early as 7 February 1603 the play had been entered in the Stationers' Register for 'Master Robertes' ('The booke of Troilus and Cresseda as yt is acted by my Lord Chamberlens men' – further proof of actual performance, almost certainly on the public stage) but 'stayed' until 'he hath gotten sufficient authority for it'. That authority would be a licence from one of the clerical licensers who, under the Archbishop of Canterbury and Bishop of London, were responsible for clearing all books for publication; it should not have been granted without the permission of the owners of the work, the Lord Chamberlain's Men and on this occasion apparently it was not. In 1606 responsibility for the licensing of play-texts for print somehow passed to Sir George Buc, who held the reversion to the Mastership of the Revels, but did not succeed to that office until 1610. Nevertheless, this change should not have affected the requirements for the granting of a licence. The 1609 entry says nothing of Robertes, but grants a licence jointly to Richard Bonian and Henry Walley, on the authority of William Segar, who was deputizing for Buc at the time.[38] Nor does this entry say anything about the acting company, by then the King's Men. This is not unusual: the majority of such entries do not mention the acting company, though its consent can usually be understood to lie behind the granting of the licence for print. It is the second state of the 1609 title-page which raises doubts here. Is it possible that Bonian and Whalley got a licence from Segar, where Robertes had failed to get one from the clerical licenser, specifically because they had conviced him that what they were printing was different in kind from the acting version? That it was expressly not 'as yt is acted by my Lord Chamberlens men' and so did not require their consent?

That such a distinction might be recognized and honoured has been given further credence in recent work by Alan Nelson on annotations by Sir George Buc in play-texts in his possession, presented in a paper at the World Shakespeare Congress (Los Angeles, 12 April 1996). The most intriguing of these, in the present context, is an inscription on the title-page of the 1600 quarto of *Henry V*, now in the Folger Shakespeare Library, which reads 'much the same with that in Shakespeare'. We do not know when Buc wrote this, but it must have been before he went insane in 1622 – and so before he could compare the quarto text with that in the Shakespeare First Folio which, as all editors of the play know, is a significantly different work. So Buc was comparing the quarto either with a performance of the play or with what he had somehow read. Of all people, the Master of the Revels was the one man who would get to read a play in manuscript, so this has no bearing on that side of my argument. But Buc's judgement here that the play as published was 'much the same with' something else he knew indicates that he recognized clearly that play-texts might exist in different states – which could open up the possibility that different licenses could apply to those different versions.

We cannot be sure if Buc made inscriptions in this way as part of his official duties as a licenser – he was a deeply learned historian and scholar, for whom it was second nature to annotate and record his opinions. But if (as I suspect) this was done in the line of duty, his perception of two versions of *Henry V* might well parallel the situation Segar faced when he was asked to licence *Troilus and Cressida* – not the version of the play 'as yt is acted by my Lord Chamberlens men', but one 'never staled with the stage, never clap-perclawed with the palms of the vulgar'. And in all this we see foreshadowings of what Moseley describes in respect of the Beaumont and Fletcher texts, where the acting versions of plays were popularly known (and indeed often available in manuscript copies), but a particular cachet attached to what the authors had originally written: that was what Moseley wanted to make a selling-point of his edition, though the carelessness of the actors with the originals made his task difficult. Bonian and Walley first advertised their text as something it was not, an acting version and then haughtily changed their tune in trumpeting a text unsullied by the common stage.

I conclude my argument with three familiar comments by con-temporaries which seem to me far more intelligible if Shakespeare were indeed circulating his plays in manuscript. First, Gabriel Harvey's comments, written in a copy of Speght's *Chaucer*, in which he observes: 'The younger sort takes much delight in Shakespeare's *Venus, & Adonis*: but his *Lucrece*, & his tragedie of *Hamlet, Prince of Denmarke*, have it in them, to please the wiser sort.'[39] One per-plexing feature of this is its dating; we do not know exactly when it was written but the wider passage in which it occurs refers to the Earl of Essex (who was executed in February 1601) as still alive, ap-parently making the play earlier than many people suppose. Equally perplexing, however, is that it seems to refer to *Hamlet* as a written text, on a par with *Venus and Adonis* and *Lucrece*, which were both in print by 1594. *Hamlet* was not printed until 1603 and then only in a text that would hardly 'please the wiser sort'; the first respectable text was printed the following year. But by then Essex was long dead and Lord Mountjoy (to whom Harvey also refers and by that style) had been created Earl of Devonshire. We are forced to the conclusion that Harvey is not talking about a printed text: so he was either referring to performances (though that option is not really in keeping with the tenor of the passage) or to the play circulating in manuscript. The Arden editor of *Hamlet*, Harold Jenkins, provides an admirable survey of these perplexities (ed. cit., pp. 3–6) but finally baulks at this last explanation: 'The possibility of its manuscript circulation is one to view with scepticism:

however appropriate it might seem for the author of the narrative poems, it is not what we think of as the way of a professional playwright and a sharer in a company jealous to protect its scripts' (p. 6). We are back to the red herring of the 'company jealous to protect its scripts', with which I dealt earlier and which is coupled with some very telling phrasing: 'it is not what we think of as the way of a professional playwright.' It has been precisely my point throughout this essay to re-think what it might have meant to be a professional playwright in Shakespeare's position which (as I have stressed) was very different from that of the playwrights employed, say, by Henslowe. By far the least problematic explanation of Harvey's reference to *Hamlet* is that versions of the play were circulating in manuscript, among 'the younger sort'.

My remaining two comments both relate directly to Shakespeare status as 'a professional playwright'. The first of these is Henry Chettle's defence, in *Kind-Heart's Dream* (1592/3), of his own role in the printing of Robert Greene's *Groatsworth of Wit, bought with a Million of Repentance*, with its bitter death-bed denunciation of fellow playwrights. This is, of course, a notorious minefield.[40] I want to draw attention only to the curiously oblique commendation of Shakespeare's writing, at the end of the passage: 'divers of worship have reported, his uprightness of dealing, which argues his honesty and his facetious grace in writing, that approves his art'. The passage as a whole, with its references to Shakespeare's civil demeanour, his 'uprightness of dealing' and 'honesty', is an attempt to convince 'Gentlemen Readers' that Shakespeare was every inch a gentleman himself, presumably to repudiate Greene's slurs ('upstart crow', 'absolute Johannes Factotum') on an actor/artisan with pretensions. What Chettle cannot vouch for personally he takes from the report of other gentleman ('divers of worship') and this includes 'his facetious grace in writing, that approves his art'. This is an oddly precise phrase, 'facetious grace' apparently echoing Cicero's praise of Plautus in *De Officiis*.[41] But to what does it refer? What had the 'divers of worship' actually seen to warrant this praise? There was certainly nothing then in print. Shakespeare's first published work, *Venus and Adonis* was entered in the Stationers' Register on 18 April 1593, some months after *Kind-Heart's Dream*. To be sure, it might already have been circulating in manuscript, as might some of the sonnets. But if the phrase really does echo Cicero on the dramatist, Plautus, it must relate to Shakespeare's plays – and all the more so, since it was those that

Greene had scorned. Chettle could have heard these in the theatre, as could anyone else. What Chettle implies, however, is that 'divers of worship' have access to written texts, where 'facetious grace' – the mark of a polished, gentleman writer – will be more apparent than in performance.

This stray remark is given substantial corroboration by those who ought to be the most authoritative of sources, the actors with whom Shakespeare worked. In prefacing the 1623 folio, Heminge and Condell pay homage to a Shakespeare 'Who, as he was a happie imitator of Nature, was a most gentle expresser of it. His mind and hand went together: And what he thought, he uttered with that easinesse, that wee have scarse received from him a blot in his papers' (A3r) – the 'gentle … easinesse' of the gentleman writer – though an 'easinesse' which they do not scruple to polish by imposing on the plays a five-act structure in imitation of classical precedents, notably Terence, though this was almost certainly alien to Shakespeare's writing practice.[42] But they also declare themselves 'so to have publish'd [the plays] as where (before) you were abus'd with diverse stolne and surreptitious copies, maimed and deformed by the frauds and stealthes of injurious impostors, that exposed them: even those, are now offer'd to your view cur'd and perfect of their limbes … as he conceived them'. As a blanket dismissal of all the earlier quartos this is less than candid. It is entirely possible that all were indeed 'stolne and surreptitious', but were they 'maimed and deformed' in the process? As we have observed, the latter may be true of the 1600 *Henry V* and the 1603 *Hamlet*; it is certainly not true of the 1604 *Hamlet* and the 1609 *Troilus and Cressida*, which modern scholars regard as at least as good as the versions in the folio.

Ironically, what tends to make them 'superior' is precisely the quality that Heminge and Condell single out for praise, the 'easiness' of expression that characteristically produced texts which, while intensely theatrical, were (if we follow Edwards) too long to use. Some folio texts – *Macbeth* and *The Tempest*, for example (significantly lacking quarto versions) – seem to reproduce what might practicably have been staged, showing distinct signs of having been cut down from longer originals. W. W. Greg long ago observed of *Macbeth* that 'there is clear evidence of cutting at some points in short abrupt lines accompanied by textual obscurities'.[43] In *The Tempest* – in so many ways admirably edited – a 'ghost' (Antonio's son) and undeveloped characters (Adrian) also suggest cutting rather than carelessness. In short, Heminge and Condell praise a quality in Shakespeare's writing which their own texts tend rather to diminish than to enhance: it is better preserved in the 'good' quartos. It may be true that the 'foul papers' they received from him contained 'scarce ... a blot'. But they say nothing about the blots needed to reduce them to playing form. As with Beaumont and Fletcher, 'When these Comedies and Tragedies were presented on the Stage, the Actours omitted some Scenes and Passages (with the Author's consent) as occasion led them'. In the case of Shakespeare it is usually assumed that there is no real distinction between 'actors' and 'author' in this way, because he was indeed an all-round man of the theatre. The issues I have raised here call that into question. We have no way of knowing what part Shakespeare had in preparing what he wrote for the stage. It may have been a considerable one and there are no grounds finally for believing that anything in the 1623 folio was not in some sense sanctioned by him.

But it also seems clear that the process was not as simple as Heminge and Condell imply, or as later ages have often taken on trust. There is substantial evidence of a Shakespeare who regularly wrote, with some facility, plays too long and complex to be staged in the theatre of his day, plays for which the only plausible audience was one of readers. The 'good' quartos provide us with the clearest evidence of what those plays were like and the sheer number of them suggests that manuscript copies were in circulation, making it possible for printers eventually to obtain them – as, without question, they did the 'sugared sonnets'. What I have argued here calls into question the primacy increasingly often accorded performance as the only true, or at least most authentic, manifestation of the Shakespeare text. The most distinguished recent contribution to that school of thought is the *Complete Oxford Shakespeare* (1986), whose general editors were Stanley Wells and Gary Taylor. The guiding principle thoughout that volume was to reproduce as nearly as possible the state of the plays as they were performed in Shakespeare's lifetime. To take only one example, this resulted in a preference for the folio *A Midsummer Nights Dream* as copy text, over the almost universal use of the 1600 quarto by earlier editors. As the general editors argued, in the *Textual Companion* to the edition, 'we have found no reason to doubt that the bulk of the Folio directions represent the play as originally and authoritatively staged. Those directions which clearly envisage a different staging from that implied in Q seem to us dramatic improvements for which Shakespeare was probably responsible.'[44] Elsewhere, other recent editors have accorded significantly more (or, at least different) authority than was traditionally allowed to the so-called 'bad' quartos, even where their printers patently did not have access to authoritative texts, on the grounds that they nevertheless embody actual stage practice, however crudely.

These are entirely legitimate and defensible editorial practices, but we must not regard them as definitive ones. What Chettle, Heminge and Condell and the evidence of the 'good' quartos tell us is that Shakespeare had readers in mind too, however much practical theatrical applications must also have shaped his thoughts. The habit of reading Shakespeare as much as we play him is not a modern, or academic, perversity. This is indirectly acknowledged in Ben Jonson's riposte to Heminge and Condell, in *Discoveries*:

> I remember the players have often mentioned as an honour to Shakespeare, that in his writing, whatsoever he penned, he never blotted out line. My answer hath been, 'Would he had blotted a thousand'; which they thought a malevolent speech ... [He] had an excellent fantasy, brave notions and gentle expressions; wherein he flowed with that facility that sometime it was necessary he should be stopped ... His wit was in his own power; would the rule of it had been so too.[45]

What grates with Jonson is the adoration of a Shakespeare who wrote like a gentleman amateur ('gentle expressions'), giving every impression that it was effortless ('flowed with ... facility') and, what was more, that he did not give what he wrote a second thought ('never blotted out line') – as much because he did not care as because he got it right instinctively. This is a Shakespeare who affects a sprezzatura, a dismissive nonchalance like that of Sir Philip Sidney commending as he devalues the *Arcadia* to his sister with the kind of self-deprecation that traditionally constitutes boasting in the English upper classes.[46] And it smacks much more of a man writing for 'gentle readers' than of one crafting texts for the stage.

It is an image of authorship that Jonson very much resisted, because it was so much at odds with his own, that of the self-made man of letters, proud of his 'laborious' art and determined to make his mark in public print. For another notable aristocratic mark was the aversion to print, with its connotation of artisan labour and writing for money.[47] Jonson does not, however, deny that Shakespeare wrote as Heminge and Condell implied; on the contrary, he confirms that they were only too right – even if their edition of the plays is not the best reflection of the qualities they claim. Between them, Chettle, Harvey, Heminge and Condell and Jonson all associate Shakespeare with this tradition – all but Jonson doing so with awed respect. So we cannot rule out the possibility that Shakespeare's apparent lack of involvement in the printing of his plays also derives from a sense of the associated social stigma (an embarrassment we repeatedly find in writers with social pretensions, like Samuel Daniel). If so, Shakespeare's lack of inhibition in printing *Venus and Adonis* and *Lucrece*, quasi-classical epyllia demonstrating 'facetious grace' in writing but in no way associated with artisan labour, suggests that different social nuances were at work there, possibly deriving from their association with a bid for Southampton's patronage. In the case of the plays, social pretensions and the pressures of corporate bonding may mutually have reinforced one another.

It is unusual, to say the least, to link together sprezzatura (generally associated with courtly lyrics, sonnets and romances) with writing for the public playhouse. But Shakespeare's career crossed many of the fault-lines of writing in early modern culture, to which Michel Foucault refers when he writes that the 'coming into being of the notion of the "author" constitutes the privileged moment of "individualization" in the history of ideas, knowledge, literature, philosophy and the sciences'.[48] Such a development was neither spontaneous, nor did it occur in a single, definitive form. The competition between the old world of courtly letters, largely wedded to manuscript culture and the new world of commercial print, played itself out over several generations. It has always been apparent that Shakespeare straddled these divides. What I have argued here is that the two sides of his career were less clearly demarcated than is usually supposed, that in writing plays which were in some respects unplayable (albeit perfect raw material for his actor colleagues) he was effectively writing for a readership no different in essence from that of his sonnets. Heminge and Condell knew this in commending his plays to a wider readership, 'To the Great Variety of Readers', but they blurred the message – perhaps, like Moseley, finding it difficult to recover some originals – in favouring texts which spoke more of the playhouse than they did of unblotted lines. Thus they gave (new) birth to an author of mixed authority, to a hybrid poet-playwright, who speaks simultaneously the different languages of which he was composed.

This has important implications for our editing and reading practices. If Wells and Taylor, for example, have gone to one extreme of the spectrum of Shakespearean language, that located as comprehensively as possible in theatrical practice, it is only fair to observe that they did so at least partly in response to centuries of editorial practice that silently privileged the 'writerly' end of the spectrum, the Shakespeare who 'never blotted line'. It has been usual, at least this century, to pay lip-service to the idea of Shakespeare as 'a man of the theatre' but at the same time to make editorial judgements on what were essentially aesthetic rather than theatrical grounds, measuring the options against an elusive ideal text, usually characterized by 'fulness' and 'facility'. Whether consciously or not, this has actually favoured the 'writerly' Shakespeare, who remains the dominant voice in the English-speaking world's construction of its definitive author – a voice essentially of pre-print culture, of closet or privileged readership, of (to a degree) social snobbery. That is not to say that the other, 'theatrical' Shakespeare is in any real sense more modern, or democratic, or egalitarian. But he is different and he speaks with a different voice, attuned to a different audience. And one of our duties as modern readers (or practitioners) of Shakespeare is to recognize the fact of multiple voices and to discriminate between them as best we can.

## NOTES

1. *Titus Andronicus* (1594); *Richard II* (1597); *Love's Labour's Lost* (1598); *I Henry IV* (1598); *Romeo and Juliet* (1599); *A Midsummer Night's Dream* (1600); *2 Henry IV* (1600); *The Merchant of Venice* (1600); *Much Ado About Nothing* (1600); *Hamlet* (1604); *King Lear* (1608); *Troilus and Cressida* (1609) and *Othello* (1622), while *Richard III* (1597) is not far behind the standard of these twelve. Dates are those of publication. I omit palpably unsatisfactory texts such as the 1600 *Henry V* and 1603 *Hamlet* from this list, as well as the problematic *Pericles* (1609).

2. See, for example, George Walton Williams, 'The Publishing and Editing of Shakespeare's Plays', in *William Shakespeare: His World, His Work, His Influence*, ed. John F. Andrews, 3 vols (New York, 1985), 3: 589–601, 589–90; Fredson Bowers, 'The Publication of English Renaissance Plays', in *Elizabethan Dramatists*, ed. Bowers, *Dictionary of Literary Biography* (Detroit, 1987), 62: 406–16, 414. The widely-held

assumption that the 1609 text of the sonnets was not sanctioned by Shakespeare and was indeed unauthorized, has been cogently challenged by Katherine Duncan-Jones: see 'Was the 1609 *Shake-speares Sonnets* Really Unauthorised?', *RES* 34 (1983): 151–71.

3. Leeds Barroll, *Politics, Plagues and Shakespeare's Theater* (Ithaca, NY and London, 1991), p. 17.

4. See E. K. Chambers, *The Elizabethan Stage*, 4 vols (Oxford, 1923), 3: 177–92; E. M. Albright, *Dramatic Publication in England 1589–1640* (1927; reprint New York, 1971), pp. 217–61; and G. E. Bentley, *The Profession of Dramatist in Shakespeare's Time* (Princeton, NJ, 1971), Chapter 10.

5. Prolonged plague and the Civil War closure of the theatres are most often cited as occasioning the sale of playbooks the actors would otherwise have preferred to retain.

6. See Bentley, *The Profession of Dramatist*, pp. 266–7.

7. Ann Haaker, 'The Plague, the Theater and the Poet', *Renaissance Drama*, n.s., 1 (1968): 283–306, 298. Text modernized.

8. See Chambers, *The Elizabethan Stage*, 3: 183, 339.

9. Thomas Middleton, *Women Beware Women*, ed. J. R. Mulryne, *The Revels Plays* (London, 1975), xxi and n. 2. In further support of Chambers, see S. Schoenbaum, *William Shakespeare: A Compact Documentary Life*, rev. edn (New York and Oxford, 1987), p. 159 and Leeds Barroll, *Politics, Plagues and Shakespeare's Theater*, pp. 16–17.

10. Cited from Joseph Quincy Adams, ed., *The Dramatic Records of Sir Henry Herbert* (New Haven, CT, 1917), p. 24. On the state of the papers left by the Masters of the Revels, see Richard Dutton, *Mastering the Revels: the Regulation and Censorship of English Renaissance Drama* (Basingstoke, 1991), pp. 15–16; on Herbert's distinctive form of entry, see p. 223.

11. See Adams, ed., *The Dramatic Records of Sir Henry Herbert*, p. 23.

12. See Dutton, *Mastering the Revels*, pp. 94–6.

13. Adams, ed., *The Dramatic Records of Sir Henry Herbert*, p. 25.

14. Adams, ed., *The Dramatic Records of Sir Henry Herbert*, pp. 55, 75.

15. References are to John Marston, *The Malcontent*, ed. George K. Hunter, *The Revels Plays* (London, 1975).

16. Quoted in Chambers, *The Elizabethan Stage*, 2: 49.

17. See Dutton, *Mastering the Revels*, Chapter 7, on the licensing of the boy companies early in the reign of James I. On tensions between actual and potential licensers, see pp. 47–9, 115–16, 148–55.

18. Albright, *Dramatic Publication in England 1580–1640*, p. 283

19. See Bentley, *The Profession of Dramatist*, pp. 267–8, 227, 281–4.

20. See Edward Arber, ed., *A Transcript of the Registers of the Company of Stationers of London 1554–1646*, 5 vols (London, 1875–94; reprinted New York, 1950), pp. 3: 36, 37, 167.

21. The Lord Admiral's Men finally came to an arrangement in 1602 with Henry Chettle (their most prolific writer for some time). Since that arrangement was directly with the company, not their financier, we know nothing of the details from Henslowe.

22. See Bentley, *The Profession of Dramatist*, ch. 5, esp. pp. 97–108, for a full analysis of the evidence on payment.

23. Andrew Gurr, *The Shakespearean Stage 1574–1642* (Cambridge, 1970), p. 46.
24. See Chambers, *The Elizabethan Stage*, 2: 256–71.
25. On the King's Revels company's Articles of Agreement, see Chambers, *The Elizabethan Stage*, 2: 65.
26. See Haaker, 'The Plague, The Theater and the Poet'.
27. Bentley, *The Profession of Dramatist*, p. 282. The gloss in square brackets is Bentley's.
28. See Andrew Gurr, 'Money or Audiences: the Impact of Shakespeare's Globe', *Theatre Notebook* 42 (1988): 3–14.
29. Barroll, *Politics, Plagues and Shakespeare's Theater*, p. 16.
30. See T. H. Howard-Hill, *Middleton's 'Vulgar Pasquin': Essays on 'A Game at Chess'* (Newark, DE, 1995) and esp. ch. 6, 'The Bridgewater Manuscript and the Evolution of the Text', for a detailed account of the production of the manuscripts of the play – an account that supposes many more copies than have actually survived.
31. See F. P. Wilson, 'Ralph Crane, Scrivener to the King's Players', reprinted in *The Seventeenth Century Stage*, ed. G. E. Bentley (Chicago 1968), pp. 137–55, 149.
32. Cited from *The Works of Francis Beaumont and John Fletcher*, ed. Arnold Glover, 10 vols (Cambridge, 1905), I: xiii.
33. The figures are based on Neil Carson, *A Companion to Henslowe's Diary* (Cambridge, 1988), pp. 82–4. The one manuscript play would be Munday's *John a Kent and John a Cumber*, but only if that is a version of what Henslowe refers to as *The Wise Man of West Chester*.
34. See S. Schoenbaum, *Shakespeare's Lives* (Oxford, 1970), pp. 125–6; Richard Wilson, *Will Power: Essays on Shakespearean Authority* (Detroit, 1993), p. 183.
35. Philip Edwards, *Shakespeare: A Writer's Progress* (Oxford, 1987), pp. 21–2. Alfred Hart computed that the average length of a Globe play *c.*1594–1603 (omitting Jonson and Shakespeare) was 2494 lines: 'The length of Elizabethan and Jacobean plays', *RES* 8 (1932): 139–54.
36. Virgil K. Whitaker, 'Note on the Text', in his Pelican Shakespeare edition of the play, in *William Shakespeare: The Complete Works*, gen. ed. Alfred Harbage, rev. edn (Baltimore, 1969), p. 979.
37. Schoenbaum, *Shakespeare: Compact Documentary Life*, pp. 267–8.
38. See Mark Eccles, 'Sir George Buc, Master of the Revels', in *Sir Thomas Lodge and Other Elizabethans*, ed. C. J. Sisson (Cambridge, MA, 1933), pp. 409–506, 462. There is no reason to suppose that Segar would have been lax or unaware of the rules because he was only a deputy; he was a herald and writer, a man of intelligence and integrity and more a friend of Buc's than his subordinate. Buc was seriously ill throughout 1608 and 1609; Segar was holding the fort for him and had been doing so for several months before he licensed *Troilus and Cressida*.
39. Quoted from *Hamlet*, ed. Harold Jenkins (Methuen, 1982), p. 573; Jenkins cites as his source *Harvey's Marginalia*, ed. G. C. Moore Smith (London, 1913), pp. 232–3.
40. See my earlier comments on the passage, in *William Shakespeare: A Literary Life* (Basingstoke, 1989), pp. 17–20 and 'Shakespeare and

Marlowe: Censorship and Construction', *Yearbook of English Studies* 23 (1993): 1–29, 6–8. See also Schoenbaum, *Shakespeare: Compact Documentary Life*, pp. 154–7.

41. See Schoenbaum, *Shakespeare: Compact Documentary Life*, p. 155 and note.

42. See T. H. Howard-Hill, 'The Evolution of the Form of Plays in English During the Renaissance', *Renaissance Quarterly* 43 (1990): 112–45.

43. W. W. Greg, *The Editorial Problem in Shakespeare* (Oxford, 1942), p. 147.

44. Stanley Wells and Gary Taylor, *William Shakespeare: A Textual Companion* (Oxford and New York, 1987), p. 280.

45. 'Timber, or Discoveries', in *Ben Jonson*, ed. Ian Donaldson (Oxford, 1985), pp. 521–94, lines 658–73.

46. See the letter of Sir Philip Sidney to the Countess of Pembroke, prefacing *The Arcadia*, ed. Maurice Evans (Harmondsworth, 1977), p. 57.

47. See J. W. Saunders, 'The Stigma of Print: A Note on the Social Bases of Tudor Poetry', *Essays in Criticism* 1 (1951): 139–59. I am aware that the notion of this 'stigma' has been challenged (see Stephen W. May, 'Tudor Aristocrats and the Mythical "Stigma of Print"', *Renaissance Papers* 1980 [1981]: 11–18), but it remains indisputable that many authors at court or on its fringes inserted apologies of some kind in works that they sanctioned for print, suggesting a degree of embarrassment (however formulaic).

48. Michel Foucault, 'What is an Author?', in *The Foucault Reader*, ed. Paul Rabinow (New York, 1984), p. 101.

# 8

# Mending and Bending the Occasional Text: Collegiate Elegies and the Case of 'Lycidas'

## Cedric C. Brown

Essays in this volume consider texts in relation to changing moments of publication, and to the different kinds of reading elicited in changing cultural and historical situations. Milton's famous elegy of 1637/8 for Edward King presents a fascinating instance of a text intricately woven into its occasion, perhaps over-ambitiously writing it into its text. It demands a reading mindful of the conventional expectations of its funerary functions as well as its institutional and political situations, and the challenges it has presented to its readers over the centuries as a particularly artful example of elegy have spelled out a wonderful story of difficulty. I shall suggest that anxieties about understanding affected not only subsequent readerships but also, perhaps, the poet himself at the most important moment of subsequent publication, in his collection of poems in 1645. That is my specific subject.

But I need first to review some features of funerary writing, especially within collegiate situations, and with this material the first parts of my essay are concerned. To begin with, we must recognize that much of the poetic output of the early modern period is occasional on character – that is a general practice within which my funerary examples are set. By the end of the seventeenth century, the familiar wording on title-pages – 'Poems written upon Several Occasions' (the formula used for Milton's volume of 1673) – had become a cliché. If we want to be good at reading much early modern English poetry, we need to be good at reading various kinds of occasional text.

Occasional poetry gives particular difficulties to later readers, who feel disempowered by lack of knowledge of the original situation or by uncertainties about long-outdated modes of address and matters of decorum. Readers do not like to be disempowered. New forms of criticism are developed in order to offer new forms of self-empowerment. In this respect, the story is no different now, with late twentieth-century critical and theoretical discourses, than it was with Dr Johnson, a notoriously problematical voice to cite on 'Lycidas', to whom I shall return. In the constant contentions between the demands of texts of yesterday and the desire of critics and readers to be empowered by the possession of some 'material' foothold, subtle occasional writing merely presents those difficulties in an acute form.

Milton's career presents an interesting case, because a great deal of the verse collected in *Poems of Mr. John Milton* in 1645 is occasional in character, though the circles in which the early poems belonged vary from domestic and social to university. In his mature ouput Milton's addresses to friends or public figures tended to be selective and to deny dependence in the addressing voice. They exhibit a mastery, the utterance of one who stands upon his own self-recognition as a culturally authorative figure. As is often observed, when he published *Paradise Lost*, he set his mark in the history of publishing by assuming a true writer's own self-sufficient ownership of his text, shorn of any patronage support other than that of God himself.[1]

But the fact is that young poets were often dependent upon given occasions, to practise upon and be noticed. The techniques they learned were connected with exploiting those opportunities. If we review the poems written by Milton, in Latin and English, from the age of about 15 through to the time of his writing for large households in the early 1630s, we find typical preoccupations for the self-reflexive verse of a grammar school poet, like an interest in the institutions of education itself and in the place of literature. Typical, also, is the playing with Ovidian myth. Certain skills are inevitably to be shown: in particular, a display of rhetorical ingenuity and an impressive familiarity with literary tradition, chiefly with the Roman poets. These are measures of distinction within an educational culture and long-established practices of training in poetry, which were immensely formative on poetic careers at the time.[2] With Milton there may be some biases, perhaps some greater than usual domestic pieties, a particular interest in literary friendship, and evidence of engagement with Protestant nationalist, anti-Catholic themes. One also sees some avoidance of expected occasions, like university tributes to royal births. Nevertheless, broadly speaking, we have a clear pattern of a poetic career developing along familiar lines of dependence on set occasions, in the verse both of his school and university years.

At Cambridge, there were numerous deaths to be used as occasions for a display of poetic talents. Death and gratulations called forth 'books' of verses, often not printed, and many of these have not survived. Those occasions we know of concern senior bishops with Cambridge connections, Nicholas Fenton of Ely, and Launcelot Andrews of Winchester; there was John Gostlin, the Vice-Chancellor; Richard Ridding, the esquire beadle who carried the mace before the Vice-Chancellor; there was an aristocratic death connected with the university, of the Marchioness of Winchester; and the legendary carrier who plied his trade between Cambridge and London, Hobson, given two comic epitaphs (in line with his lower social status). The undergraduate Milton's dependence on death for subject is typical for the period.

With funerary elegy in mind I would like to make some comparisons with Milton's younger grammar school rival, Abraham Cowley. Some have suspected that Cowley was among the 'more timely-happy spirits' alluded to in Milton's sonnet 'How soon hath time'.[3] It is unlikely: the sonnet is probably of late 1631 and Cowley's first book did not appear until 1633. But we may put the elegies of two grammar school poets together, though they stand in these examples at opposite ends of the educational experience.[4] 'Lycidas' is written beyond the end of the poet's university life, whereas the Cowley poems come from the very outset of his career, from his school years.

Abraham Cowley's first collections, *Poetical Blossoms* (1633) and *Sylva* (1636), furnish a spectacular case of a precocious, very well tutored child-poet . He was a son not of Milton's St Paul's but of Westminster School, famous for its poetry training. Accordingly, *Blossoms* includes a poem to his master Lambert Osboldston and two dedicatory verses by schoolfellows, Benjamin Masters and Robert Mead.

*Blossoms* begins with two narrative poems written very young: 'Pyramus and Thisbe', fashioned largely out of Golding's Ovid

when Cowley was only 10; and 'Constantia and Philetus', showing
the influence of Spenser and the Ovidian poems of Shakespeare
and Marlowe, composed when he was 12. The rest of the poems in
the little volume 'were made since upon severall occasions'.⁵ Of
these, the last is 'A Dreame of Elysium', which like much else in
the volume is about the idea of being a poet, but two are funerary
elegies, one on Lord Dorchester, the statesman and former pupil of
Westminster who died in February 1631/2, the other on 'my loving
Friend and Cousen, Mr Richard Clerke' of Lincoln's Inn, who probably died in 1632. These elegies show how an ambitious grammar
school-trained boy-poet could face the mature task of contemplating life in death.

The Dorchester elegy invents a new myth to explain the statesman's death as a hellish design against virtue and innocence; narrative invention thus fulfils the duty of praise. Appropriately, in a
tribute to a grandee, the close does not express personal grief but
states that mourning this death is the general duty of the country:

> Sol's Chorus weepes, and to adorne his Herse
> Calliope would sing a Tragicke verse.
>    And had there bin before no Spring of theirs,
>    They would have made a Helicon with teares.

A. C.⁶

As in 'Lycidas' the social convention is alluded to of attaching
verses to the coffin. Cowley's poem also faces the epideictic task:
the boy-poet works within a ritual organized through the school, is
governed by a sense of *pietas*, and there is an allowed space in
which forward talent can show itself. There is in fact a tell-tale sign,
which we will see in another elegy: 'Weepe with mee each who
eyther reads or heares, / And know his losse deserves his
Countries teares.' Whatever literary tradition is behind it, 'heares'
implies oral delivery, not so much rhetoric on the page as oration.
Funerary orations took place in halls of collegiate societies, and the
line between funerary oration and funerary elegy can be thin.

The Clerke elegy, seemingly a family tribute, begins by rehears-
ing the inevitability of death even for the gifted, naming Cicero (for
eloquence), Solon (for wisdom) and Virgil (for poetry). The terms of
praise have been set out . Then, as expected, this very fluent poem
for a 14-year-old asks for mourning:

Who would not therefore now, if Learnings friend,
Bewayle his fatall and untimely end:
Who hath such hard, such unrelenting Eyes,
As would not weepe when so much Vertue dyes?

(*Works*, p. 62)

Again, not a simple weeping but a call for general weeping. As in the Dorchester elegy, the point is illustrated by reference to the functions of poetry itself:

The God of Poets doth in darknesse shrowd
His glorious face, and weepes behind a Cloud.
The dolefull Muses thinking now to write
Sad Elegies, their teares confound their sight:
    But him to Elysium's lasting Joyes they bring,
    When winged Angels his sad Requiems sing.

(pp. 62–3)

In this apprentice volume, in which, to use Cowley's words, his 'Quill ... relisheth a Schoole' (*Works*, p. 77), the main endeavour has been to proclaim a childhood ambition to become a poet, but when the boy faces occasions of death, he seems most of all to rehearse the duty which his poetic gift might serve in the rituals of the occasion. These poems are keyed into the community: the school encourages the poetic practice, which is an illustration of its own educational endeavour, and thus points towards the kinds of 'public' use which such a talent might subsequently serve. Both Cowley and Milton, pre-eminently, are products of such training.

*Sylva or Divers Copies of Verses Made upon sundry occasions by A. C.* was a new set of poems added for the second edition of *Blossoms* in 1636. Again, the context is often Westminster School up to the point at which university attendance was imminent for Cowley and the poems begin to suggest wider horizons. The first item is a prime example of a school production. 'On his Majesties return out of Scotland', with the song following, was part of a manuscript collection of poems by Westminster pupils presented at court and now in the British Library, on Charles' return to London after the Scottish coronation in 1633 (*Works*, pp. 68–9, 307). The last part of *Sylva* is composed of Horatian or quasi-Horatian odes, assuming a persona which was to become habitual in later years. Here, too, the occasions spread into the familial, and in general there is as with Milton's 1645 volume the display of a facility in different kinds. There are two further elegies, on Mrs Anne Whitfield, an unidentified courtier perhaps known to Cowley's family, and John Littleton, a 17-year-old Oxford student drowned while trying to save his younger brother from the river by Magdalen Bridge.

The Whitfield elegy (*Works*, pp. 77–8) stands out for the directness of its approach: it offers a way of turning grief into communal celebration. Here grief is not to be evaded, but embraced and turned to new use: 'thus wee must dull griefes sting, / And cheate the sorrow that her losse would bring.' The not-forgetting amounts to a repeating and celebrating of the name of Whitfield, perhaps playing on the associations of white/whit and purity. The aim is to make a monument in the heart:

> Thus in our hearts wee'l bury her, and there
> Wee'l write, Here lyes Whitfield the chast, and faire.
> >  Art may no doubt a statelier Tombe invent,
> >  But not like this, a living Monument.

We might dwell on the authority granted the speaking voice. The community of mourners is explicitly included in the 'we', yet the teenage poet is given licence to command and teach the mourners hieratically. The poem is a pretence at didactic oration, parading authority beyond any boy's years. Here, too, the idea of speaking and hearing is included as well as of writing and reading:

> Wee'l tell how love was dandled in her eye,
> Yet curb'd with a beseeming gravity,
> And how (beleeve it you that heare or reade)
> Beauty and chastity met and agreed
> In her, although a Courtier: we will tell
> How farre her noble spirit did excell
> Hers, nay our Sexe: wee will repeate her Name,
> And force the Letters to an Anagrame.

We need to understand the cultural practices that allowed this boy-poet such presence in the communal rituals of death.

The Littleton elegy (*Works*, pp. 78–80) is even more precocious. It may be that a witty youthfulness together with the newsworthy

nature of the death of the brothers combined to draw attention to
the elegy. Surviving Oxford copies of *Sylva* record circumstantial
information, and in *Remarks and Collections* Thomas Hearne singles
this poem out, explaining the occasion (see *Works*, p. 313). Thoughts
of 'Lycidas' come to mind when reading the 'dramatic' nature of
the utterance in this elegy. The speaker begins by angrily blaming
the river for the deaths, before finding a more considered approach.
The poem then tells of the heroic death of the elder brother, gives
high-termed but generalized praise of his character, and ends with
self-advertizing paradoxical wit by addressing the river again:

> Weepe then, sad Floud; and though thou'rt innocent,
> Weepe because fate made thee her instrument:
> And when long griefe hath drunke up all thy store,
> Come to our eyes, and wee will lend thee more.

What does the 'we' stand for in this poem, which seems to be a
more general offering upon a sensational item of news? Whatever
the answer, the matter of decorum appears again: with how much
wit and ingenuity is decorum satisfied, in the funerary ritual?

It is clearly important to register that there is a communal dimension to such poems. Even in more private cases or of familial affection there are conventions which identify a community of
mourners, and if the elegy is very rhetorically conceived it manifestly addresses an audience. With collegiate writing, there can be
an extra sense of community, a speaking on behalf of the school or
college, which might present its 'book of verses'. But these writings
involved fine-judged distinctions of tone and address. Different
kinds of elegy also need to be distinguished, and even the four ado-
lescent examples of Cowley furnish a range: from the more domestic and intimate, to the more distanced, or school-sponsored,
communal text. The expression of grief is also not a simple or
uniform matter. There is always a duty to ask for mourning, even
when the deceased is not known to the writer, but the pretence of
deep grief might in some cases be as indecorous as the failure to
show enough grief in others. (English funerary writing tended, in
any case, towards a Stoic containment or Christian redirection of
feeling.)[7] Each case must be judged against the particularities of the
situation. Similarly problematical is the need for rhetorical distinction, which amounts to display: it is never absent, because the provision of a fine speaking monument is expected,[8] even in cases of

friendship; but in collegiate sets of elegies, it is of prime concern. The school or college is expected to show itself as a learned and ingenious body.

When boys were trained to write verse at school, they were often competing on given themes. The result was the development of a craft which could encourage, on one hand, many look-alike neo-Latin poems, or it might on the other produce complex ingenuity, something which marked out the quality of one such poem on a theme over another on the same theme. There is a relationship between this kind of training and the ingenuity of a John Donne, and some of the characteristics which later embarrassed generations were negatively to call 'metaphysical' are connected to this kind of hothouse competition, the ability to treat set themes in clever, eye-catching ways.[9]

As far as the development of careers was concerned, for those young men who wished to make a mark in poetry, the occasions which presented themselves for such displays of rhetorical skill tended to be of certain kinds, and deaths provided many opportunities. Young poets could launch reputations on deaths, especially when memorial volumes were in prospect. John Milton, another grammar school poet, found himself caught up in the some of the same practices which can be seen so clearly with the precocious Abraham Cowley.

When Milton published a collection of his verse in 1645, amongst similar author-centred volumes published by Humphrey Moseley, he displayed the progress of his poetic development and that involved showing what he evidently regarded as choice productions of his formative years. His impulse to demonstrate how well he had performed within the educational culture in which he had grown up, whatever his critical thoughts about that culture, continued to the end of his life, when he offered to the public selected academic exercises from his Cambridge years.[10] As far as his funerary elegies are concerned, those written in Latin about university notables are impressive impositions upon the occasions, with easy recall of Roman myth and phrase, contrived dramatic gesture or the creation of some new narrative, rounded out piously with visions of heaven.

Some similar features are easily visible in an early English example, 'On the Death of a Fair Infant ...', which forms a good comparison with the youthful elegies of Cowley. The opening stanzas give clear signals:

O fairest flower, no sooner blown but blasted,
Soft silken primrose fading timelessly,
Summer's chief honour if thou hadst outlasted
Bleak winter's force that made thy blossom dry;
For he being amorous on that lovely dye
    That did thy cheek envermeil, thought to kiss
But killed alas, and then bewailed his fatal bliss.

For since grim Aquilo, his charioteer,
By boisterous rape the Athenian damsel got,
He thought it touched his deity full near,
If likewise he some fair one wedded not,
Thereby to wipe away the infamous blot
Of long uncoupled bed, and childless eld,
Which 'mongst the wanton gods a foul reproach was held.[11]

In his 1673 collection Milton duly registered his age at the time of composition: 'Anno aetatis 17'. The poem was to be judged not against expectations of maturity, but as the kind of composition which early training encouraged. The creation of a story and the broadly post-Ovidian mythology are expected features; it is evident that young Milton, like young Cowley, knew notable English examples of Ovidian narrative poems – Shakespearean language, in particular, is unmissable. Also, the elaborate length of the poem hangs upon a series of dramatizing questions from the singer, of just the kind that practice on such themes encourages. What is more, although the end of the poem defers the writing of fame to the dead girl herself in heaven, it is obvious that a hopeful young poet is contributing to his own potential fame by demonstrating the ability to sustain a considerable poetic structure within the bounds of decorum. There is an understanding that the tribute might fall short if there is not a sufficient degree of self-display, in a mode appropriate both to offerer and occasion (female subjects tended to receive playfully narrative treatments), just as if some ritual had been curtailed.

    The problems of critical assessment here are similar to those famously posed by 'Lycidas' itself, and they are highlighted by Dr Johnson's tart remark that where there is leisure for such artifice as 'Lycidas' displays, there can be no room for grief.[12] Johnson was rejecting a whole cultural tradition, and empowering his own voice with a different critical perspective. In these schoolboy exercises the issues were really about rhetorical distinction, to be judged according to the age and experience of the rhetor. This was part of the due dignity of the rituals, which should manifest itself in what Daniel Featley, giving a funeral sermon in 1613, referred to as the necessity to do everything, if funds and connections permitted, 'decently and in due order'.[13] The organizers of *Justa Edouardo King* would have expected that Milton, like others, would display his educated talent in a best tribute, and a first-person voice might well appear with some self-representational distinctiveness, as long as it served the institutional functions of the volume. But, if we look ahead to the history of Milton's famous elegy for King in printings subsequent to *Justa*, we can see that once the poem is printed in an authorially centred collection, such mutual serving can only be reconstructed by providing contextualizations for the reader. All occasional poetry is inevitably construed differently, when it is decontextualized.

Although 'Lycidas' is most unusual in some things, as can be seen by comparing it with other poems within *Justa Edouardo King*, its basic procedures are in line with the kind of poetic practice I have been sketching in the schoolboy productions of Cowley and Milton – it is a more mature, virtuoso development of such poetic practice, written by one who has several years of experience beyond Cambridge. The *re-entry* into this kind of writing is in fact the subject of the opening of Milton's post-university poem. Notoriously, Milton's elegy begins with a bold, oblique and compressed opening which shows a developed interest in rhetorical, perhaps even oratorical, practice. A singer reluctantly rouses himself to song, with an attitude which is within a few lines to be put aside as 'denial vain, and coy excuse':

> Yet once more, O ye laurels, and once more
> Ye myrtles brown, with ivy never sere,
> I come to pluck your berries harsh and crude,
> And with forced fingers rude,
> Shatter your leaves before the mellowing year.
> Bitter constraint, and sad occasion dear,
> Compels me to disturb your season due ...

Milton had distinguished himself in academic exercises at Cambridge and had also produced good verses for various university occasions and collections. That is presumably why he was being asked, five years after leaving Christ's College, to contribute to *Justa*. According to his announced ambition to become an English poet, he chose to produce a substantial poem for *Obsequies* rather than write, more academically, in Latin or Greek. Reading this book of elegies for a King's Fellow, the Cambridge community – the first audience for the poem – was likely to see in 'once more' an allusion to the fact that John Milton, at Cambridge and now after Cambridge, was in demand as occasional rhetor.

The reluctance to write, though quickly placed as a gesture lacking decorum, seems also to confide an ambition which had been confessed before to Cambridge audiences: to prepare himself for a major role in English poetry, one self-determined rather than subject to the demands of occasional writing. The grounds for the reluctance – not being able to sing well enough as yet – are paradoxically a sign that only the best offerings should be countenanced by a serious Protestant-humanist community. We might note, too, that the device of beginning orations, as he often had at university, with an indecorous gesture which would then serve to define appropriate gestures, was to produce the Attendant Spirit's momentarily ungracious entry into the Ludlow masque, before he settled to that 'task'. The opening is a response to the request to contribute, like an answer to a letter. The poet dramatizes his coming to terms with the communal enterprise, admitting nervousness about the performance expected of him. The organizers were giving space to John Milton poet, in which to display his dignifying skills; he must respond by richly serving the occasion.

This is not an eager entrance, like Cowley's, into the opportunities offered in collegiate and similar exercise, but the case of one who has in his own estimation produced enough occasional university verse – 'once more ... and once more' – and whose prepara tions are for less constrained occasions. Indeed, the general tendency of critics, aware of patterns of literary tradition and Virgilian imitation, to present 'Lycidas' as a last pastoral poem, after which the poet will graduate from the pastoral mode, though understandable is too simple a reading of the situation. Milton seems to be signalling to his former university that *he has already passed on*: his perspectives are now broader, beyond the college, or, perhaps, he is placing the university experience in some greater context.

Indeed the whole evocation of collegiate experience in 'Lycidas' has the feel of retrospective construction. This poet only re-enters collegiate poetic production because of the call of a special duty:

> For Lycidas is dead, dead ere his prime,
> Young Lycidas, and hath not left his peer:
> Who would not sing for Lycidas? he knew
> Himself to sing, and build the lofty rhyme.
> He must not float upon his watery bier
> Unwept, and welter to the parching wind,
> Without the meed of some melodious tear.

Grief and consolation are a part of the ritual, as they must be, but it is not simply or even centrally a matter of personal grief:[14] it is a commission to make the best funerary tribute, to speak with what he conceives to be the highest considerations of education and shepherdly calling: it is an instructional laying to heart. Seen in a collegiate context, the transition is deft from the first section, expressing reluctance to compose, to the taking to heart of the occasion to which he will rise – 'For Lycidas is dead, dead ere his prime' – there are other premature matters to consider, and 'he well knew / Himself to sing ...', so that within the context of academic versifying, at least, King and Milton are fellows.

The promise is of a virtuoso performance; the poem will have all the oratorical power of a monody. The duty expressed, though couched in Virgilian reminiscence – 'Who would not sing for Lycidas?' ... 'neget quis carmina Gallo?'[15] – is the kind of expression one expects on such occasions, and such as Cowley produced in his call for mourning: 'Who would not therefore now, if Learnings friend,/ Bewayle his fatall and untimely end...'. The ambitiousness of Milton's elegy, however, with its sophisticated technique and highly politicized uses of the mourning occasion, demands a special kind of hearing, and by implication, a special kind of audience.

Reviewing the shared but lost experience of study at the university, the singer gives a description of a regime of life. Early Milton texts abound in pastoral ingenuity, and this passage is wrapped up in terms of sheep watching and song, but it is clear that from 'Together both, ere the high lawns appeared / Under the opening eye-lids of the morn' down to 'And old Damaetas loved to hear our song' Milton is depicting, fancifully but instructionally, an idealized rhythm of hard study from early morn until dusk in an institution liberal enough to delight in the uses of poetry and song. (As we know, that is more Milton's *idea* of a university, than what he actually met; but this former scholar instructs his instructors.) Such a description could also be said to define the kind of readership that 'Lycidas' demands.

The poem demonstrates qualities which should match the educative achievements of such a university. It demands recognition of educational attitudes, to do with the best preparation for and execution of the offices of a pastor – because the two universities were largely training colleges for the ministry. It also asks for recognition of an astounding variety of literary references, moving comfortably between English, Latin, Greek and biblical formulations. Where the other elegies in *Justa* do not, this poem shows a knowledge of the best genre, the pastoral elegy, in its Greek, Latin and Italian examples. Its sudden changes of voice and mood are demanding, and the identity of its speaker is confirmed only after the process of the poem. The reader is asked to observe and interpret the reactions of the swain and the other voices, and much lateral thinking is called for, as the sense of loss is expanded from personal, collegiate, and institutional to that for the nation at large, at a time when the university should be championing reform against a background of sliding discipline or betrayal at the centre. The poems in *Justa* exploit similar opportunities, loss of colleague, loss to the university, and several build on the symbolism of water or the sea, but no one composed in such multi-layered fashion as Milton, or used the national dimension to make the elegy into an admonishing laying to heart.

And yet what we have come to think of as the 'political' dimensions of 'Lycidas' are themselves part of a funerary ritual, not an intrusion into it.[16] 'It is the dutie of those that live, to lay to heart the death of others ...', explained a funeral sermon, and laying to heart meant, in the case of the death of a admirable, godly person, solemn consideration of the significance of the loss to the community and what that loss might portend: 'Some times, wee see an apparent judgement of God in the death of some.' In the case of a bad person, it might be a 'judgement of God upon themselves'; but with the death of a righteous person:

Sometimes againe it is a judgement of God upon others. Thus God takes away divers of his servants, because the world is not

worthy of them... . God in mercy taking them away from the
evill to come, and from the evill present ... . Righteous and mer-
ciful men are taken away, and no man layeth it to heart ... . A
Land, a Kingdome, a State, a People, a place is much weakened,
when those that are righteous ... are taken away. The house will
certainly fall, when the pillars are removed.[17]

So, too, in Milton's elegy the 'loss to shepherd's ear' is developed
into thoughts of the vocations of learned ministers and instructive
poets, and is related to Cambridge and 'the faithful herdsman's art'
in the national church. The preacher's allusion, in the 'fallen
pillars', is to the Samson story; in 'Lycidas' the imminent collapse,
deserving judgement, is in the failure to feed the 'hungry sheep',
who are given insubstantial (i.e. formalist) and even superstitious
teaching, while Catholic infection ('the grim wolf') spreads un-
halted. The judgement is promised in the 'two-handed engine' 'at
the door', waiting to be revealed. By the time of the headnote to the
poem as later printed in 1645 that judgement had been seen in the
fall of the bishops. To that headnote and the 'grim wolf' I shall be
returning.

It is an extraordinary poem which dramatizes loss of the body
by scanning the western shores from the Hebrides to Lands End,
then reveals at the southern end of that sweep an allusion to the
Armada of 1588, another storm causing wreck down western
shores, brought to memory by the vision of Michael on the mount,
protector of Protestant England, looking out towards Spain. The
terms of reference are familiar enough in popular national consciousness, through the mythologies of 1588 and 1605. What this
amounts to is another aspect of the community of interests in a
proper 'laying to heart' which Milton shares with his readers, a
recognition of ideologies as well as of sophisticated literary
means. So what we have in 'Lycidas' is a combination of factors
defining challenges for readers and to do with a sense of community value. With one or two other features of the poem, it may be
that some of the features which prove problematic in readings
after 1638 are in fact symptoms of a hoped-for communality of
understanding in 1638.

I have in mind to begin with the extraordinary passage describing the imaginary strewing of flowers on the hearse of Edward
King:

> return Sicilian muse,
> And call the vales, and bid them hither cast
> Their bells, and flowrets of a thousand hues.
> Ye valleys low where the mild whispers use,
> Of shades and wanton winds, and gushing brooks,
> On whose fresh lap the swart star sparely looks,
> Throw hither all your quaint enamelled eyes,
> That on the green turf suck the honied showers,
> And purple all the ground with vernal flowers,
> Bring the rathe primrose that foresaken dies,
> The tufted crow-toe, and pale jessamine,
> The white pink, and the pansy freaked with jet,
> The glowing violet
> The musk-rose, and the well-attired woodbine,
> With cowslips wan that hang the pensive head,
> And every flower that sad embroidery wears:
> Bid amaranthus all his beauty shed,
> And daffadillies fill their cups with tears,
> To strew the laureate hearse where Lycid lies.
> For so to interpose a little ease,
> Let our frail thoughts dally with false surmise.

These lines were much expanded in the Trinity Manuscript.[18] In some ways, the decision to build them up needs little explanation. After the stern prophetic warning of Peter, this imagined flower-strewing offers the relief of a familiar ritual, before the recollection that the body is irretrievably lost. In the first manuscript version the valleys were asked to throw vernal flowers, but the respite lasted just a few lines. It is easy to see that the eight new lines are more engrossing and therefore a better 'false surmise'.

But the flower-strewing as expanded also appeals to communal experience. After the corruption of Church and Court, the freshness of the valleys implies an uncorrupted place. This pastoral site must bring funerary tributes, and they sound more and more like elegiac offerings towards the end – not just early blooms that fade but pensively inclined cowslip heads, flowers with 'sad embroidery', the traditional funerary amaranthus, and daffadillies filled with tears. In floral form, these are the offerings within the volume of obsequies, and, as I have said, such expression is underpinned both by literary tradition and the convention of attaching verses to the coffin, strewing or adorning the hearse. Expressing that communal-

ity in ritual mourning there is a plural at the end – 'For so to inter-
pose a little ease / Let our frail thoughts dally with false surmise'.
The swain speaks for all the shepherds.

With this passage, as with the passage about the life of study at
Cambridge, the sense of community would have been much easier
to maintain in the context of the university collection itself. Ever
since eighteenth-century editions, there have had to be *explanations*
of passages which give pastoral figuration to university life and interests. There is an amusing instance with Warton in 1785, as he
annotates 'Together both, ere the high lawns appear'd...' By then,
the main frame of reference shared by editor and reader is the idea
of the great poet, so Warton's first annotations are about the habits
of John Milton's life: 'From the regularity of his pursuits, the
purity of his pleasures, his temperence, and general simplicity of
life, Milton habitually became an early riser ...' He cites proof from
autobiographical passages in later prose works, and mentions
early rising in 'L'Allegro'. Then, as if conscious that such biographical matters are really digressive, he pulls himself together:
'In the present instance, he more particularly alludes to the stated
early hours of a collegiate life, which he shared, *on the self-same hill*,
with his friend Lycidas at Cambridge.'[19] So the sense which could
easily have been taken by the university community in 1638 has by
now, against the pull of other priorities and interests, to be re-
trieved by guiding paraphrase. By the time of the New Critical
account of the poem in Brooks and Hardy, a decontextualized interpretation, imbued with ideas of the self-sufficiency of poetic
texts, we reach a stage at which the university is not mentioned at
all – the account has absolutely no sense of the delicate negotiations of occasionality.[20]

Another key feature in focus here is the uncouth swain himself.
He is a construct allowing the singer to be both John Milton, poet,
with all his vocational allegiances showing in the presentation of
the ethos of the speaker, and a spokesman for the university community, one who can call legitimately for 'our' thoughts to dally
with false surmise. To understand the give-and-take between
singer and university audience, the reader needs a sense of that
'we'. One finds many predictable bendings of the negotiations of
the swain in later editions, for example, noting what happens to the
wonderful multifaceted ending, as he signs off: 'Tomorrow to fresh
woods, and pastures new.' Here Verity, in his late nineteenth- and
early twentieth-century editions, serves splendidly for the tradition

centred on the biography of a great poet: 'It is usual to find here an allusion to Milton's tour in Italy.'[21] Oh yes? What is expressed in the continuation of pastoral is that there are different fields of experience and activity, the collegiate life, friendship within that life, the communities of learning and of poetry, and the responsibilities of true pastors in the university and out in the nation. Is it not likely that the ending is meant to draw the community together? As John Milton, Cambridge shepherd out in the world, moves on to his next tasks, so too the other shepherds who belong or belonged to the university, who form that ideal audience for his poem, may move on to their new tasks and responsibilities as well. The whole community can move forward, with a prescribed sense of vocation.

We can define more of the differences of context in *Justa* and Milton's own volume of 1645, and the way Milton seems to have responded to the different later occasion. With regard to the political climate of November 1637, when 'Lycidas' was being composed, much has been written about the time of radical opposition and debate recorded in the poem. I wish here only to repeat what I have said elsewhere about the exact timing and precise occasionality, of the crucial line 129: '...what the grim wolf with privy paw / Daily devours apace, and nothing said.'[22] 'And nothing said' was the first reading in the manuscript. It was then changed to 'and little said' in the manuscript and *Justa*, only to revert to 'nothing' in *1645*.

The immediate context was worship at the Catholic chapel of the Queen at Somerset House and the notable converts to Catholicism being made through the Queen's circle. The fresh opportunity for controversy came with the conversion of the Countess of Newport in October 1637, following which the Earl complained to Laud, who put pressure on the King. It was a test case. Ardent Protestants hoped to force some anti-Catholic measures out of the King, to stop the daily devouring. Everyone expected *something* to be said. By November, as Milton was writing his vocational poem, nothing had been said: hence the original reading. By the end of December something had been said, but the royal proclamation on the matter of conversions was so anodyne that it was as good as nothing. Hence Milton's patronizing 'little'. In *1645*, all sensitivity past, 'nothing' was restored as the accurate assessment. This crux indicates such an urgent sense of occasion that the word changed back and forth with the political action of a few weeks. Here we can see a peculiarly intense sense of occasionality, which amounts to the feeling that there were moments when God meant John Milton to speak out.

When texts are republished, such occasionality is liable to fade as surely as the original social negotiations. We know how the elegy for King was headed in 1645:

In this monody the author bewails a learned friend, unfortunately drowned in his passage from Chester on the Irish Seas, 1637. And by occasion foretells the ruin [that is, the fall] of our corrupted clergy then in their height.

The first sentence appears in the Trinity Manuscript, but in a later hand than the main text and squeezed into the space – it probably dates from after the Cambridge volume. The second sentence appears only in the printed text of 1645.

How do you give readers a sense of fading occasions? I used to think of this headnote as triumphant, at least in the second part; that it says, look what I prophesied in my poem of 1637, during all that trouble about the Church and Court, and did not a divine judgement occur? By the time Milton printed this in 1645, the bishops had fallen, and he was reviewing the past and relocating his poem within a present time, in which he had a leading part in arguing for the abolition of episcopacy. But one might read the headnote less simply. The poem has been given a new life by the events of a new time, eight years later. Contextualizations have had to be given, and readers had to use their memories to recognize the issues which arose when the clergy were 'in their height' but not yet fallen. A poet publishing his occasional text in a different collection, remote from its original contexts, might need to contextualize for his readers. In fact, apart from that opportunistic note of triumph, one could say that the headnote is a damage limitation exercise. The readers needed to know that this is an elegy for 'a learned friend', so that they could be prepared for the kind of discourse which a showcase university volume required. They needed to know the date, 1637, or they would have no handle on the political context. They needed to know that it was a death by drowning from shipwreck, and the place of death, or they would be puzzled by many details in the poem, including some political opportunism about western shores, and would not understand why water is so important a motif.

The fact is that poems which closely negotiate with their occasions, politically, or with the social constraints, fade all the time, like yesterday's conversations. Poets sometimes try to mend their ageing occasional texts, or prank them out anew, but for all that later readers will always relocate, or bend, those occasional texts. Occasionality and the supposed immortality of verse sit uneasily together. But historicizing attempts to understand the nature of the original negotiations, and indeed of subsequent negotiations, speculative though they must be, open up areas of interest, indeed unlock whole systems of communication in early modern poetry.

## NOTES

1. On this issue see, for example, Peter Lindenbaum, 'John Milton and the Republican Mode of Literary Production', in *Patronage, Politics, and Literary Traditions in England, 1558–1658*, ed. Cedric C. Brown (Detroit, 1991), pp. 93–108.
2. Donald Lemen Clark, *John Milton and St Paul's School* (1948: reprint, New York, 1964). On the idea of a poetic career, see especially Richard Helgerson, *Self-Crowned Laureates: Spenser, Jonson, and Milton and the Literary System* (Berkeley, 1983); John Guillory, *Literary Authority: Spenser, Milton, and Literary History* (New York, 1983); Dustin Griffin, 'The Beginnings of Modern Authorship: Milton and Dryden', *Milton Quarterly* 24.1 (1990), pp. 1–7.
3. Reported in *The Collected Works of Abraham Cowley*, vol. 1, ed. Thomas O. Calhoun, Laurence Heyworth and Alan Pritchard (Newark, NJ, London and Toronto, 1989), p. 297. Hereafter cited as *Works*.
4. It is for this reason that I put them together, not because Dr Johnson happens to mention Cowley in his denunciation of 'Lycidas' in his *Life* of Milton and *Life* of Cowley.
5. 'To the Reader', *Works*, p. 17.
6. *Works*, p. 61. Here and in later quotations some features of capitalization and italicization have been normalized.
7. One of the themes of G. W. Pigman III in *Grief and Renaissance Elegy* (Cambridge, 1985), in which a general shift is traced from sixteenth-century containments of grief to greater allowance of expressions of grief in seventeenth-century elegy. Hereafter cited as Pigman.
8. On the whole epideictic tradition in relation to elegy, see Barbara K. Lewalski, *Donne's Anniversaries and the Poetry of Praise: The Creation of a Symbolic Mode* (Princeton, NJ, 1973); and O. B. Hardison, *The Enduring Monument: A Study of the Idea of Praise in Renaissance Literary Theory and Practice* (Chapel Hill, NC, 1962); on funerary poems see, for example, Eric Smith, *By Mourning Tongues* (London, 1977); Pigman; Peter M. Sacks, *The English Elegy: Studies in the Genre from Spenser to Yeats* (Baltimore, MD, 1985); Joshua Scodel, *The English Poetic Epitaph: Commemoration and Conflict from Jonson to Wordsworth* (Ithaca, NY,

1991). All these studies, however, tend to treat elegiac expression in a personal rather than community framework.

9.  Material of this kind forms the groundwork for a forthcoming book by John Dolan on rhetoric and poetic occasion in the early modern English lyric. I am grateful to him for sharing them with me.

10. Milton published his academic exercises and familiar letters in 1674, at the very end of his life, having also published or republished a lot of other educational works in the last years and augmented his collection of poems: *1645* was expanded as *Poems etc ... Upon Several Occasions* in 1673 and the tractate *Of Education* was reprinted with it; his *Artis Logicae* was published in 1672, his school-grammar *Accidence Commenc't Grammar* in 1669, and the incomplete *History of Britain* in 1670.

11. Quotations of Milton's poems from *Milton: Complete Shorter Poems,* ed. John Carey (2nd edn 1997), pp. 15–18 (hereafter cited as Carey).

12. Samuel Johnson, *Lives of the English Poets,* ed. G. B. Hill (Oxford, 1905) vol. 1, pp. 163–5.

13. '... might not the money have been better expended in charitable almes ...? I answer in the words of our Saviour, *Haec oportet facere, & illa non omittere*; Those workes of charitie they spake of, ought to be done; and these of decent Rites and ceremonies not to be left undone: ... if all things must be done decently, and in order, in the State and Commonwealth, much more in the Church ...; and if all things in the Church must bee so carried then Funeralls as well as Nuptialls, Burialls as well as Christenings; and if so, then ought they to bee celebrated not after the preposterous manner of some in the night as workes of darknesse; but in the day as workes of Pietie, in honour of them who have received the inheritance of Saints in light, not perniciously and basely, but nobly and liberally; where the qualitiy of the dead requireth it, and the estate will beare it.' *Iter Novissimum. Or, Mans Last Progress. A Sermon Preached at the Funerall of the Right Worshipfull Sir Thomas Thinne, Knight ...,* published in the collection of funeral sermons by different hands called *Threnikos. The House of Mourning* (London, 1640), pp. 817–34 (hereafter cited as *Threnikos*). Featley's sermon has been noted by various scholars, including Pigman (p. 136), and I am also grateful to Ralph Houlbrooke for discussing this and other material with me from his forthcoming book on the social history of death.

14. To see the comparison with a monumental elegy for a close personal friend, 'Lycidas' should be compared with 'Epithaphium Damonis', Milton's specially printed elegy for Charles Diodati.

15. Virgil, Ecl. x 3.

16. Probably the most influential acount of the structure of the poem as one of three movements, in which there is a 'return' to pastoral after the outbursts of Phoebus and St Peter (see 'The Pattern of Milton's Nativity Ode', *UTQ* 10 (1940–1): 167–81, an account which itself picked up on that of Tillyard (*Milton* [London, 1930], pp. 79–85, in which it was explicitly stated that the real subject of the poem was Milton himself.

17.  In the sermon *The Praise of Mourning, or Mourning preferred before Mirth in Threnikos*, pp. 27–52, here pp. 46–7. See similar material adduced in my earlier essay 'The Death of Righteous Men: Prophetic Gesture in Vaughan's "Daphnis" and Milton's "Lycidas"', *George Herbert Journal* 7 (1983–4), 1–24. The key phrase about laying to heart is biblical, as in Isa. 57.1: 'The righteous perisheth, and no man layeth it to heart.' See also, for example, the sermon *The Worlds Losse; and the Righteous Man's Gain* in *Threnikos*, pp. 147–74: 'And mercifull men are taken away, none considering that the Righteous is taken from the evill to come' (p. 151); 'When a Saint is removed, a Pillar is removed ... there is a losse every way: to the Church, to the State ...' (p. 167); '... The reason why men goe on in excess and riot, and continue in drunkennesse, is nothing but this, *they lay it not to heart* ...' (p. 169).

18.  *John Milton: Poems, Reproduced in Facsimile from the Manuscript in Trinity College, Cambridge, with a Transcript* (Menston, 1972), p. 30.

19.  *John Milton, Poems upon Several Occasions ... by John Milton*, ed. Thomas Warton (London, 1785), p. 7.

20.  *Poems of John Milton: the 1645 Edition, with Essays in Analysis*, ed. Cleanth Brooks and John Edward Hardy (New York, 1951), pp. 169–86.

21.  *Milton's Ode to the Morning of Christ's Nativity ... and Lycidas*, ed. A. W. Verity (Cambridge, 1891), p. 163.

22.  The material in this paragraph follows that in my *John Milton: A Literary Life* (Basingstoke, 1995), pp. 51–2. Amongst various contextualising accounts of 'Lycidas' in 1637, see David Norbrook, *Poetry and Politics in the English Renaissance* (London, 1985), pp. 275–85.

# 9

# Between the 'Triumvirate of wit' and the Bard: The English Dramatic Canon, 1660–1720

## Paulina Kewes

> They have each their proper graces ... which makes every one appear that individual Poet He is.
>
> *The Moderator*, 23 June 1692

> It is agreed, I think, by all that understand our Language, that we have equall'd, if not surpass'd all other Nations in *Dramatic Poetry*; and that our *Tragedies* excel those of other Countries, both in Majesty of Style, and Variety of Incidents: And that this Part of the *Drama* is a Sort of Poetry peculiarly adapted to the *Martial* Genius of the *British* Nation ...
>
> *Thesaurus Dramaticus* (1724)[1]

Modern literary historians, much exercised by questions of canonicity, have dwelt on the ascendency of the 'Triumvirate of wit' in the seventeenth century and of Shakespeare in the eighteenth. Several recent studies have emphasized the construction of the triumvirate through the publication of the Jonson, Shakespeare, and 'Fletcher' folios in 1616, 1623, and 1647 respectively.[2] Shakespeare is believed to have outflanked the others by the late 1730s, and to have become the nation's cultural icon by the time of the Stratford Jubilee in 1769.[3] This perspective, though not incorrect, is seriously incomplete. It overlooks the hierarchy of esteem that prevailed in the late seventeenth and early eighteenth centuries. In that period, which had its own concern with canonicity, the pre-eminence of the triumvirate waned and the solitary greatness of Shakespeare was by no means assured. Shakespeare did not simply displace Fletcher and Jonson in the national pantheon. The critical evaluation of drama after the Restoration was, I shall argue, both more complex and more appreciative of contemporary achievement than has hitherto been realized. The new generation of playwrights – Dryden, Otway, Lee, Shadwell, and others – enjoyed a high reputation. Their plays proved enduringly popular on the stage and won critical acclaim when printed. These modern bards, I shall show, were widely thought to have equalled, if not surpassed, the 'Gyant Race ... before the Flood'.[4]

How were playwrights ranked in the Restoration? How were plays classified, assessed and judged? What was the correspondence, if any, between critical acclaim and theatrical success or failure? In order to recover the contemporary outlook we have to go beyond clichés about the supremacy of the triumvirate of wit. Equally, we have to avoid undue reliance on two famous critical documents, which, for all their distinction, are unrepresentative of the tastes and preferences prevalent in our period: Dryden's *Essay of Dramatick Poesie* (1668) and Rymer's *Tragedies of the Last Age* (1678).[5] A more dependable guide is provided by the ranking of writers and plays that was built into and disseminated by successive dramatic catalogues. Those documents advertised, assessed and classified the growing profusion of printed drama. They not only told prospective buyers what was on offer, but also instructed them how to read and judge the plays they purchased. The aesthetic outlook embodied in them was consensual; they purported to reflect and propagate a universally accepted critical standard. These compendia are an invaluable record of cultural change. Published over a period of time, they registered the shifts within the hierarchy of older and current writers.

What was the critical hierarchy of plays and authors towards the end of the seventeenth century? How did contemporaries judge and define it? To reconstruct their criteria and order of preference we look to performance, publication and critical commentary. Performance records prior to about 1703 are too scanty for the analysis to yield meaningful results. Commercial publication of plays is a more reliable, if a limited, index of current tastes. The pattern of publication of collected editions after the Restoration evinces the temporary ascendency of the aristocratic amateurs in the 1660s, Dryden's achievement of celebrity status in the 1690s and 1700s, and the prominence of contemporary dramatists in the early decades of the eighteenth century. The folios of Shakespeare (1663, 1685), Beaumont and Fletcher (1679), and Jonson (1692) had been eclipsed, in the later seventeenth century, by the folio collections of plays by genteel authors: Margaret Cavendish, Duchess of Newcastle's *Playes* (1662) and her *Plays, Never before Printed* (1668), Thomas Killigrew's *Comedies, and Tragedies* (1664), Sir Robert Howard's *Four New Plays* (1665), Sir William Killigrew's *Four New Playes* (1666), and the Earl of Orrery's *The History of Henry the Fifth. And the Tragedy of Mustapha, Son of Solyman the Magnificent* (1668) and his *Two New Tragedies* (1669).[6] In the early eighteenth century, collected editions of the triumvirate in octavo and duodecimo were outnumbered by collections of post-Restoration playwrights. Between 1700 and 1720, there were only two collected editions of Shakespeare (1709 and 1714),[7] one of Beaumont and Fletcher (1711) and two of Ben Jonson (1715 and 1716–17). By contrast, we have four collections of Farquhar ([1708], [1711], 1714, 1718), three each of Behn (1702, 1711, 1716) and Congreve (1710, 1712, 1719), two each of Etherege (1704, 1715), Otway (1712, 1717–18), and Vanbrugh 1719,[8] and one each of Wycherley (1713), Lee (1713), Dryden (1717), Shadwell (1720) and Rowe (1720).[9] The reputation, and therefore the economic viability, of Jonson and Beaumont and Fletcher had dwindled; and the boom in Shakespeare publishing only began in the 1720s. Early eighteenth-century readers would have been far more familiar with the collected output of contemporary playwrights than with the *œuvre* of the antediluvian giants.

Print consolidated the emerging canon by making the work of popular dramatists increasingly accessible as reading matter. What then were the grounds of their popularity? Why did some plays enjoy lasting success and others fail? Prologues, epilogues, prefatory epistles and critical pamphlets are useful in assessing what appealed to late seventeenth-century audiences. Personal correspondence and diaries too can be of help. They register individual likes and dislikes, and occasionally offer an insight into the views of a family, a professional group or social class. Yet such sources are by definition partial and incomplete. Our most systematic evidence of critical commentary and judgement comes from play catalogues and dictionaries of dramatic biography. These compendia set out to list and attribute all extant English plays. From mere mechanical lists they evolved into well-considered guides. Their changing format and organization reflected a new understanding of the territory, and communicated this new understanding to a growing audience. Dramatic catalogues sought to define the standard of literary judgement, and by assessing and ranking the mass of printed plays showed how this standard could be applied in practice. To extrapolate and analyse the evaluative criteria embodied in successive catalogues is to recover the conceptual basis on which the contemporary dramatic canon was formed.

The urge to judge and evaluate was already implicit in the play catalogues prepared by Francis Kirkman. Though his aim in *A True, perfect, and exact Catalogue* of 1661 was to advertise the commodities for sale at his and his partners' shops, and though he retained the alphabetical arrangement of plays typical of the commercial listings of the 1650s, Kirkman made his notion of dramatic hierarchy plain by placing Shakespeare, Fletcher and Jonson at the head of each alphabetical entry.[10] The prominence of Shakespeare was further underscored in the revised and expanded edition of the catalogue ten years later. Kirkman now purposed to list the most prolific playwrights first.[11] In failing to remove Shakespeare from the initial position in each consecutive entry, he conspicuously violated this design, for according to his own count Shakespeare had written fewer plays than either Fletcher or Jonson.

The typographical layout of entries could only go so far in signalling precedence. And Kirkman felt that his familiarity with all the plays included in the catalogue qualified him to comment on their relative merits. 'I have not only seen, but also read all these Playes', he wrote, 'and can give some account of every one; but I shall not be so presumptuous, as to give my Opinion, much less, to determine or judge of every, or any mans Writing, and who writ best.' He promptly contradicted this profession of restraint by declaring that 'in my Opinion, one *Thomas Meriton*, who writ two Pamphlets, which he calls Playes … was the worst [*English* Playwriter].' With a perfunctory nod towards well-born amateurs 'the *English* Stage is much improved and adorned with the several Writings of several persons of Honour' – Kirkman proceeded to state his genuine preference: 'but, in my Opinion chiefly with those of the most accomplished Mr. *John Dreyden*.'[12]

Kirkman did not articulate the grounds for his dismissal of Meriton, for his respect for the aristocratic dabblers or for his admiration for Dryden. Edward Phillips was more explicit. He was much exercised by the rise and fall of literary reputations. '[I]n the

State of Learning, among the Writers of all Ages', he observed in the Preface to *Theatrum Poetarum* (1675), 'some deserve Fame, & have it; others neither have nor deserve it; some have it, not deserving, others though deserving, yet totally miss it, or have it not equall to their deserts.'[13] Phillips took linguistic change to be the main reason for the lapse of older works from the canon. He also noted that plays were more likely to live beyond their time than other compositions. '[L]et us look back as far as about 30 or 40 years', he wrote, 'and we shall find a profound silence of the Poets beyond that time, except of some few Dramatics, of whose real worth the Interest of the now flourishing Stage, cannot but be sensible.'

'Is Antiquity then a crime?', he exclaimed, 'no certainly, it ought to be rather had in veneration, but nothing it seems relishes so well as what is written in the smooth style of our present Language taken to be of late so much refined' (sig. **2ʳ). Phillips was uncomfortable about the arguments of Dryden, Sprat and others concerning the spectacular improvement of the English tongue as both a communicative tool and poetic medium. He condemned his contemporaries' excessive regard for new literary fashions and means of expression, and deplored the resulting shifts in the canonical hierarchy. This hostility to change and a yearning for stability originated in a conviction that 'what was *verum & bonum* once, continues to be so always' (sig. **3ʳ).

Phillips undertook to specify the '*verum & bonum*' in all of the world's poetry and drama; his compilation was promoted as a 'Compleat Collection of the Poets, Especially The most Eminent, of all Ages'. Phillips largely recycled and rearranged information culled from continental encyclopedias and dictionaries of literary biography, and was at his most original in the entries on English authors. His particular judgements were often commonplace. What was truly new about the enterprise was Phillips' attempt to convey a sense of a hierarchy beyond the triumvirate, and to spell out some of the criteria for its differentiation.

Shakespeare was afforded pre-eminence over Jonson and Fletcher. Phillips recognized 'his unfiled expressions, [and] his rambling and indigested Fancys' (sig. **9ᵛ), and allowed that 'some others may perhaps pretend to a more exact *Decorum* and *OEconomie*, especially in Tragedy'. Even so, he averred that 'never any expres't a more lofty and Tragic heighth; never any represented nature more purely to the life.' For 'where the polishments of Art are most wanting', Shakespeare 'pleaseth with a certain wild and native Elegance; and in all his Writings hath an unvulgar style' (p. 194, second pagination).

Second in rank to the triumvirate of 'the Chief Dramatic Poets of our Nation, in the last foregoing Age' were James Shirley, Richard Brome and Thomas Middleton. Phillips compared Shirley to Fletcher: 'by some he is accounted little inferiour to *Fletcher* himself' (p. 80, second pagination), Brome to Jonson: 'not many parasangues inferior to him in fame by divers noted Comedies' (p. 157, second pagination), and Middleton to both those poets: 'a copious Writer for the English Stage, Contemporary with *Johnson* and *Fletcher*, though not of equal repute, and yet on the other side not altogether contemptible' (p. 180, second pagination). At the bottom of the scale he placed Thomas Nash, 'one of those that may serve to fill up the Catalogue of English Dramatics [sic] Writers' (p. 181, second pagination).

Phillips' rating of pre-Restoration playwrights was superficial and conventional.[14] He was more outspoken in his criteria for assessing recent English plays. His cardinal objection was that they unthinkingly imported imperfect French models. In the entry on Corneille, Phillips sarcastically noted the Frenchman's exceptional following 'both among his own Countrey-men, and our *Frenchly* affected *English*, fot [sic] the amorous Intreagues, which if not there before, he commonly thrusts into his Tragedies and Histories', and castigated 'the Imitation whereof among us, and of the perpetual Colloquy in Rhime, [which] hath of late very much corrupted our *English* Stage' (p. 28, second pagination). He was more appreciative of Molière, 'the pleasantest of French Comedians, for smart Comic wit and Mirth; and to whom', he admitted with embarrassment, 'our English Stage hath within a few years been not a little beholding' (p. 230, second pagination).

The taste of audiences must be vitiated, Phillips thought, if they applaud the 'Dramatic Histories' of the Earl of Orrery, with their 'continual Riming, and love and honour way of the French' (pp. 165–6, second pagination). He was likewise sceptical about Dryden's two-part *The Conquest of Granada*, 'in which … he have indulg'd a little too much to the French way of continual Rime and interlarding of History with ascitious [sic] Love and Honour' (p. 108, second pagination). Phillips's patriotic resistance to the encroachment of Gallic fashions was not a new departure; similar sentiments had been voiced before. His was the earliest sustained endeavour to use the bias against French influence as grounds for discrediting specific English plays and playwrights.

The embryonic hierarchy of pre-Civil War dramatists discernible in Phillips' *Theatrum Poetarum* was reproduced virtually intact by William Winstanley in his *Lives Of the most Famous English Poets* (1687).[15] Winstanley was less overtly critical of native writers than his predecessor. His more extreme brand of literary patriotism prompted him to delete both Phillips' harsh dismissal of minor old writers such as Nash and his reservations about the infiltration of the fabric of recent English drama by foreign accretions. To allow them to stand would have undermined the jingoistic manifesto with which Winstanley launched his volume, namely, that 'we come not behind any Nation in the World, both in Grandity and Gravity, in Smoothness and Propriety, in Quickness and Briefness.'[16]

The work of Phillips and Winstanley belonged in the tradition of collective literary biography, to which they brought rudiments of critical judgement. Gerard Langbaine's *Momus Triumphans: or, The Plagiaries of the English Stage* (1688) descended from an alternative tradition, that of the commercial play list. Langbaine proposed to do more than advertize available titles. His ambition was to teach his readers, the '*Nobility* and *Gentry*, who delight in Plays', how properly to judge of what they see on the stage and read in the privacy of their closets.[17] He encouraged them to become acquainted with criticism of the drama, and recommended relevant texts accessible in English. Among them were Jonson's *Timber*, Roscommon's translation of Horace's *Ars Poetica*, Rymer's translation of Rapin and his *Tragedies of the Last Age*, Dryden's *Essay of Dramatick Poesie*, Hédelin's *The Whole Art of the Stage*, Longinus' *On the Sublime* and Boileau's *Art of Poetry* (sigs. a3v–a4r).[18] Reading criticism enhances understanding, he claimed, and to understand drama is better to appreciate and enjoy it. The audience 'would have the greater satisfaction in seeing a *correct Play*', Langbaine affirmed, 'by how much they were capable … to discern the *Beauties* of it; and the greater value for a *good* Poet, by how much they were sensible of the Pains and Study requisite to bring such a Poem to perfection' (sig. a4r).

What is 'a *correct Play*'? How to recognize 'a *good* Poet'? There is a universal standard of judgement, Langbaine intimated, a set of prescriptive and descriptive criteria, which help distinguish good plays from bad ones. Spectators and readers would become more competent judges once they learnt and absorbed these criteria as expounded in the critical texts he recommended. Langbaine, however, had his own distinct notion of what a play should be, and of how dramatists ought to be assessed, which went beyond any putative critical consensus. His major concern was with artistic self-sufficiency.

In the Preface to *Momus Triumphans*, Langbaine laid out his views of plagiarism and appropriative licence in drama.[19] He exhorted readers to compare plays and their sources in order to appraise the writer's achievement, and, by way of illustration, offered a review of Dryden's thefts and Shadwell's legitimate borrowings. To enable his readers to carry out such comparisons for themselves, he cited the sources which he had been able to identify in footnotes appended to individual titles. His own valuation was transparent in the terms he used to express the debt. Most footnotes simply indicated the origin of the plot; others designated translations; but there were also damning ones which marked out plays stolen verbatim.[20] Ultimately, the reader was led to conclude that that play was best for which no sources had been specified.

Langbaine's Preface represents a very early instance of reader-oriented criticism. It was meant to advise readers how to read, not to instruct writers how to write, even if dramatists were expected to learn from his castigation of plagiarists. Though furnished with a critical introduction and suggestive footnotes, *Momus Triumphans* was still an inventory of titles. As such it was unlikely to have much effect on what people thought of plays. *An Account of the English Dramatick Poets* (1691) was a vastly more substantial work. Situated at the intersection of two or perhaps even three traditions, it combined the comprehensiveness of a play catalogue, and the interest in the lives of authors typical of biographical dictionaries, with the urge to issue value judgements intrinsic to criticism.

The distinctive feature of Langbaine's critical enterprise in the *Account* was its scope. Treatises such as Dryden's *Essay of Dramatick Poesie* and Rymer's *Tragedies of the Last Age* tended to mention relatively few names of authors and titles of plays except the best known, or the ones they set out to discuss in detail. In making value judgements they resorted to general categories based on historical epoch or genre: the moderns, the ancients, tragedies of the last age. By contrast, Langbaine undertook systematically to compare, assess and rank all extant English plays and authors. He proposed to render verdicts on hundreds of plays which were related to what he saw as their innate merits, and not necessarily or exclusively to their success in the theatre. However unfavourable some of his opinions may have been, such retrospective evaluation did treat plays as serious literary productions of individual authors.

Langbaine often mentioned that he had seen plays, and commented on their fortunes on the stage, but the reception of a play was not for him an index of its quality. He was prepared to admit that 'a Play *Read* ... wants the Greatest Ornament to a Play, *Gracefulness of Action*',[21] but this did not prevent him from lavishing praise on closet drama. Milton's *Samson Agonistes* was for him 'an Excellent Piece' (p. 376); and he used the same words to describe Dryden's unacted opera *The State of Innocence* (p. 185). He could be equally appreciative of plays for which there was no record of performance. 'I know not how it succeeded on the Stage', he remarked of James Carlile's *The Fortune-Hunters*, 'but if it be consider'd as the First Play of a young Poet, I think it deserv'd Applause, and exceeds several Comedies printed in this Age' (p. 50). At times he commended plays which had failed in the theatre. 'This Play notwithstanding it was decryed on the Stage', he said about the anonymous *Belphegor*, 'I think far surpasses many others, that have lately appear'd there' (sig. Oo5r).

Langbaine constructed several canons or hierarchies. First, he formulated two fairly discrete ratings based on the time in which the authors lived and worked: one of the 'Ancients', as he called pre-Restoration playwrights, and a separate one of the 'Moderns', that is, those who wrote since the Restoration. Secondly, subsumed by this chronological classification was a ranking of plays belonging to a given type or genre. Thirdly, Langbaine assessed each individual writer's output and judged which was his or her best or worst production. If less consistently, he also compared and ranked successive translations of foreign works into English,[22] and weighed the achievement of native plays *vis-à-vis* their foreign sources or analogues.[23] How then did he justify his good or bad opinion? What were his terms of praise and blame?

Langbaine tended to confine his judgemental comparisons to writers of a specific historical period. On occasion he might proclaim an old play to be superior to current stage fare, as he did in the case of Richard Brome's *Novella* ('This I take to exceed many of our modern Comedies', p. 37). But overall old writers were for

Langbaine hardly comparable with the moderns. Even his assertion of the timeless supremacy of the triumvirate was no more than a repetition of a hackneyed trope. Beaumont and Fletcher, he wrote, 'succeeded in Conjunction more happily than any Poets of their own, or this Age, to the reserve of the Venerable *Shakespear*, and the Learned and Judicious *Johnson*' (p. 203). Elsewhere he described 'these three [sic] Great Men' as 'the most Correct Dramatick Poets of the last Age' (pp. 136, 138), thus leaving open the possibility that their achievement might now be surpassed.

In his 'Vindication of the Ancients', Langbaine responded to censures which, he felt, Dryden had unfairly and erroneously advanced against them. He was particularly incensed by Dryden's claim that the works of Shakespeare, Fletcher and Jonson are structurally incorrect and derivative. Langbaine's apology was an attempt to attenuate rather than deny this and other charges. Instead of exonerating the ancients, he accused Dryden of like trespasses. Admitting Jonson's substantial borrowings from the classics, he pointed out that 'our late *Laureat* has far out-done him in Thefts, proportionable to his Writings' (p. 145). Similarly, even as he conceded Fletcher's appropriation of Spanish plots and frequent breaches of decorum, Langbaine maintained that the fault was more excusable in the earlier poet than in Dryden, 'who pretends so well to know it, and yet has offended against some of its most obvious and established Rules' (p. 143). He attempted to counter Dryden's attack on Shakespeare's irregularities of form and dramatization of trivial stories by explaining that Shakespeare had not known Aristotle or Rapin (p. 142). Whatever his provisos and qualifications, Langbaine as good as acknowledged that in some respects Dryden had outdone Shakespeare and, by implication, the two less exalted triumvirs, Fletcher and Jonson. If Dryden 'exceed Mr. *Shakespear* in Oeconomy, and Contrivance', he wrote 'tis that Mr. *Dryden*'s Plays owe their Advantage to his skill in the French Tongue, or to the Age, rather than his own Conduct, or Performances' (p. 141). By framing his vindication in so accusatory a mode, and by placing it in the entry on Dryden, which thereby grew to be the longest one in the book, Langbaine foregrounded both the now precarious position of the triumvirate and the authority of their modern detractor.

Individual entries on Shakespeare, Fletcher and Jonson were ridden with tensions. Langbaine sought to endorse the triumvirate's transcendence. His efforts, however, were undercut by an unwelcome, if inescapable, recognition that neither author's *œuvre* had survived the rupture of the Civil War intact. For how to uphold Shakespeare's – and Fletcher's, and Jonson's – status as poets 'not of an age, but for all time' when so many of their productions had either slipped from active repertory, or, in the case of Shakespeare and Fletcher, had been given, in revivals, new garbs? How to stop the erosion of these writers' reputations and protect them from the recent assaults of Dryden, Rymer and others? Langbaine wavered in his resolve. He vacillated between rating Shakespeare only against his own contemporaries and affirming his priority over both ancients and moderns. Having described him, in the opening sentence of his sketch, as 'One of the most Eminent Poets of his Time' (p. 453), Langbaine proceeded to extol Shakespeare's plays as timeless masterpieces: 'I esteem his Plays beyond any that have ever been published in our Language' (p. 454).

Langbaine's prime concern was with plays as printed artifacts. He none the less took care to record the theatrical currency of some of Shakespeare's remains, whether unaltered like *Othello* ('an Admirable Tragedy ... and is still an Entertainment at the Theatre-Royal', p. 461), or adapted to present taste like *The Tempest* ('How much this Play is now in Esteem, tho' the Foundation were *Shakespear's*, all People know', p. 463). Langbaine was equally mindful of the continued appeal of a few pieces by Fletcher and Jonson. He portrayed the former's *The Bloody Brother* as 'a Tragedy much in request', which 'notwithstanding Mr. *Rymer's* Criticisms on it, has still the good fortune to Please' (p. 207), and cited the 'extraordinary applause' with which the audience had received Buckingham's 'very much improv'd' version of *The Chances* (p. 207). Jonson's *Volpone*, he noted, 'is still in vogue at the Theatre in *Dorset-Garden*' (p. 298), and both *Bartholomew Fair* and *Everyman in his Humour* had been successfully revived since the Restoration (pp. 287–8, 290).

These were isolated triumphs. As the title-by-title survey of the triumvirate's productions made plain, the bulk of their output was now dead to the stage. Langbaine did not advocate unconditional revival; at most, he recommended that certain pieces be revised and made fit for presentation, with due credit given to the original author. Nor did he elaborate on the aesthetic merit of individual plays by Shakespeare or Fletcher. Their innate worth, he maintained, was sufficiently demonstrated by the propensity of the moderns to plunder them. Conversely, the claims of modern writers to excellence were rendered void, he argued, by their extensive reliance on old English masters and on the more recent work of foreign dramatists.

Beyond the triumvirate, whom he treated as a law unto themselves, Langbaine's hierarchy of pre-Restoration playwrights contained two more distinct levels or classes. Presided over by Shirley, Langbaine's second class included Heywood, Middleton, Chapman, Webster and others. Among 'Poets of the Third-rate', by far the most numerous, he counted writers like Nabbes, Dekker, Glapthorne, Manuche and others. Following the example of Kirkman, he decried Thomas Meriton as 'certainly the meanest *Dramatick* Writer that ever *England* produc'd' (p. 367), and placed him in an underclass of his own.

While fitting old playwrights into one class or the other, Langbaine styled himself a chronicler rather than a judge. He affected to convey inherited valuations, not to issue new ones. Having nominated Shirley as 'the Chief of the Second-rate Poets', Langbaine noted that 'by some' he 'has been thought even equal to *Fletcher* himself' (p. 474).[24] He also pointed out that Heywood's plays 'were in those Days accounted of the Second-Rate' (p. 256). When departing from received opinion, as he did by situating an obscure amateur, Cosmo Manuche, alongside professionals such as Dekker and Glapthorne, Langbaine felt that justification was required. 'If it be consider'd that our Author's Muse was *travesté en Cavileer*', he pleaded, 'that he made Writing his Diversion, and not his Business; that what he writ was not borrow'd but *propriâ Minervâ*, I hope the Criticks will allow his Plays to pass Muster amongst those of the third Rate' (p. 339). He believed that Manuche, though not an accomplished writer, deserved recognition for his invention.

By analogy with the ancients, Langbaine envisaged several orders of Restoration playwrights. Uppermost in his hierarchy were Lee, Wycherley, and Etherege. Banks and Tate were among those assigned to the second rank; Duffet to the third. These assignments were explicit. Langbaine averred that Lee's 'Dramatical Pieces ... gave him a Title to the First Rank of Poets', and remarked on how 'soft and passionately moving, are his Scenes of Love written' (p. 321). 'I may boldly reckon [Wycherley] amongst the Poets of the First Rank', he wrote, 'no Man that I know, except the excellent *Johnson*, having outdone him in Comedy' (p. 514), a ruling which implied that Shakespeare's comedies were inferior to both

Jonson's and Wycherley's. Duffet, he said, is 'An Author altogether unknown to me, but by his Writings; and by them I take him to be a Wit of the third Rate' (p. 177). Unspecified 'pitiful *Poets* of the Fourth-Rate' (p. 452) were relegated to the bottom of the scale.

Parallel to this ranking of authors was Langbaine's classification of plays. Though first-rate plays were largely those by first-rate poets, a few pieces held in utmost esteem by Langbaine were the work of little-known figures. He regarded the Dryden-Lee *Oedipus* as 'one of the best Tragedies we have extant' (p. 167), and was equally impressed by Lee's independent pieces: *Theodosius*, *The Rival Queens*, and *Mithridates*, the last of which, he said, 'may be reckon'd amongst those of the First-Rank, and will always be a Favourite of the Tender-hearted Ladies' (p. 324). But he also warmly commended the sole production of an academic amateur, William Joyner's *The Roman Empress* (1671), for being 'writ in a more Masculine, and lofty Stile than most Plays of this Age; and Terror and Compassion being the chief hinges on which he design'd his Tragedy should turn' (pp. 308–9). Langbaine's choices in comedy, too, included theatrical obscurata alongside perennial favourites. Not surprising was his celebration of Etherege's *The Man of Mode* ('as true Comedy, and the Characters as well drawn to the Life, as any Play that has been Acted since the Restoration') and *She Wou'd if She Cou'd* ('This Comedy is likewise accounted one of the first Rank', p. 187), or of Tuke's *The Adventures of Five Hours* ('One of the best Plays now extant, for Oeconomy and Contrivance', p. 505). He was more singular in his praise of Shadwell's unsuccessful *A True Widow* ('This Play I take to be as True [sic] Comedy; and the Characters and Humours to be as well drawn, as any of this Age', p. 451) or St. Serfe's *Tarugo's Wiles* ('This Comedy if not equal with those of the first Rank, yet exceeds several which pretend to the second; especially the *third* Act, which discovers the several Humours of a *Coffee-house*', p. 434).

The frame of reference for such judgements was extensive. Each play was assessed against all other plays of 'this Age', which had dawned at the Restoration. Langbaine made more local comparisons too. Indeed, he routinely looked at individual titles in the context of the author's dramatic *œuvre*. Edward Howard's *The Womens Conquest* was, according to Langbaine, 'the best Play our Author has publisht' (p. 274), and Aphra Behn's comedy, *Feign'd Curtezans*, 'One of the best she has written' (p. 20). These pronouncements did not carry the same weight. The top production of a professional writer like Behn, 'sufficiently Eminent ... for her Theatrical Performances' (p. 17), was of a different order from the foremost composition of a 'Gentleman ... who has addicted himself to the Study of Dramatick Poetry' (p. 274).

The qualitative criteria by which Langbaine judged of plays were essentially aesthetic and structural, though a few pieces attracted his censure on account of bawdy and anti-clerical sentiment. In tragedy, he favoured lofty style, adherence to dramatic decorum, and the propensity to move passions. He clearly enjoyed an occasional political allusion. His opinion that the anonymous *Edward III* 'exceed[s] most of the Plays that have been lately publisht' was not unrelated to his perception that 'in the Characters of *Tarleton*, Chancellor of *England*, and Serjeant *Etherside*, [the author] has somewhat detected the Misdemeanours of some Great Men in the last Reign' (sig. Oo5$^v$). In comedy, Langbaine prized humours and skilful handling of plot (in his nomenclature, 'Oeconomy and Contrivance'). For farce and low comedy he had little but contempt.

In contrast to his successors, who wrote after the appearance of Jeremy Collier's *A Short View of the Immorality, and Profaneness of the English Stage* (1698), Langbaine tended to eschew moral judgements. He abandoned his customary neutrality only in a handful of cases. Unruffled by the witty indecencies of Etherege or Wycherley, he nonetheless condemned the 'Libertinism' of Otway's comedies (pp. 395–6) and the 'Scurrility' of Duffet's burlesques (p. 177). He also decried Shadwell's satire of the church in *The Lancashire Witches*, with its biting portrayal of the Anglican minister, Smirk, 'for 'tis evident that ... the Clergy, are abused in that Character' (p. 447). Langbaine advised the author 'to treat serious things with due Respect; and not to make the *Pulpit* truckle to the *Stage*; or Preface a Play, with a Treatise of Religion'. '[E]very Man has his Province', he insisted, and to engage in religious controversy is not a task fit for a playwright.

Besides judging the dramatist's individual productions, Langbaine issued succinct appraisals of his or her personal talents and aptitudes. The key concept he used to denote these special faculties was 'Genius', always spelled with a capital 'G'. 'His Genius', he wrote of Dryden, 'seems to me to incline to Tragedy and Satyr, rather than Comedy: and methinks he writes much better in *Heroicks*, than in *blank Verse*' (p. 131). By contrast, he thought Crowne's 'Genius ... fittest for Comedy; tho' possibly his Tragedies are no ways contemptible' (p. 90). Banks's *forte* was, in his view,

serious drama: 'His Genius lays [sic] wholly to Tragedy' (p. 7).
Through a different choice of words in his entry on Settle – 'An
Author ... whose *Muse* is chiefly addicted to Tragedy' (p. 439)[25] –
Langbaine conveyed this writer's lack of the innate gift which
makes for a good tragedian. Others of lesser note were similarly
dismissed. Here is Langbaine on D'Urfey: 'In my Opinion he is a
much better Ballad-maker, than *Play-wright*' (p. 179); on Duffet:
'One whose Fancy leads him rather to Low-Comedy, and Farce,
than Heroic Poetry' (p. 177); on Flecknoe: 'he had a greater
propensity to Riming, then a Genius to Poetry' (p. 199).

Langbaine's various rankings purported to measure and reflect
artistic merit. His purely aesthetic valuations, however, were complicated and qualified by his assessment of the playwright's invention and the extent to which he or she relied on sources. To judge a
play, he reasoned, is distinct from judging a playwright. For the
play may be excellent, but the individual named on the title-page
may not deserve all or even part of the credit. Thomas D'Urfey, for
example, 'is accounted by some for an Admirable Poet, but it is by
those who are not acquainted much with Authors, and therefore
deceiv'd by Appearances, taking that for his own Wit, which he
only borrows from Others' (p. 179). Likewise, Edward Ravenscroft
'with the Vulgar passes for a Writer: tho' I hope he will pardon me,
if I rather stile him in the Number of Wit-Collectors; for I cannot
allow all the Wit in his Plays to be his own' (p. 417). John Leonard
was for Langbaine no more than 'A Confident Plagiary, whom I
disdain to stile an Author' (p. 319). Even as he acknowledged the
value of the final product, Langbaine frequently voiced reservations about the integrity of its self-styled maker. Contrariwise, he
might commend the invention of a writer for whose productions
he had slight regard. Langbaine's preoccupation with authorial
self-sufficiency destabilized the aesthetic hierarchy embodied in the
*Account*, and made a playwright's position within a given class
quite precarious.

No problems arose when his aesthetic and ethical judgements coincided. He genuinely appreciated the affective power of Lee's
tragedies which, he noted, 'have forc'd Tears from the fairest Eyes
in the World' (p. 321); and he had no objections to Lee's use of plots
from chronicles and romances. He was only slightly less impressed
by the plays of John Banks: 'if he be not accounted a Poet of the
first form, yet he bears up with his Contemporaries of the second'
(p. 7). Not having detected any thefts, Langbaine contented himself

with listing the putative sources of Banks's plays without comment. If Banks was in the upper echelon of the second class, Tate barely attained to the lower stratum. '[F]or Dramatick Poetry', Langbaine opined, 'he is not above the common Rank'. Tate's artistic ineptitude was, in Langbaine's view, matched by his proclivity toward recycling extant plays: 'generally he follows other Mens Models, and builds upon their Foundations: for of Eight Plays that are printed under his Name, Six of them owe their Original to other Pens' (p. 500). His verdict on Thomas Thompson was yet more blunt. Since anything of worth in Thompson's plays had been stolen, Langbaine dismissed him as yet 'Another Author of the meanest Rank, and a great Plagiary' (p. 503).

Most cases were less clearcut. All too often, Langbaine found, gifted dramatists appropriated heavily while mediocrities trusted to their own barren fancies. How was he to rate prolific and successful professionals such as Dryden, Shadwell, or Behn who ranged far and wide in search of usable materials? How to accommodate pathetic, if doggedly self-reliant, amateurs such as Edward Howard or the Duchess of Newcastle? Langbaine faltered. Though he might explicitly rank several of their productions against other modern plays, he did not assign any of these writers to a specific category. Even as he conceded that 'in *Epick Poetry* [Dryden] far exceeds ... most, if not all the Poets of our Age' (p. 452), Langbaine could not bring himself to designate that arch-plagiarist as a first-rate author. However much he wished to assert Shadwell's superiority as a comic writer – 'I like *His* Comedies better than Mr. *Dryden*'s; as having more Variety of Characters, and those drawn from the Life; I mean Men's Converse and Manners, and not from other Mens Ideas, copied out of their publick Writings' – Langbaine was candid enough to take notice of Shadwell's thefts: 'I cannot wholly acquit our *Present Laureat* from borrowing; his Plagiaries being in some places too bold and open to be disguised' (p. 443). He was equally conscientious in detailing Aphra Behn's debts (pp. 18–22). Yet he was convinced that Behn 'has borrow'd from others Stores, rather of Choice than for want of a fond [sic] of Wit of her own', since, he said, 'whatever she borrows she improves' (p. 18). By contrast, his tentative plea on behalf of the 'Admirable Dutchess' whose 'Language and Plots ... are all her own' (pp. 390–1) was singularly unconvincing.

Langbaine's primary concern was that the language of a play be new. He was ready, as we have seen, to accept the lifting of a story from another genre, such as a novel, a romance or a history (p. 162). He nevertheless believed that inventing one was preferable. 'I know not any One Play, whose Plot may be said to be the Product of Mr. *Dryden*'s own Brain' (p. 148), he complained. As his appraisal of the Duchess of Newcastle shows, Langbaine knew that to think up a plot was not necessarily to write a good play. The ultimate achievement and test of a writer, he thought, is to produce plays that are both aesthetically pleasing and entirely original in their plots and words. No dramatist treated in the *Account*, whether ancient or modern, fully satisfied Langbaine's demands.

In 1699 Charles Gildon revised and expanded *An Account of the English Dramatick Poets*. He published this new compilation under the title *The Lives and Characters of the English Dramatick Poets*. Gildon challenged and discarded a number of Langbaine's valuations. He accused his predecessor of personal bias ('Mr. *Langbain* seems ... seldom to regard the Merit of the Person he reflects upon')26 and lack of critical discrimination ('he seems ... to have had little or no Taste of Dramatick Poetry'). He also contested the ranking of authors and plays built into the *Account*, and claimed that 'a Stranger to our Stage wou'd from [Langbaine's] Recommendation make a very odd and ridiculous Collection of our English Plays' (sig. A6v).

Langbaine, we have seen, had taken care to distinguish his rating of pre-Restoration playwrights from the modern canon. Even as he included Shirley or Heywood in the second rank of poets, he made clear that they were so classed only *vis-à-vis* their contemporaries. His apology for the triumvirate was a sign of their loss of reputation rather than continued ascendency. Gildon misunderstood the separation between the two hierarchies implicit in the *Account*, and assumed that Langbaine had sought to elevate the ancients at the expense of the moderns. 'Mr. *Langbain* ... often commends, *Shirley*, *Heywood*, *&c.* and will scarce allow Mr. *Dryden* a Poet', he complained, 'whereas the former have left us no Piece that bears any Proportion to the latter' (sig. A6v). His own sketches on older writers were brief and matter-of-fact, if not downright dismissive.27 Less prone to defer to the past than Langbaine, he sided firmly with the moderns.

The survival of old drama in active repertory was for Gildon a measure of its canonicity. 'Their Comedies are much the best', he observed in the entry on Beaumont and Fletcher, 'yet of them take away five or six, and they will not bear Acting, scarce reading by a nice Judge' (p. 57). His contempt for these writers was manifestly due to the lapse of so many of their plays from the repertory. The survival-rate of Jonson's productions was, by Gildon's computation, even lower (pp. 77–81). If he was less disparaging about Shakespeare, this was because some of his plays remained in stock throughout the Restoration while others proved enduringly popular when 'reviv'd with Alterations', like Shadwell's *Timon*. The latter, Gildon noted with visible respect, was 'for a few Years past, as often acted at the Theatre Royal, as any Tragedy I know' (p. 129).

Gildon was readier than Langbaine to take success on the stage and continued public approbation as evidence of quality. '[T]ho' a bad Play may take', he wrote, 'yet we hear very few Instances that a good one miscarried' (p. 121). He was convinced that spectators, if left to themselves, were perfectly able to appreciate what they saw. When an undeserving piece succeeded, he maintained, the fairness of theatrical reception was likely to have been vitiated by advance publicity which the author had secured through his personal contacts and connections.[28]

Gildon was also more explicit about his evaluative criteria. The aesthetic standards he propounded were not very different from Langbaine's; the one notable discrepancy was his preference for wit over humour in comedy. Nor was he unmindful of the importance of invention and novelty.[29] '[T]he Duty of this Undertaking', he observed in his account of Congreve, 'and the Foundation I build on, obliges me to examine what he may have borrowed from others' (p. 24). Gildon sought to locate the sources of all plays which appeared since the publication of the *Account*, and in each case to determine the degree of verbal and thematic debt. Like Langbaine, he commended authors who admitted their borrowings, and who transformed and enriched the borrowed matter. Gildon quoted in full Southerne's grateful acknowledgement that he had drawn the plot of his tragedy, *Oroonoko* (1696), from Mrs Behn's novel of the same title, 'because 'tis very uncommon with Authors to speak well of those they borrow from in their Writings'. Gildon considered *Oroonoko* an exemplary dramatization of a novel in terms of its artistic and structural autonomy. '[T]he Play had not its mighty Success without an innate Excellence', he opined, and 'the necessary regularities a Dramatick Poet is obliged to observe, has [sic]

left many Beauties in the Novel, which our Author cou'd not transfer to his Poem' (p. 136).

What set Gildon apart from the earlier commentator was his
concern about the moral function of drama. Adopting the concept
from Rymer, he asserted that 'Poetick Justice … ought ever to be
observed in all Plays' (p. 91). The lesson imparted through the
outcome of the action should be fortified, he thought, by aptly
drawn passions. To elicit excessive sympathy for the culprit was,
according to Gildon, a risky enterprise since the emotion might
detract from, or even subvert, the edifying message. '[T]ho' it is an
extraordinary thing to make us pity the Guilty, (which I know none
but *Otway* could do)', he wrote in his appraisal of Ravenscroft's *The
Italian Husband*, 'yet the Audience must be very Compassionate, to
pity so willing an Adultery as this' (p. 116).[30] Gildon took exception
to Dryden's representation of the 'famous patterns of unlawful
love', Antony and Cleopatra, on similar grounds.[31] '*All for Love*', he
said, 'were it not for the false *Moral*, wou'd be a Masterpiece that
few of the Ancients or Moderns ever equal'd' (sig. A6v). If Dryden's
artistic achievement is somewhat compromised by the 'false *Moral*'
of his tragedy, the improbable climax of Colley Cibber's *Love's Last
Shift*, when Loveless fails to recognize his wife Amanda after a
period of separation, is, for Gildon, 'abundantly outweigh[ed]' by
'the Excellent Moral that flows from it' (p. 20).

These moralizing professions had little or no effect on the canon
of modern English drama constructed in *Lives and Characters*. The
most highly rated tragedians, Dryden, Otway and Lee, were far
from model adherents to the principle of poetic justice. Among
comic writers, Gildon accorded priority to Etherege, Wycherley,
and Vanbrugh. The title of 'Master of Farce' went to Thomas
D'Urfey, one of the smuttiest writers in the period (p. 48).

Gildon identified what he considered to be the best English
tragedies in his discussion of Congreve's *The Mourning Bride*.
Although he agreed that this play, which 'had the greatest Success,
not only of all Mr. *Congreve*'s, but indeed of all the Plays that ever I
can remember on the English Stage', deserved 'a Place in the first
Form' (p. 23), Gildon added the following proviso:

> … yet I can never prefer it to the *All for Love* of Mr. *Dryden*, *The
> Orphan*, and *Venice Preserv'd* of Mr. Otway, or the *Lucius Junius
> Brutus* of Mr. Lee, either in true Art in the Contrivance and
> Conduct of the Plot; or the Choice and Delineation of the

Characters for the true End of Tragedy, *Pitty* and *Terror*; or the *true* and *natural Movement* of the Passions, in which Particular, none of the Ancients (I was going to say equal'd, but I will boldly say) surpass'd our English dead Bards in those Plays, and our living Poet in this of his that I have mention'd. Or the *Diction*, either in regard to its *Propriety, Clearness, Beauty, Nobleness,* or *Variety.* (pp. 23–4)

This proud assertion of native achievement in tragedy was matched by Gildon's appraisal of comic drama. Wycherley, he declared, 'excell'd all Writers in all Languages, in Comedy' (p. 150). More recently, Vanbrugh's productions 'have got him the Preference to all our Modern Writers of Comedy, since Mr. *Wycherly,* and Sir. *George Etheridge* have left the Stage' (p. 142). The encomium on Vanbrugh was profuse. Gildon praised his wit, spirited dialogue, lively action and characters. Vanbrugh's comedies are not only superb stage vehicles, he claimed; they are also good literature, for the author 'puts Folly into such a Light, that it is as diverting to the Reader as Spectator' (p. 143).

In Gildon there is no 'anxiety of influence', no sense that classical or older English drama is in any way superior to the plays written since the Restoration. Neither Shakespeare nor Jonson nor 'Fletcher' receives special treatment; the overriding impression is that Dryden, Lee, Otway, Wycherley and other contemporary playwrights are not only as good but better. Notwithstanding his attempted defence of the triumvirate and occasional praise of minor Renaissance writers, Langbaine's canon had been at core a modern one; Gildon's was more fully so.[32]

I have, in essence, been analysing the 'literary' canon as recorded in publication history and play catalogues. Granting the difficulties imposed by close to nonexistent performance records prior to about 1703, we must ask to what extent the 'literary' canon mirrors or contradicts the playhouse repertory. One useful and practicable test is to look at those plays which are known to have received at least ten performances between 1700 and 1711. Only a dozen pre-1642 plays meet this test.[33] Three unaltered plays by Shakespeare qualify (*Hamlet,* which received 37 performances; *1 Henry IV,* 19; *Othello,* 19); four of Jonson's plays received between 13 and 24 performances; three plays by 'Fletcher' were shown from 13 to 20 times.

The total number of performances of these popular Renaissance plays is 253. They contrast with 32 modern classics which received 654 performances, the most popular of them being Farquhar's *The Recruiting Officer* at 55. Only 14 plays by living and active authors achieved ten performances or more, the total coming to 284 performances. Seven adaptations from 'Fletcher' and Shakespeare enjoyed a total of 159 nights, the most popular of them being Davenant's alteration of *Macbeth*. My point here is simple: the theatrical canon of *c*. 1710, though quite different in content from the 'literary' canon to be deduced from Langbaine or Gildon, projects a very similar pattern. A relatively small number of pre-1642 plays appear, and only two of them are by any writer other than the triumvirate of wit.[34] Shakespeare is an important presence on the stage, but on the basis of only three plays (together with four alterations, three of them radical). Jonson is at least as canonical as Shakespeare; 'Fletcher' is much less visible. But for a regular play-goer of the first decade of the eighteenth century, Dryden, Cibber, Shadwell and Vanbrugh are more conspicuous a feature of the repertory than Shakespeare. And Farquhar, with 106 performances of three celebrated plays, was yet more visible.[35] Obviously performance influences publication; likewise publication can influence performance. But the 'literary' canon does not simply reflect performance history. Wycherley makes a good example: his critical reputation stood high, but between 1700 and 1711 we find only five known performances of *The Country Wife* and nine of *The Plain Dealer*. Plays may be revived because they are good vehicles for performers (which accounts, I suspect, for the 30 recorded performances of Dryden's *The Spanish Fryar*). What creates 'literary' reputation is harder to judge. At all events, the slowness with which more than a few plays by Shakespeare entered the repertory between 1700 and 1740 is powerful evidence of the degree to which offerings in the theatre remained independent of critical evaluations. We are, I believe, justified in concluding that the 'literary' canon was only tangentially influenced by popularity in the theatre. A more rewarding subject than the ultimately unresolvable question of 'influence' is the correspondence that can be seen between 'literary' and theatrical canons: the critical hierarchy of plays and authors is tilted far more in favour of contemporary work than one might expect. Shakespeare is far from a towering and dominant figure prior to the appearance of the Rowe edition in 1709, and not much more so for a good many years after that. As

Bate, Dobson, Hume and others have argued, the forces that created the Bard were nugatory until the 1720s and only began to achieve major influence in the 1730s. Accustomed to obeisance to Shakespeare, modern scholars have been slow to acknowledge the degree to which late seventeenth- and early eighteenth-century critics had faith in the refinement of culture and believed that, great as Shakespeare, 'Fletcher', and Jonson might be, they could be surpassed. A strong sense of hierarchy does indeed inform the dramatic catalogues published after the Restoration. Yet it is by no means a hierarchy that privileges the 'Gyant Race ... before the Flood'. Patriotic sentiment breeds reverential statements about the triumvirate of wit, but the 'literary' canon of the time implies quite different valuations of English playwrights. To make sense of the state of drama at the beginning of the eighteenth century, one must confront the surprising comprehensiveness and modernity of the dramatic canon.

## NOTES

1. *Thesaurus Dramaticus. Containing all the Celebrated Passages, Soliloquies, Similies, Descriptions, and Other Poetical Beauties in the Body of English Plays, Antient and Modern*, 2 vols (London, 1724), Preface, I, iii–iv.

2. See Gary Taylor, *Reinventing Shakespeare: A Cultural History from the Restoration to the Present* (New York, 1989), pp. 27–33; Margreta de Grazia, *Shakespeare Verbatim: The Reproduction of Authenticity and the 1790 Apparatus* (Oxford, 1991), pp. 32–48; Michael Dobson, *The Making of the National Poet: Shakespeare, Adaptation and Authorship, 1660–1769* (Oxford, 1992), pp. 29–30. Jonson, Shakespeare and Fletcher were described as 'the Triumvirate of wit' by Sir John Denham in the commendatory poem which he prefaced to the Beaumont and Fletcher folio of 1647. Shakespeare embodied Nature, Jonson Art, while Fletcher's work exemplified a perfect blending of Nature and Art ('On Mr John Fletcher's Workes', in *Comedies and Tragedies* (London, 1647), sig. b1ᵛ).

3. Jonathan Bate, *Shakespearean Constitutions: Politics, Theatre, Criticism, 1730–1830* (Oxford, 1989), pp. 22–7; Dobson, *Making of the National Poet*, pp. 134–222. For a valuable reassessment, from an angle different from mine, of the status of Shakespeare in the early eighteenth century, see Robert D. Hume, 'Before the Bard: "Shakespeare" in Early Eighteenth-Century London', *ELH*, 64 (1997), 41–75.

4. John Dryden, 'To my Dear Friend Mr. Congreve, On His Comedy, call'd, *The Double-Dealer*', in *The Works of John Dryden*, ed. E. N. Hooker et al., 20 vols (Berkeley, 1956–), IV, 432, l. 5.

5. Though useful as a close reading, Howard D. Weinbrot's chapter on Dryden's *Essay* in *Britannia's Issue: The Rise of British Literature from Dryden to Ossian* (Cambridge, 1993) does not address the change of attitude towards native, foreign and classical drama that occurred in the decades following the *Essay*'s appearance.

6. Some of these collections were reissued and/or reprinted. Orrery's two folio volumes of 1668 and 1669 respectively came to be marketed as a single item: a nonce collection of *Four New Plays* (1670). With the addition of *Guzman* (1693) and *Herod the Great* (1694), Orrery's *Four New Plays* were metamorphosed into *Six Plays* in 1694 (see Appendix B of *The Dramatic Works of Roger Boyle, Earl of Orrery*, ed. William Smith Clark II, 2 vols (Cambridge, MA, 1937), II, 954–62). Howard's folio too was reprinted. It was redone as *Five New Plays* in 1692 (*The Great Favourite* was the fifth 'new' play). *The Gentleman's Journal* for May of that year carried an advance notice of the edition: 'Sir *Robert Howard*'s Plays, which have been so scarce, are reprinting' (p. 25). In 1700 the same sheets were re-issued as 'The Second Edition Corrected' (see Montague Summers, *A Bibliography of the Restoration Drama* (New York, 1935, rpt. 1970), p. 79).

7. For a comprehensive survey of the publication of Shakespeare's work in the eighteenth century see H. L. Ford, *Shakespeare, 1700–1740: A Collation of the Editions and Separate Plays with Some Account of T. Johnson and R. Walker* (Oxford, 1935, rpt. 1968).

8. Two distinct collections of Vanbrugh appeared in 1719.

9. My calculations are based on the Eighteenth-Century Short-Title Catalogue available on CD-ROM in the Bodleian Library.

10. See *A True, perfect, and exact Catalogue of all the Comedies, Tragedies, Tragi-Comedies ... that were ever yet printed and published, till this present year 1661*, which was bound with copies of the second impression of *Tom Tyler and His Wife* (London, 1661). For a general bibliography of play catalogues see Carl J. Stratman, *Dramatic Play Lists, 1591–1963* (New York, 1966).

11. See his 'Advertisement to the Reader': 'Although I took care and Pains in my last Catalogue to place the Names in some methodical manner, yet I have now proceeded further in a better method, having thus placed them. First, I begin with *Shakespear*, who hath in all written forty eight. Then *Beaumont* and *Fletcher* fifty two, *Johnson* fifty, *Shirley* thirty eight, *Heywood* twenty five, *Middleton* and *Rowley* twenty seven, *Massenger* sixteen, *Chapman* seventeen, *Brome* seventeen, and *D'Avenant* fourteen; so that these ten have written in all, 304. The rest have every one written under ten in number, and therefore I pass them as they were in the old Catalogue, and I place all the new ones last' (*A True, perfect, and exact Catalogue of all the Comedies, Tragedies, Tragi-Comedies ... that were ever yet Printed and Published, till this present year 1671*, appended to John Dancer's translation of Pierre Corneille's *Nicomede. A Tragi-Comedy* (London, 1671), p. 16). On Kirkman's career see R. C. Bald, 'Francis Kirkman, Bookseller and Author', *Modern Philology*, 41 (1943), 17–32; and Strickland Gibson, 'A Bibliography of Francis Kirkman with his Prefaces, Dedications, and Commendations

(1652–1680)', *Oxford Bibliographical Society Publications*, New Series, 1 (1947 [1949]), 47–148.

12. 'An Advertisement to the Reader', in *A True, perfect, and exact Catalogue* (1671), p. 16.
13. *Theatrum Poetarum, or A Compleat Collection of the Poets, Especially The most Eminent, of all Ages* (London, 1675), sig. *4r.
14. On Phillips' methods in compiling *Theatrum Poetarum*, especially his misuse of reference works, see Sanford Golding, 'The Sources of *The Theatrum Poetarum*', *PMLA*, 76 (1961), 48–53.
15. For a general discussion of Winstanley's borrowings from Phillips, see William Riley Parker, 'Winstanley's *Lives*: An Appraisal', *Modern Language Quarterly*, 6 (1945), 313–18; and his Introduction to a facsimile edition of *The Lives Of the most Famous English Poets (1687) by William Winstanley* (Gainesville, FL, 1963), pp. v–viii.
16. *The Lives Of the most Famous English Poets, or The Honour of Parnassus* (London, 1687), sig. A2v.
17. *Momus Triumphans: or, The Plagiaries of the English Stage* (London, 1688), Preface, sig. a3v.
18. For those well-versed in foreign tongues, Langbaine adds a more challenging reading-list which includes Vossius, Heinsius, Scaliger, Plutarch, Athenaeus, Cinthio, Castelvetro, Lope de Vega, Corneille and Menadière.
19. See Paulina Kewes, 'Gerard Langbaine's "View of *Plagiaries*": The Rhetoric of Dramatic Appropriation in the Restoration', *The Review of English Studies*, n.s. 48 (1997), 2–18.
20. For instance, Behn's *Emperour of the Moon* was glossed as 'Stollen from *Harlequin, Emperur [sic] dans le Monde de la Lune*' (p. 3n).
21. *An Account of the English Dramatick Poets* (Oxford, 1691), p. 202.
22. He considered Charles Cotton's version of Corneille's *Horace* at least as good as the one supplied by Katherine Philips and far better than Sir William Lower's (p. 75).
23. He thought that John Lacy's *The Dumb Lady* was an improvement upon Molière's *Médecin malgré lui* (p. 318), and maintained that Thomas Jevon's farce, *The Devil of a Wife*, 'If compar'd with our *French* Farces so frequent on our *English* Stage ... may deserve the Preheminence' (p. 280).
24. Cf. Phillips, *Theatrum Poetarum*, p. 80, second pagination.
25. This phrase was subsequently inserted by Anthony à Wood into his entry on Settle in *Athenae Oxonienses, An Exact History of All the Writers and Bishops Who Have Had Their Education in the University of Oxford*, ed. Philip Bliss, 5 vols (London, 1813–20), IV, 684.
26. Gildon repeatedly mocked Langbaine's 'furious Tender for Quality' (*The Lives and Characters of the English Dramatick Poets* [London, 1699], p. 177).
27. See, for instance, the entries on Heywood (p. 70) and on Shirley (p. 131).
28. See his jaundiced accounts of such publicity which ensured the success of plays by Cibber (p. 20) and Congreve (p. 22). Twenty years later, in his proposal for a Royal Academy, Gildon advocated that 'No

Play … be acted whose Author is known before; because Party and Interest else may give a Run to a bad Play, or stifle a good one' (*The Post-Man Robb'd of his Mail: or, The Packet broke open* [London, 1719], p. 335).

29. See, for instance, his derisive review of *The Novelty* (1697), a five-act hybrid of old and new pieces put together by Peter Motteux (p. 101).

30. Gildon here questions Ravenscroft's fulfilment of his aim as expressed by his mouthpiece, the Poet, in 'The Prælude' to the play: 'The great design being to bring a guilty person to be pity'd in her circumstances' (*The Italian Husband. A Tragedy* [London, 1698], sig. A3r).

31. See Dryden's Preface, where he holds up 'the excellency of the Moral' (*Works*, XIII, 10).

32. This modern bias was firmly in place twenty years later when Giles Jacob brought out *The Poetical Register: or, The Lives and Characters of the English Dramatick Poets* (1719), for which living authors such as Congreve and Granville provided their own biographical sketches.

33. I have made my performance counts from the draft calendar for the new version of *The London Stage, 1660–1800*, Part 2: 1700–1729, ed. Judith Milhous and Robert D. Hume (printout on deposit in the Bodleian Library).

34. Brome's *The Jovial Crew* (17) and *The Northern Lass* (29).

35. At the same time, the publication of Farquhar's plays was booming. For a review of the popularity of Farquhar and other turn-of-the-century playwrights later in the period see Shirley Strum Kenny, 'Perennial Favorites: Congreve, Vanbrugh, Cibber, Farquhar, and Steele', *Modern Philology*, 73 (1976), S4–S11.

# 10

# Friends or Lovers? Sensitivity to Homosexual Implications in Adaptations of Shakespeare, 1640–1701[1]

## Paul Hammond

On 1 July 1663 Samuel Pepys recorded in his diary:

> Sir J. Mennes and Mr. Batten both say that buggery is now almost grown as common among our gallants as in Italy, and that the very pages of the town begin to complain of their masters for it. But blessed be God, I do not to this day know what is the meaning of this sin, nor which is the agent nor which the patient.[2]

Pepys's ignorance about the meaning of 'buggery' may strike us as endearingly naïve, but a version of his puzzlement is current today as scholars seek to understand the meaning of sexual relations between men in the early modern period. Our own ignorance concerns the ways in which homosexual[3] relationships were understood and represented within the epistemological structures (and therefore also the ideological and political structures) of seventeenth century England. Part of the problem for modern interpreters is that homoerotic desire is rarely made articulate unambiguously in texts from this period, and instead often speaks the same language as passionate friendship. At a time when the death penalty was in force for sodomy, it was obviously expedient for writers to deploy various kinds of indefinition, using a language which permitted multiple interpretations and allowed scope for denying dangerous constructions. But it also seems likely that distinctions between friendly and erotic feelings were not always required, and social relations between men could be coloured by a warmth of affection and expression which in later periods might be interpreted as improper. In such circumstances it is difficult enough to understand the representation of homoerotic desire in Renaissance texts and its relation to homosocial[4] feeling; it is doubly difficult to understand the cultural change which took place during the seventeenth century which resulted in the emergence of an urban homosexual subculture by around 1700. Moreover, it is far from clear that 'cultural change' is an appropriate term for alterations in sensibilities, practices and texts which may not have been part of a coherent culture: homoerotic desire inhabited other discourses (the vocabularies and narratives of male friendship, or of heterosexual encounters) in opportunistic and discontinuous ways, so that individual readers often selected meanings from among a range of possibilities or made readings at a tangent to the signals provided by the texts. One might, for example, have read Shakespeare's *Sonnets* as expressing passionate homosexual love, although that is by no means the only reading which they permit; or have taken homoerotic pleasure in Shakespeare's description of the young male body in *Venus and Adonis*, so turning a narrative of heterosexual desire into a series of discontinuous opportunities for homoerotic pleasure. Discontinuity seems to have been crucial, for it was the capacity of writers and readers to refuse definition that created and protected the textual spaces in which homoerotic pleasure became possible. The task, then, of writing a narrative of the changing representation of homoerotic desire in the seventeenth century may be impossible, but some purchase on the problem may be obtained by examining how texts from the Renaissance became unacceptable to subsequent generations: in so doing we would be allowing writers' sensitivities to the implications of language and incident to alert us to changes in the social perception of desire between men.

According to the map of homosexual relations in early modern England which has been drawn by historians and literary critics, there is a marked contrast between the period *circa* 1600 and the period *circa* 1700.[5] Alan Bray, in his pioneering book *Homosexuality in Renaissance England*, argued that legal and theological discourse in the Renaissance period demonized sexual relations between men as 'sodomy', which was consigned to a category of otherness and subversion: sodomites were bracketed with Jesuits, Spanish spies and werewolves as agents of social and moral subversion. This way of thinking provided no resources for self-definition, for a man who enjoyed sex with other men would hardly place himself in such a category. Nor did it speak of erotic desire, only of immoral acts. Sodomy was part of the shadow-side of human existence, a sign of moral depravity and alienation from God, an activity of which anyone might be capable if only they were sufficiently depraved. According to Bray, sexual relations between men were nevertheless common, but only became visible as 'sodomy', attracting that label, when some political or social pressure shifted the way in which they were seen: for example, a close friendship between powerful courtiers who shared a bed might be labelled 'sodomy' if the political interests of others made that expedient. But the implication in Bray's thesis that there was a whole range of strong sexual and emotional feelings which lacked any vocabulary except the condemnatory language of officialdom does not quite ring true, and one needs to qualify his otherwise compelling argument by taking account of the work of Bruce Smith. In his valuable book *Homosexual Desire in Shakespeare's England*, Smith charts a whole repertoire of literary modes through which readers were able to explore homosexual desire: these motifs included pastorals which celebrated the love between shepherds, stories of military comradeship, cross-dressing at carnival time, the relationship of master and minion, and, finally, the subjectivity of the desiring poet fashioned in Shakespeare's *Sonnets*. This literature offered a gamut of imaginative possibilities, a range of social and erotic roles which a reader might try out in the private world of his imagination. It offered a world of free play, with the possibility of discontinuous identity, resources for temporary and shifting modes of self-definition. For the most part these texts invite and satisfy a desiring homoerotic gaze which is part of a continuum of masculine emotional interests, creating textual spaces for homoerotic pleasure within works which principally satisfy homosocial and heterosexual interests. What these texts do not invite the reader to do is to label himself as a man with exclusive or unusual sexual preferences.

The late seventeenth and early eighteenth centuries, by contrast, have been identified as the point when homosexual self-definition began to take place through an emerging subculture, in clubs and meeting houses which permitted the private and collective exploration of sexual role-playing, cross-dressing, parodic rituals and specialized slang. These 'molly houses' were secret establishments, but their existence was known, and observers remarked with alarm on the contrast between some men's behaviour in the public, social world and their activities in private. Thus secrecy shared between men came to have 'sodomy' as one of its possible significances. Alan Bray's book began to map this subculture, and his work has been extended by Rictor Norton in *Mother Clap's Molly House*, and by other social historians. But this leaves the perplexing question of how this later culture could have arisen from the former: how a Renaissance world of polymorphous male sexuality, in which sodomy was demonized and occasionally punished, but where varieties of homoerotic texts flourished, gave way to the eighteenth-century world of homosexual self-definition and even a limited degree of communal self-assertion. This is too large and intricate a topic to be tackled in one essay, but an approach to the problem suggests itself. If we set some of Shakespeare's texts alongside the adaptations of them which were made in the late seventeenth and early eighteenth centuries, what can we learn about changing sensitivities in the area of relations between men? Could these texts contribute to our understanding of the larger change which the social historians have sketched?

One of the earliest signs of anxiety about homoeroticism in Shakespeare's work is the reshaping of the *Sonnets* in the generation after Shakespeare's death. First published in 1609, the *Sonnets* were reissued by the bookseller John Benson in 1640.[6] It is well known that Benson rearranged the poems, ran several sonnets together to form new poems, gave them titles which referred to the poet's mistress, and altered the wording in several places to make the poems address a female lover. Some of the new titles, such as 'Love-sicke' (added to sonnets 80–1), or 'A good construction of his Loves unkindnesse' (sonnet 120), or 'An intreatie for her acceptance' (sonnet 125), implicitly create miniature narratives from among the recognizable scenarios of heterosexual love and courtship, whereas in their original form the *Sonnets* had largely eschewed a legible narrative sequence, and had instead presented readers with various forms of discontinuity: the *Sonnets* as printed in 1609 never quite let us see consequences and conclusions, and such a concern to avoid narrative connection and closure is an understandable caution if writing of homoerotic desire, whose ends must at this period elude representation. Other of Benson's titles present the sonnets as poems of unambiguous friendship, as in 'The

benefit of Friendship' (sonnets 30–2) or 'Two faithfull friends'
(sonnets 46–7). Such explicit references to friendship serve to define
and contain the otherwise fluid meanings of the words 'friend',
'love' and 'lover' which occur, for instance, in sonnets 30–2:

> Then can I drowne an eye (vn-vs'd to flow)
> For precious friends hid in deaths dateles night,
> And weepe a fresh loues long since canceld woe...
>> But if the while I thinke on thee (deare friend)
>> All losses are restord, and sorrowes end.

> (30. 5–7, 13–14; 1609 text)

> Thou art the graue where buried loue doth liue,
> Hung with the trophies of my louers gon...

> (31. 9–10; 1609 text)

> These poore rude lines of thy deceased Louer...
> Reserue them for my loue, not for their rime...
> Oh then voutsafe me but this louing thought...

> (32. 4, 7, 9; 1609 text)

By labelling these poems as articulating 'The benefit of friendship',
Benson ensures that their usages of 'love' are understood to refer
not to passionate erotic feelings but to that exchange of benefits
between male friends which is not merely acceptable and
profitable, but necessary for the smooth running of the social order.

Textual alterations also limited and redefined the feelings: in
sonnet 101 Benson prints:

> Excuse not silence so, for't lies in thee,
> To make her much out-live a gilded tombe:
> And to be prais'd of ages yet to be.
>> Then doe thy office muse, I teach thee how,
>> To make her seeme long hence, as she showes now.

Benson has 'her' and 'she' where the original *Shake-speares Sonnets*
had printed 'him' and 'he'. In another case, where the 1609 edition
had referred to the addressee as 'sweet boy' (sonnet 108. 5) the 1640

edition changes this to 'sweet-love'. In sonnet 104 the male 'faire friend' of 1609 becomes the implicitly female 'faire love' of 1640.

We might pause over Benson's alteration of 'friend' to 'love'. The young man of the *Sonnets* is generally referred to by modern critics as the 'friend', but this is often done in order implicitly to remove any suggestion that the passionate relationship described in the *Sonnets* could be thought of as homoerotic. We are told that Renaissance friendships between men were often passionate and deployed a passionate vocabulary – with the implication that all such passionate language therefore points only to non-sexual friendship. Leaving aside the lack of logic in this argument, we may note the dubious assumptions that erotic desire plays no part in male friendship, and that the distinction between manly friendship and homosexual desire is clear. In the case of the *Sonnets* there is a further difficulty in maintaining such an insistence on simple friendship. Renaissance ideals of male friendship drew upon the classical (particularly the Ciceronian) model which expected these bonds to be between men who were roughly equal in social stand-ing, who would share their goods, and would enjoy a relationship of reciprocity and trust. But it is remarkable that in all the areas where this ideal would require stability, the *Sonnets* register insta-bility. There is a difference of age between poet and friend, and probably a difference of social status; the feelings are not reciprocal, or at least not reciprocated consistently or in their intensity; the ex-changes of gifts between the two (far from being signs of equality and security in friendship) are occasions of anxiety and signs of an uncertainty which is not only emotional but even existential: the friend's apparent theft of the poet's mistress is rewritten as an ex-change of gifts between the three, but this triangular relationship throws up searing anxieties about the stability of the poet's 'self', a self which in turn becomes part of the traffic between the two men (sonnets 133–6). The *Sonnets* are almost an extended definition of what classic Renaissance friendship was *not*.

Benson was right to be sensitive about the possible implications of 'friend', and I should like to sketch briefly the semantic field which this word occupies in Renaissance usage by citing some examples from Shakespeare's plays. The word could be used to greet a stranger, particularly a social inferior, as Viola greets the Clown in *Twelfth Night* (III. i. 1). It could mean 'relation' (*OED* 3): a lady in *The Two Gentlemen of Verona* (III. i. 106–7) has been promised in marriage 'by her friends/ Vnto a youthfull Gentleman'. It could mean

someone of the same sex with whom one is specially intimate, a relationship implying comradeship, loyalty and trust (the word
echoes through *The Two Gentlemen of Verona* as Valentine is betrayed
when his friend Proteus steals his girl). The word can be used
between men and women who are in love, but not yet married or
sexual partners: thus the virginal Perdita calls Florizel 'my fairest
friend' and 'my sweet friend' (*The Winter's Tale* IV. iv. 112, 128). But
'friend' can also mean 'sexual partner' (*OED* 4): Caesar says that
Antony is Cleopatra's 'Friend' (*Antony and Cleopatra* III. xii. 22); in
*Measure for Measure* Claudio 'hath got his friend with childe' (I. iv.
29); and Juliet – aching with love and longing as Romeo is forced to
leave after their first and only night together – calls him 'love, Lord,
my husband, friend' (*Romeo and Juliet* III. v. 43), where the last of
those names is evidently no anticlimax. The shifting meanings of
this word are exploited in *Othello* to mark out the shifting relationships within and between the sexes: when Iago assures Roderigo
that he is his 'friend' (I. iii. 336) the two are of similar social status,
and partners in skulduggery; but when Othello calls Iago – who is
his military subordinate – 'My Friend' (V. ii. 161) this signifies the
depth of dependency into which Othello has sunk. And when Iago
tells Othello that Desdemona has been 'naked with her friend in
bed/ An houre, or more' (IV. i. 3–4), he can be sure that Othello will
understand what sort of 'friend' to his wife Cassio has become. As
these usages map the changing bonds within the play, something
similar (though much more complex) happens in the *Sonnets*, which
exploit these ambiguities, defining and redefining the word 'friend'
through the extended play of longing, assurance and betrayal.

What of the word with which Benson replaced it, the word 'love',
or its cognate 'lover'? He presumably thought that his readers,
prompted in part by his new titles, would take the word to refer
unambiguously to a beloved woman. But the semantic range which
'lover' had in Shakespeare overlaps to a considerable degree with
that of 'friend'. It can simply mean 'well-wisher' (*OED* 1): when
Ulysses says to Achilles 'I as your louer speak' (*Troilus and Cressida*
III. iii. 207) he is only claiming to be giving him helpful advice.
More strongly, 'lover' can mean 'one in love with someone' (*OED*
2), which according to the *OED* only happens between people of
opposite sexes. In Shakespeare's comedies the mooning lover is a
familiar dramatic type. Could the word also mean 'sexual partner',
as it does today? The *OED* is innocent of this usage at any period,
but 'lover' is moving towards its modern sense in *Measure for*

*Measure*, when Isabella is told 'Your brother, and his louer haue embrac'd' (I. iv. 39) and that the lover is consequently pregnant. In this instance 'lover' might still mean only 'one who is in love' or 'one who is being courted', but it clearly has a sexual meaning when Antony says that he will run towards death 'As to a louers bed' (*Antony and Cleopatra* IV. xv. 101), or when Juliet longs for the night which will bring her first love-making with Romeo, and says: 'Louers can see to do their amorous rights/ By their owne bewties' (*Romeo and Juliet* III. ii. 8–9).

Though the choice of an appropriate sense from among these possibilities may be a reasonably simple matter in the context of routine social exchanges, or emotional relationships between men and women, the uses of 'friend' and 'lover' when applied emotively between *men* operate in a field where ambiguity may be necessary, and definition may be undesirable or even dangerous. In which of the possible senses is the young man of the *Sonnets* the poet's 'friend' (sonnets 30, 42, 104, 111, 133)? Is it the same sense in which the young man and the dark lady are 'both to each friend' (sonnet 144. 11), a phrase which occurs in an account of what is clearly a sexual relationship? When the poet refers to himself as the young man's 'louer' (sonnet 32. 4), or to the young man as his 'louer' (63. 12), in which of its possible senses is that word being used? And does it mean the same in both cases? Perhaps the poet is in love with the young man, whereas the young man is only a well-wisher towards the poet, and they are not sexual partners: but that is only one possible scenario which could be constructed out of the permutation of possible meanings, and every reader is liable to feel the nuances of 'friend' and 'lover' differently. The words 'love', 'lover' and 'friend' in the *Sonnets* have no single or unambiguous meanings, but are continually being redefined, refelt, re-imagined. The vocabulary which was available to Shakespeare for describing sexual relations between men consisted primarily of pejorative labels for particular sexual roles, such as 'sodomite', 'catamite' or 'ingle' – none of which Shakespeare used, though he did make Thersites say that Patroclus was Achilles' 'male varlot' and 'masculine whore' (*Troilus and Cressida* V. i. 15–17): Thersites is the only person in the Shakespeare canon who makes such sneering definitions. The poet who would write about bonds between men which are fashioned by reciprocal emotion and desire had only the words of another world at his disposal. The literature which exploits the multiple meanings of such words as 'friend' and 'lover', and insists upon *in*definition, may be carefully avoiding the kind of precision which would lead a man to execution; but it may also be exploring desires which found expression and acceptance within a continuum of masculine relationships. So long as sexual exchanges between men reinforced rather than endangered the social fabric, why seek to define, to label and to judge?

Shakespeare's *Sonnets* explore the half-open, half-secret domain in which a male 'friend' might also be a 'lover' in all the available senses of that word. The intricately interwoven ecstasy and desolation of the *Sonnets* are manifested partly through the poet's realization of how transitory are the appropriate senses of 'lover', as one meaning becomes applicable only to turn a moment later into a marker of betrayal or self-deception. The anxiety over the vocabulary of friendship and love which Benson displayed in his textual alterations to the *Sonnets* may signal a new need for the kind of social assurance which craves secure definition, foreshadowing a move away from a world in which masculine friendship and desire formed a continuum, towards one where the admission of sexual attraction between men was taboo, or confined to a special subculture, so requiring that expressions of ordinary male friendship be purged of any over-intense emotion or gesture which might imply a sexual motivation, and requiring that 'love' be confined safely to heterosexual relations.

In *The Merchant of Venice* Antonio is described as Bassanio's 'friend', but also as his 'deere... louer' and even his 'bosome louer' (*The Merchant of Venice* III. iv. 7, 17). Modern critics have devoted much anxious discussion to defining exactly what the bond is between Antonio and Bassanio[7] – but this is an anxiety which the play itself seems not to share. *The Merchant of Venice* may be anxious about several kinds of social and emotional relationship, but it shows no interest in categorizing the association between Antonio and Bassanio. It is a passionate friendship with emotional intimacy, but there is no indication that the relationship is unusual or needs explanation. If an erotic colouring was one of the interpretations available to Shakespeare's audience, that did not prevent the men's relationship from standing as the epitome of the male bonding which makes Venetian society work.

However, there are manifest tensions and anxieties around the Antonio/Bassanio friendship in the adaptation of the play which was made in 1701 by George Granville under the title of *The Jew of Venice*,[8] and this reworking of the story may help to bring into focus the differing sensitivities about male/male relationships which prevailed at the beginning of the seventeenth century and at the end.

The prologue to *The Jew of Venice*, contributed by Bevill Higgons, is spoken by the ghosts of Shakespeare and Dryden, who rise crowned with laurel. After the two playwrights have lamented the debased judgement of audiences who are unmoved by passion, and are 'deaf indeed to Nature and to Love', deserting true drama for French farce, 'Dryden' complains:

> *Thro' Perspectives revers'd they Nature view,*
> *Which give the Passions Images, not true.*
> Strephon *for* Strephon *sighs; and* Sapho *dies,*
> *Shot to the Soul by brighter* Sapho's *Eyes:*
> *No Wonder then their wand'ring Passions roam,*
> *And feel not Nature, whom th' have overcome.*
> *For shame let genal Love prevail agen,*
> *You Beaux Love Ladies, and you Ladies Men.*
> Shakes. *These Crimes unknown, in our less polisht Age,*
> *Now seem above Correction of the Stage;*
> *Less Heinous Faults, our Justice does pursue.*

(sig. [A]4r)

So English society in 1701 is thought to be deserting the natural in pursuit of the unnatural, and not only when it comes to theatrical preferences: men are now in love with other men, and women with other women. The ghost of Shakespeare says that such behaviour was unknown in his day, admitting to a lack of refinement, but exculpating himself, his plays and his contemporaries from any imputations of unnatural behaviour. Although the prologue says that Granville's play is not concerned to punish these deviations from nature and from 'genal' (i.e. 'genial', procreative) love, it is striking that Higgons should think it appropriate to raise this issue in relation to an adaptation of *The Merchant of Venice*. A recent essay on this adaptation claims that 'the suspicion that constant companions of the same sex who continually show signs of affection may well be homo-erotically involved never appears to have crossed Granville's mind.'[9] On the contrary, I think that this is exactly the possibility that Granville understands

and is at pains to avoid, as his play drives home a clear and em-
phatic distinction between friendship and love, and consistently
excises lines which might suggest an exclusive and possibly physical union between the two men. As he stresses in his preface, 'the
judicious Reader will observe... many Manly and Moral Graces in
the Characters and Sentiments' (sig. [A]3ʳ), and it is into the extended definition of moral manliness that Granville's play puts
much of its energy.

The adaptation opens without any trace of Antonio's melan-
choly: there is no secret here to be read or guessed at. Whereas in
Shakespeare's play he had defined his role in life as a sad one, in
Granville's version it is merely 'serious'. When he offers to help
Bassanio, he does not say (as Shakespeare's character does):

> My purse, my person, my extreamest meanes
> Lie all vnlockt to your occasions.

> (I. i. 138–9)

but:

> My Purse, my Person, my extreamest Means,
> Are all my Friend's.

> (p. 2)

In Shakespeare, what is locked away from others lies all unlocked
to Bassanio. Granville's erasure of these implications of a shared
secrecy may reflect unease about the new connotations which
secrecy shared between men was acquiring with the arrival of the
secret molly houses, while the idea that Antonio's person might 'lie
all vnlockt' to Bassanio's needs may now have acquired too clear a
sexual invitation. To avoid any doubt, Granville makes his Antonio
define friendship:

> Is this to be a Friend? With blushing Cheek,
> With down-cast Eyes, and with a faltring Tongue,
> We sue to those we doubt: Friendship is plain,
> Artless, familiar, confident and free.

> (p. 2)

Friendship is open, unblushing; to be a man of silence and secrecy would run the risk of being interpreted as a man with something unmanly to hide, perhaps like the new kind of Strephon.

Friendship involves openness in asking and in granting, but Granville carefully stresses that although Antonio may give his body for his friend, this gift has no erotic significance; instead it is an example of that generosity and benevolence which is character- istic of manly and moral virtue:

> what is a Pound of Flesh,
> What my whole Body, every Drop of Blood,
> To purchase my Friend's Quiet! Heav'n still is good
> To those who seek the Good of others...
> Of all the Joys that generous Minds receive,
> The noblest is, the God-like Power to give.

                                                    (p. 9)

If Antonio's offering of his body for Bassanio is pure benevolence, Shylock's obsession with Antonio's flesh is perhaps motivated by something more than the stereotypical malevolence of the Jewish usurer. Shylock himself protests that his proposals can 'bear no wrong/ Construction' (p. 9), thus alerting the audience to the poss- ibility that more than one construction might be placed on them. Whereas Shakespeare's Shylock simply says:

> let the forfaite
> Be nominated for an equall pound
> Of your faire flesh, to be cut off and taken
> In what part of your bodie pleaseth me.

                                                (I. iii. 147–50)

Granville's Shylock takes pleasure in contemplating which part of Antonio's body he will cut off:

> Let me see, What think you of your Nose,
> Or of an Eye —or of — a Pound of Flesh
> To be cut off, and taken from what Part
> Of your Body — I shall think fit to name.

                                                    (p. 8)

The play pauses over the possibility that the as yet unnameable part of Antonio's body represented here only by dashes is an object of Shylock's perverse sexual interest.[10] In any case, he clearly represents the opposite of Antonio and Bassanio's form of manliness.

Manliness, in Granville's view, does not require that displays of affection and emotion be suppressed, but it does require that these be carefully defined and not left open to misconstruction. When Antonio and Bassanio part for the latter to go to Belmont, Bassanio exclaims:

> One more Embrace: To those who know not Friendship
> This may appear unmanly Tenderness;
> But 'tis the frailty of the bravest Minds.

(p. 20)

For Granville there is no blurring of friendship and love, nor is there any conflict of interest between the friendship of Antonio and Bassanio on the one hand, and the love of Bassanio and Portia on the other; indeed, he is careful to stress that friendship and love are at once distinct and allied. Antonio urges Bassanio not to give 'your Heart so far away,/ As to forget your Friend' (p. 20) when courting Portia, but at the same time he urges Bassanio to make haste to Belmont. Bassanio is eager to board ship, but at the same time reluctant to leave Antonio. The friendship is entirely reciprocal and unselfish. When Antonio at a banquet proposes a toast to 'immortal Friendship', Bassanio responds with 'Let Love be next, what else should/ Follow Friendship?' (p. 12). Portia for her part sees Bassanio's concern to rescue Antonio from the consequences of the bond as a sign of those very qualities which will make him a good husband: 'as you prove,/ Your Faith in Friendship, I shall trust your Love' (p. 28).

Granville will not allow us to think that the male association between Antonio and Bassanio might have priority over the marriage of Portia and Bassanio. In Shakespeare's play, Portia and Lorenzo discuss the deep bond between the two men: Lorenzo tells Portia that she would be proud of Bassanio's prompt desertion of her in order to rescue Antonio if she knew 'How deere a louer of my Lord your husband' Antonio is: the implication seems to be that this is a man's world, understood by Lorenzo but not shared by Portia. She replies that she realizes how the two 'beare an egall yoke of loue' and that Antonio is 'the bosome louer of my Lord' (III. iv. 13, 17). But this scene in which Lorenzo and Portia discuss the primacy of the male bond is trimmed by Granville, leaving simply Portia's comment that 'I never did repent of doing good' (p. 28), so that she now shares that overriding concern for beneficence which Antonio and Bassanio have stressed in their speeches to each other: thus she is linked to them, instead of being excluded from their world.

In Shakespeare's trial scene Antonio describes himself as 'a tainted weather of the flocke' (IV. i. 113), but Granville cuts this, for he will admit nothing which suggests that Antonio is anything other than the perfect gentleman. In the adaptation, Antonio's speech of farewell to Bassanio when Shylock is about to cut out his heart omits the lines in which Shakespeare's character asks Bassanio to tell Portia how much Antonio loved him:

> Say how I lou'd you, speake me faire in death:
> And when the tale is told, bid her be iudge
> Whether *Bassanio* had not once a loue:
> Repent but you that you shall loose your friend...

> (IV. i. 272–5)

(In the Oxford and Arden editions,[11] the word 'love' here is glossed 'friend', with a cross-reference to the *Sonnets*, thus neatly saving both texts from any suspicion of impropriety.) Is there an imbalance in Antonio's phrasing, implying that he has loved Bassanio, while Bassanio has only thought of him as a friend? If so, it is not present in Granville's equivalent speech, where Antonio says 'Grieve not my Friend, that you thus lose a Friend' (p. 35): here the balanced phrasing marks out an entirely mutual friendship, in which there is no place for the word 'love', at least, not as a noun meaning 'lover'. This moment of self-sacrifice is made into a moment of total openness, for Antonio says:

> Now, do your Office,
> Cut deep enough be sure, and whet thy Knife
> With keenest Malice; for I would have my Heart
> Seen by my Friend.

> (p. 35)

His heart is to be disclosed to his friend, but this happens in a public arena for all to see. Antonio's heart evidently harbours no secrets: there is nothing suspect, embarrassing or dangerous in this male bond.

In Shakespeare, Bassanio and Gratiano both say that they would willingly sacrifice their wives so as to redeem Antonio's life. Granville cannot permit such an assertion of the male bond over the obligations of love and marriage, and cuts out these speeches, replacing them with an offer from Bassanio to die in Antonio's place. There then follows a contest between Antonio and Bassanio as to which of them is to die for the other, so that the focus is not on the primacy of male friendship over marriage, but on which of the two men is to have the opportunity to make the ultimate demonstration of friendship. Then Bassanio draws his sword to kill Shylock, and although the Duke is outraged at this violation of the court, he does admit that he admires Bassanio's virtue more than he blames his passion: thus the passion is clearly virtuous, not excessive or suspect.

At the end of the trial scene Bassanio embraces Antonio, but at the same time celebrates his love for Portia; these are the twin guarantors of his existence:

> Once more, let me embrace my Friend, welcom to Life,
> And welcome to my Arms, thou best of Men:
> Thus of my Love and of my Friend possess'd,
> With such a double Shield upon my Breast,
> Fate cannot peirce me now, securely Blest.

> (p. 38)

The play's conclusion seems to be that love and friendship are complementary, but also that successful marital love needs that solidity of trust, benevolence and reciprocity which one finds in friendship:

> Love, like a Meteor, shows a short-liv'd Blaze,
> Or treads thro' various Skies, a wond'ring Maze;
> Begot by Fancy, and by Fancy led,
> Here in a Moment, in a Moment fled:
>> But fixt by Obligations, it will last;
>> For Gratitude's the Charm that binds it fast.

> (p. 46)

This seems to be the voice of companionable marriage, founded on sentiment, reason and interest, in which the relationship of husband and wife has some of the qualities provided by male friendship. The two bonds are not merely compatible, but mutually reinforcing, and understood through reciprocal definition.

Granville's play, written at the very point when a homosexual subculture emerges in London, takes considerable pains to define the relationship between Antonio and Bassanio as friendship, and to define the meaning of friendship as mutual benevolence; it makes the relationship open to the view, avoids places of secrecy, and calls attention to how any displays of emotion or offerings of the body are sure tokens of moral manliness. In the light of the anxieties voiced so clearly in the prologue, it is hard to avoid concluding that Granville is taking great pains to remove from Shakespeare's text any emotion which in the new climate could be construed as suggesting covert homosexual bonding.[12]

One particular kind of friendship which often entails close emotional bonds is that between soldiers, and whereas Shakespeare seems to have permitted a vein of homoeroticism to colour his depiction of military comradeship, his adaptors sought to purge comradeship from any sexual implication. The principal example here is *Coriolanus* and the adaptation of it by Nahum Tate in 1682 as *The Ingratitude of a Commonwealth*.[13] Tate's handling of the meeting between Coriolanus and Aufidius alters or removes some of the lines which most suggest that there is an erotic charge to the martial bond between the two men, at least on Aufidius' side. Shakespeare's Aufidius greets Coriolanus with a speech heady with emotion and excitement:

> Let me twine
> Mine armes about that body, where against
> My grained Ash an hundred times hath broke,
> And scarr'd the Moone with splinters: heere I cleep
> The Anuile of my Sword, and do contest
> As hotly, and as Nobly with thy Loue,
> As euer in Ambitious strength, I did
> Contend against thy Valour. Know thou first,
> I lou'd the Maid I married: neuer man
> Sigh'd truer breath. But that I see thee heere
> Thou Noble thing, more dances my rapt heart,
> Then when I first my wedded Mistris saw

Bestride my Threshold. Why, thou Mars I tell thee,
We haue a Power on foote: and I had purpose
Once more to hew thy Target from thy Brawne,
Or loose mine Arme for't: Thou hast beate mee out
Twelue seuerall times, and I haue nightly since
Dreamt of encounters 'twixt thy selfe and me:
We haue beene downe together in my sleepe,
Vnbuckling Helmes, fisting each others Throat,
And wak'd halfe dead with nothing.

(IV. v. 107–27)

Here Shakespeare makes the feeling of Aufidius for Coriolanus an ecstatic fusion of enmity, rivalry, comradeship and sexual desire, but Tate removes some of the more extravagant expressions and the suggestions of erotic interest. In Tate's version the words 'Let me twine/ Mine armes about that body' become, more soberly, 'Let me embrace that Body' (p. 39). The lines in which Aufidius compares his excitement at meeting Coriolanus with his rapture on his wedding night (running from 'Know thou first...' to 'Bestride my Threshold') are removed altogether. In Shakespeare, Aufidius has repeatedly dreamt of encounters with Coriolanus, but in Tate's adaptation this obsession is played down: 'nightly' becomes 'might'ly', and 'fisting' becomes 'grasping'. When the servants are discussing Aufidius' reception of Coriolanus at the banquet, one of them comments in Shakespeare:

Our Generall himselfe makes a Mistris of him, Sanctifies himselfe with's hand, and turnes vp the white o'th'eye to his Discourse.
(IV. v. 199–202)

Tate's servant simply says, 'My Lord himself makes a very Mistress of him' (p. 41), and Tate cuts out the description which suggests that Aufidius is hanging on Coriolanus' person and words like a besotted lover. Tate implies that Aufidius has been unmanned by his over-ready reception of Coriolanus, but this is envisaged not as an effeminization of Aufidius, rather as a loss of political status and individual selfhood: Nigridius tells him that he has reduced himself 'To Less, than Man, the Shaddow of your self' (p. 42), while Aufidius himself realizes that his standing has been diminished by Coriolanus' arrival.

Tate steers away from any suggestion that Aufidius' revenge may be motivated in part by a spurned homoerotic desire for Coriolanus: instead, Tate's scenario is that Aufidius had previously been in love with Virgilia, and when he sees her again in the scene where the women plead for Rome, his desire for her is rekindled. He plans to kill Coriolanus, and then rape Virgilia:

> For soon as I've secur'd my Rivals Life,
> All stain'd i' th' Husbands Blood, I'll Force the Wife.

(p. 57)

Aufidius and Coriolanus fatally wound each other, but Tate omits the stage direction which in Shakespeare's text calls for Aufidius to stand on the body of Coriolanus – a gesture of military triumph which (given Aufidius' earlier speeches) cannot be without some erotic overtones, and which is evidently alien to Tate's purposes. When Virgilia arrives on stage she is seen to be wounded by an attempt which she has made to commit suicide in order to avoid rape. Aufidius is overcome with remorse, and dies. One could construe Aufidius' grotesque plan to rape Virgilia before the eyes of her dying husband as in part a displaced manifestation of a desire to possess Coriolanus himself, yet Tate's plot provides ample motivation for Aufidius in his renewed passion for Virgilia and his resentment at being overshadowed by Coriolanus. The homosocial bond between the two soldiers has been purged of homosexual implications, and the rivalry of Aufidius and Coriolanus has become the classic paradigmatic plot of Restoration tragedy.

So too in Thomas Otway's adaptation of *Romeo and Juliet* as *The History and Fall of Caius Marius* (1680),[14] much of the possibly homoerotic bawdy in which Mercutio teases Romeo about his sexual activities has been removed. Mercutio has been transformed into a military leader who fears that the Romeo figure has turned effeminate – in the seventeenth-century sense that his passion for women has led him to neglect his manly public duty. In Otway's adaptation the bond between the equivalents of Mercutio and Romeo is purged of any homoerotic element, so that the problem of manliness can be represented in its familiar Restoration form as a need to reconcile the demands of marital passion and martial responsibilities. The Restoration counterparts of Aufidius and Mercutio can be acceptable examples of soldierly masculinity only if they show no erotic interest in the bodies of other soldiers.

A comparable sensitivity can be seen at work in Dryden's *Troilus and Cressida* (1679).[15] In the second scene of Shakespeare's play, Pandarus appraises the military and sexual prowess of the Trojan warriors as they pass over the stage, and although he is doing this for the benefit of Cressida there is a homoerotic undertow to this sexually aware gaze of male on male. Dryden does not remove this scene, but he does modify it in some details: Aeneas is no longer 'one of the flowers of Troy' (I. ii. 183) but, more robustly, 'a swinger' (I. ii. 176). Pandarus no longer vows that he could 'liue and die i' th' eyes of *Troylus*' (I. ii. 239–40), like the protagonist of an Elizabethan sonnet sequence pining for a glance from his mistress; instead, in Dryden's version he claims that he 'cou'd live and dye with *Troilus*' (I. ii. 225), like a comrade in battle.

There is also a marked difference in the way that Shakespeare and Dryden imagine the relationship of Achilles and Patroclus. In Shakespeare, Thersites explicitly accuses Patroclus of being Achilles' sexual partner:

> *Thersites*... . thou art thought to be *Achilles* male varlot.
> *Patroclus*. Male varlot you rogue whats that.
> *Thersites*. Why his masculine whore.
>
> (V. i. 15–17)

It is remarkable that Shakespeare's play neither confirms nor refutes this suggestion, leaving it as a possibility, an imaginable element in this comradely association. But it is not imaginable to Dryden, who removes this exchange altogether. When Patroclus reminds Achilles that his refusal to participate in the war is damaging his reputation, the speech runs thus in Shakespeare:

> To this effect *Achilles* haue I moou'd you,
> A woman impudent and mannish growne,
> Is not more loath'd then an effeminate man
> In time of action: I stand condemnd for this
> They thinke my little stomack to the warre,
> And your great loue to me, restraines you thus,
> Sweete, rouse your selfe...
>
> (III. iii. 209–15)

In Dryden's adaptation the speech becomes:

> 'Tis known you are in love with *Hector*'s Sister,
> And therefore will not fight: and your not fighting
> Draws on you this contempt: I oft have told you
> A woman impudent and mannish grown
> Is not more loath'd than an effeminate man,
> In time of action: I'm condemn'd for this:
> They think my little appetite to warr
> Deads all the fire in you: but rowse your self...

> (IV. ii. 35–42)

At the beginning of the speech Dryden carefully establishes
Achilles' love for Polyxena rather than Patroclus' influence as the
reason for Achilles' withdrawal from the war; the importance of
Patroclus is also lessened by the excision of the phrase 'your great
loue to me' and of the epithet 'sweete'. Similarly, Dryden's
Achilles calls his companion 'My dear *Patroclus*' (IV. ii. 205)
instead of 'My sweet *Patroclus*' (V. i. 34). It is not that Dryden
recoils altogether from using the word 'sweet' for a male comrade,
for he introduces it later in a new speech which he writes for
Achilles lamenting the death of Patroclus and swearing revenge,
but here it is used as part of a careful definition of the friendship
between the two men:

> O thou art gone! thou sweetest, best of friends;
> Why did I let thee tempt the shock of war
> Ere yet thy tender nerves had strung thy limbs,
> And knotted into strength! Yet, though too late,
> I will, I will revenge thee, my *Patroclus*!

> (V. ii. 142–6)

Here the attention to the male body focuses on the youth's physical
unreadiness for the strains of combat, and the feeling in these lines
seems more like pity than desire. The personal investment is clear
from the emphasis on 'I' and 'my' in the last line, but the parallel
which suggests itself is not with (say) Venus lamenting the dead
body of Adonis in Shakespeare's poem, but Dryden himself
lamenting his young fellow-poet John Oldham, while recognizing

the ineffectual belatedness of his own understanding, and his inca-
pacity to make amends:

> Farewel, too little and too lately known,
> Whom I began to think and call my own...

('To the Memory of Mr Oldham', ll. 1–2)

In such examples from Dryden, the intense feelings which arise
between men have no erotic colouration.

In adaptations of Shakespeare during the seventeenth century we
can see a shift in the way that passionate male relationships are
conceptualized. To Shakespeare, homoerotic desire could form part
of male friendship: the intimate bond between men is threatened
not by homosexual feelings but by heterosexual ones, as *Othello* or
*The Two Noble Kinsmen* demonstrate in tragic mode. His comedies
often promise marriage rather than deliver it, ending just on the
brink of making an irrevocable exit from the comfortable all-male
milieu; and in the occasional reminders (for instance in *Twelfth
Night*) that the 'women' to whom the men are joined are actually
boy actors there may even be an element of reassurance, a translation of women back into boys which permits a final lingering in
that imaginative world where homosocial and homoerotic possibilities coexist. Restoration comedy, on the other hand, is more interested in the sexual arrangements which adult men and women
fashion: several plays end with explicit negotiations about the
terms on which marriage will be conducted. In such a world there
is no room for the ambiguities of Shakespeare's erotic imagination,
his pursuit of multiplicity, and his desire to blur definitions, to
postpone the moment at which choices have to be made. I would
not claim that all of the changes which I have highlighted were motivated consciously or exclusively by a fear of homosexual implications: some of the highly charged language between Shakespeare's
male characters may have offended Restoration adapters by its
poetic rather than its emotional excess, and the removal or
curtailment of speeches might result from other dramaturgical considerations. But there is a sufficiently coherent pattern here to
suggest that these Restoration adaptations were motivated partly
by a concern to protect male friendship from the suspicion of

homosexual desire, and to perserve the clarity and stability of the definition of masculinity in the face of a new world of homosexual self-definition.

## NOTES

1. Some portions of this essay have appeared in abbreviated form in my book *Love between Men in English Literature* (Basingstoke, 1996).
2. *The Diary of Samuel Pepys*, ed. Robert Latham and William Matthews, 11 vols (London, 1970–83), IV. 210.
3. 'Homosexual' is an anachronistic term, since it entered the language in the late nineteenth century and carried with it psychological, medical and moral connotations quite different from those which obtained in the late seventeenth century. There is, however, no simple seventeenth-century vocabulary which could be used instead, and while it would be a serious distortion to use 'homosexual' as a noun in this context, I see no alternative to 'homosexual' and 'homoerotic' as adjectives, if cumbersome periphrases are to be avoided. The distinction between those two word is not exact, but I would tend to use 'homoerotic' to describe feelings of sexual desire for, or erotic pleasure in the contemplation of, other men (and hence to describe texts which articulate or invite such feelings); and to reserve 'homosexual' for physical sexual contact between men. The two terms would thus distinguish between longing and looking on the one hand, and possessing and acting on the other. However, this is offered merely as a convenience for the present discussion.
4. I take the word 'homosocial' from Eve Kosofsky Sedgwick's *Between Men: English Literature and Male Homosocial Desire* (New York, 1985), where it is applied to strong social bonds between men.
5. The most important accounts of the late sixteenth and early seventeenth centuries are Alan Bray's *Homosexuality in Renaissance England* (London, 1982), supplemented by his 'Homosexuality and the signs of male friendship in Elizabethan England', *History Workshop*, 29 (1990) 1–19; and Bruce Smith's *Homosexual Desire in Shakespeare's England* (Chicago, 1991). For the late seventeenth and early eighteenth centuries, see Rictor Norton's *Mother Clap's Molly House: The Gay Subculture in England 1700–1830* (London, 1992). My book *Love between Men in English Literature* covers this period and includes a more detailed bibliography.
6. Shakespeare is quoted from *William Shakespeare: The Complete Works: Original-Spelling Edition*, ed. Stanley Wells and Gary Taylor (Oxford, 1986), though with act, scene and line references supplied from the modernized spelling version of that edition. Benson's edition of the *Sonnets* appeared as *Poems: Written by Wil. Shake-speare. Gent* (1640), from which my quotations are taken. Information about Benson's changes is also provided conveniently in *The Sonnets*, ed. Hyder Edward Rollins, New Variorum Edition of Shakespeare, 2 vols

(Philadelphia, 1944), II. 18–28. Recent discussions of Benson's edition include Arthur F. Marotti, 'Shakespeare's Sonnets as Literary Property' in *Soliciting Interpretation: Literary Theory and Seventeenth-Century English Poetry*, ed. Elizabeth D. Harvey and Katharine Eisaman Maus (Chicago, 1990) pp. 143–73, and Margareta de Grazia, 'The Scandal of Shakespeare's Sonnets', *Shakespeare Survey*, 46 (1994) 35–49.

7.  See, for example, Joseph Pequigney, 'The two Antonios and same-sex love in *Twelfth Night* and *The Merchant of Venice*', *English Literary Renaissance*, 22 (1992) 201–21.

8.  [George Granville], *The Jew of Venice. A Comedy* (London, 1701).

9.  Ben Ross Schneider, 'Granville's *Jew of Venice* (1701): A close reading of Shakespeare's *Merchant*', *Restoration*, 17 (1993) 111–34, at p. 119.

10. It is also possible that Granville is drawing upon the common association of the Jewish rite of circumcision with castration: for a suggestion that this fear is already implicit in Shakespeare's play, see Lorna Hutson, *The Usurer's Daughter: Male Friendship and Fictions of Women in Sixteenth-Century England* (London, 1994), pp. 226–7.

11. *The Merchant of Venice*, ed. Jay L. Halio (Oxford, 1994), p. 202; *The Merchant of Venice*, ed. John Russell Brown (London, 1955), p. 115.

12. Similarly, performance versions of *Twelfth Night* in the eighteenth and nineteenth centuries display considerable unease over the relationship between Antonio and Sebastian, often shifting or cutting their scenes; the Inchbald version, for example, makes Orsino carefully explain the terms of Antonio's proximity to Sebastian in a closing speech: 'Thou hast a noble spirit,/ And, as Sebastian's friend, be ever near him'. See Laurie E. Osborne, 'The Texts of *Twelfth Night*', *ELH*, 57 (1990) 37–61, especially pp. 52–3.

13. Nahum Tate, *The Ingratitude of a Common-Wealth: or, The Fall of Caius Martius Coriolanus* (London, 1682).

14. Thomas Otway, *The History and Fall of Caius Marius. A Tragedy* (London, 1680).

15. Quoted from *The Works of John Dryden*, ed. H. T. Swedenberg *et al.*, 20 vols (Berkeley, 1956– ) vol. XIII.

# Index